Philosophers and Their Poets

SUNY series in Contemporary Continental Philosophy

Dennis J. Schmidt, editor

Philosophers and Their Poets

Reflections on the Poetic Turn in Philosophy since Kant

Edited by

Charles Bambach and Theodore George

Published by State University of New York Press, Albany

© 2019 State University of New York

All rights reserved

No part of this book may be used or reproduced in any manner whatsoever without written permission. No part of this book may be stored in a retrieval system or transmitted in any form or by any means including electronic, electrostatic, magnetic tape, mechanical, photocopying, recording, or otherwise without the prior permission in writing of the publisher.

For information, contact State University of New York Press, Albany, NY
www.sunypress.edu

Library of Congress Cataloging-in-Publication Data

Names: Bambach, Charles and Theodore George, editors.
Title: Philosophers and Their Poets: Reflections on the Poetic Turn in Philosophy since Kant / Charles Bambach and Theodore George, editors.
Description: Albany : State University of New York Press, 2019. / Includes bibliographical references and index.
Identifiers: ISBN 9781438477039 (hardcover : alk. paper) / ISBN 9781438477022 (pbk. : alk. paper) | ISBN 9781438477046 (ebook)

Further information is available at the Library of Congress.

10 9 8 7 6 5 4 3 2 1

Contents

ACKNOWLEDGMENTS vii

INTRODUCTION
Poetizing and Thinking 1
    Charles Bambach and Theodore George

CHAPTER 1
On the Poetical Nature of Philosophical Writing: A Controversy over Style between Schiller and Fichte 21
    María del Rosario Acosta López

CHAPTER 2
Fichte and Schiller Correspondence, from *Fichte's Werke*, Vol. 8 (De Gruyter) 47
    Christopher Turner, translator

CHAPTER 3
Hegel, Romantic Art, and the Unfinished Task of the Poetic Word 65
    Theodore George

CHAPTER 4
Who Is Nietzsche's Archilochus? Rhythm and the Problem of the Subject 85
    Babette Babich

CHAPTER 5
Untimely Meditations on Nietzsche's Poet-Heroes 115
    Kalliopi Nikolopoulou

Chapter 6
Heidegger's *Ister Lectures*: Ethical Dwelling in the (Foreign) Homeland   139
   Charles Bambach

Chapter 7
Remains: Heidegger and Hölderlin amid the Ruins of Time   159
   William McNeill

Chapter 8
The Poietic Momentum of Thought: Heidegger and Poetry   185
   Krzysztof Ziarek

Chapter 9
Learning from Poetry: On Philosophy, Poetry, and T. S. Eliot's *Burnt Norton*   201
   Günter Figal

Chapter 10
An "Almost Imperceptible Breathturn": Gadamer on Celan   215
   Gert-Jan van der Heiden

Chapter 11
Hölderlin's Empedocles Poems   239
   Max Kommerell, trans. Christopher D. Merwin and Margot Wielgus

Contributors   263

Index   267

Acknowledgments

Chapter 1, María Acosta, "On the Poetical Nature of Philosophical Writing: A Controversy over Style between Schiller and Fichte." This is a revised version of an article originally published as part of a special issue on Friedrich Schiller edited by Laura Anna Macor for *Philosophical Readings* 5 (2013): 172–93. I would like to thank Kevin Thompson and Rachel Zuckert for inviting me to discuss this paper in the context of Chicago's 2015 meeting of the German Philosophy Consortium. The comments and questions that came up during that session were essential for my revision and rewriting of this paper. I would also like to thank Christopher Eagle for being such a patient reader of several versions of this paper, and for helping me to produce a more refined account of my philosophical ideas as well as a better translation of this text into English. I also want to thank Colin McQuillan for copyediting the final version of this paper for publication in this volume.

Chapter 2, "Fichte and Schiller Correspondence, from *Fichte's Werke*, Vol. 8 (De Gruyter)," translated by Christopher Turner. The editors would like to thank the Glassock Center for Humanities Research at Texas A&M University for generous support of this translation.

Chapter 4, Babette Babich, "Who Is Nietzsche's Archilochus? Rhythm and the Problem of the Subject." This essay has been presented in Scarborough, Freiburg, and Copenhagen as well as Dallas, Texas. I am grateful, first and foremost to Christian Benne in addition to Anke Bennholdt-Thomsen who discussed some of these concepts with me, in addition to my gratitude to Andreas Urs Sommer. I am also grateful to Charles Bambach and Theodore George. A German version has been published as "Nietzsches Lyrik. Archilochos, Musik, Metrik" in Christian Benne and Claus Zittel, eds., *Nietzsche und die Lyrik. Ein Kompendium* (Frankfurt am Main: Springer, 2017), 405–29.

Chapter 11, Max Kommerell, "Hölderlin's Empedocles's Poems," from *Spirit and Letter of Poetry*, trans. Christopher Merwin and Margot Weiglus. The editors would like to thank the Glassock Center for Humanities Research at Texas A&M University for generous support of this translation.

Introduction

Poetizing and Thinking

CHARLES BAMBACH AND THEODORE GEORGE

The very gesture of thinking, Plato tells us in *Theatetus*, finds its origin in the experience of wondering (θαυμάζειν).¹ But to wonder at or about something is to experience its strangeness, its irregularity, or its difference. It is with the other that philosophy begins. What confronts us as other brings us to a perplexity that opens us to the experience of questioning as the very movement and dynamic of thinking itself. Pondering such strangeness, interrogating its anomalous disparity, we see how thinking not only begins in wonder at the other, but its every turn toward questioning is borne by such wondering as what makes it at all possible. In his 1955 Cerisy lecture "What Is That—Philosophy?" Heidegger put forward the claim that "the pathos of wonder, does not simply stand at the beginning of philosophy. . . . Wonder bears and thoroughly governs philosophy."² But if otherness belongs to such wonder, then we might also say that otherness—in the sense of ineradicable alterity—likewise bears and thoroughly governs whatever philosophy might undertake. What is other belongs to philosophy as its ἀρχή and ruling origin, one that it does not, however, leave behind as it makes its way within the world. Rather, in recognizing what is other as intimately belonging to its origin, philosophy confronts otherness as having an essential relation to whatever constitutes its own and proper task. In this sense, philosophy not only requires its other in order to be itself, but it is precisely this relation to its other that allows philosophical questioning to attend to the questionability of all that is.

In this same Cerisy lecture about the sense and origin of philosophical thinking—and not by accident—Heidegger takes up the question about the relationship between thinking (*Denken*) and its other—poetizing (*Dichten*). He writes:

> But since poetizing, when compared with thinking, stands in the service of language in a wholly other and exemplary way, our conversation, which thoughtfully pursues philosophy, is necessarily led to discuss the relation of thinking and poetizing. Between both, thinking and poetizing, there prevails a hidden affinity since in the service of language both use and squander language. At the same time, however, between both thinking and poetizing there subsists a chasm—for both "dwell on mountains farthest apart."[3]

To think the chasm "between" thinking and poetizing means that we attune ourselves to the disparateness that attends this separation. Here, poetizing confronts thinking as its other. And yet in coming to experience the separation between them, we cannot help but encounter a certain affinity between thinking and poetizing as well, an affinity that emerges in and through the chasm that divides them. As Heidegger expresses it, "[W]hat is said in poetizing and what is said in thinking are never identical; but they are at times the same—namely, when the chasm between poetizing, and thinking gapes purely and decisively."[4] Both poetizing and thinking open a pathway into being, letting the unconcealment of being happen precisely in and as a concealment and a withdrawal. Moreover, both poetizing and thinking open us to language in an originary way, whereby we come to experience language less as a tool or as an instrument for communication than as "the clearing-concealing advent of being itself."[5] Yet here we also come to see that poetizing makes communication ever more difficult, since its very manner of presenting words undermines their clarity and stability and renders them ever more obscure. In this way, we can perhaps find an echo of the original sense of the German term *dichten* (poetizing) with its roots in the adjective *dicht*. Poetry "thickens" language, making it "dense" and difficult to penetrate (*dicht machen*), sometimes closing off its meaning in dense clusters that become almost watertight (*dichthalten*).

Yet at the same time poetry beckons us to tarry awhile amid its dense, impenetrable word clusters, offering its hospitality to those readers/listeners who are patient enough to attend to its playful commerce with language. We might even say that in the experience of its thick, dense, or close-grained (*dicht*) dictions, we begin to let go of our ordinary relationship to language in its instrumental properties and prepare ourselves for a more fundamental experience with the essence of language. To be able to enter into this experience, however, signifies that we refrain from collapsing language into "meaning" so that we might begin to hear the soundings of its rhythms, modulations, resonances, tones, and timbres. Responding to these soundings, entering into the sheer strangeness of their inflections, we resist the impulse to flatten out the difference enunciated in poetic speech and instead begin to attend to what Heidegger calls "the thrust into the extraordinary" (*Un-geheuere*).[6] It is in this space of difference cleaved out by the soundings of poetic speech that we begin to hear "the speaking of language" (*das Sprechen der Sprache*). But again, to hear such speaking in its proper and authentic sense means to liberate language from mere grammar, logic, and communicative expression. Such an experience with language, attuned to both its poetic and thinkerly resonances, likewise means that we grasp Heidegger's insight that "it is not we who have language; rather, language has us, in a certain sense."[7] When we attempt to think poetizing as mere poesy and reduce it to a literary genre or a historical style, we miss the full force of language's originary power. But it is precisely poetry's relation to the origin that thinking brings into question. Heidegger holds that "language is the supreme event of human existence" and it is in the poem that language properly occurs (*ereignet sich*).[8] He goes on to relate: "Poetizing is the saying of the un-concealment of beings."[9] In thus making manifest the hidden realm of being's appearance in the world, poetizing opens us to the "world-forming power" of the word. For Heidegger, "originary language is the language of poetry."[10] In its essence, language is poetry and poetry in its essence is the fundamental happening of language.[11] In a word, "poetizing is the origin of language."[12]

In his very first lecture course on Hölderlin from WS 1934/35, Heidegger finds a "clue" to the meaning of poetizing as a "making manifest." Going back to the semantic field of the Old High German term *tithon*, which he traces back to the Latin word *dicere*, Heidegger maintains that *dichten* shares "the same root as the Greek *deiknymi*. It means to show, to make something visible, to make it manifest—not just in general, but by way of a specific pointing."[13] Only later does *dichten* get narrowed down to mean "writerly composition" or "versifying according to poetic conventions." But what does *dichten* come to mean philosophically? And how might reflecting on its essential meaning help to open philosophy's own relation to language? Within the German philosophical tradition since Kant there emerges a profound and compelling dialogue about the meaning of poetic language for philosophy. In the work of Hölderlin, Schiller, Fichte, Hegel, Nietzsche, Kommerell, Gadamer, and Celan, we come to encounter many different pathways into the question of poetry's significance for philosophical thinking. In their different ways these philosophers keep alive the differences that separate poetry and philosophy, even as they try to preserve these differences as the site for a more originary consideration of their sameness. Following Heidegger, we could even go so far as to say that it is precisely the chasm between poetry and philosophy that opens us to the need for a thoughtful dialogue about their relation. Any attempt to define each—either apart from or in harmony with the other—would prove fruitless, since it is the impossible con- and dis-junction of this pair that commands our attention. Any attempts to explain "poetry" or "philosophy," "as if they were fixed domains in themselves," shatter against the sheer questionability and enduring mystery of their relation.[14] In Heidegger's words, "[T]here is to be sure, something ambiguous and obscure concerning the inner, essential relation between poetizing, and thinking."[15] We could then say perhaps that there can be no external measure by which to gauge the proper relation between poetizing and thinking. On the contrary, it is by attending to the chasm, *Kluft*, cleft, or *Spalte* that separates them, that we come to reflect upon the enigma of what Hölderlin terms their "harmonious contrariety" (*Harmonischentgegensetzung*).[16]

If there could be something like a poetic measure for thinking, then perhaps we might situate it in an abyssal separation that would allow for a disjunctive unity that might abide between thinking and poetizing. Such a measure would attend to what remains unsaid—perhaps even what remains unspeakable—in the language spoken by poetry. In his ode "Rousseau," Hölderlin comes to understand poetizing as the beckoning intimations (*Winke*) of the gods.[17] Following the trace of Hölderlin's insights, Heidegger imagines "poetizing as the beckoning shrouded in the word."[18] Here, we might warrant that it is in poetic language that the gods beckon us to heed what remains unsaid in that which comes to be said poetically. Poetic language brings us into the sphere of mystery, ambiguity, and enigma—but not as a mere gesture of obstruction or oblivion concerning what always remains obscure. In Heraclitus Fragment B 93, we find a hinting intimation of such mysterious beckoning, one that belongs preeminently to the gods themselves:

ὁ ἄναξ οὗ τὸ μαντεῖόν ἐστι τὸ ἐν Δελφοῖς οὔτε λέγει οὔτε κρύπτει ἀλλὰ σημαίνει

(The Lord, whose oracle is at Delphi [the god Apollo], neither says, nor does he conceal, but rather intimates in beckoning [*winkt*]).[19]

As Heidegger understands it, "originary saying neither renders things immediately manifest nor does it simply conceal them altogether. Rather, this saying is both together in one, and as this one is a beckoning where . . . the conflictual sways to the harmony, which it is, and the harmony to the conflict within which it alone sways."[20]

When we here try to offer some modest thoughts on the relation of poetry and philosophy in terms of poetizing and thinking, then it can only be understood against this Heraclitean insight about the unity-in-conflict that echoes in each. We do not take poetry or philosophy as different expressions of language with their own regional domains, but rather as manifestations or ways of revealing the very event of language (*Ereignis*) that appropriates us (*uns an-eignet*) to how being occurs (*sich ereignet*). Here language neither describes this event, nor prepares it; neither does it speak to the event itself. Rather, poetic language speaks out of the event (*vom Ereignis*), from it, and of it as being's proper (*eigene*) way of essencing. As such, language is not a human invention, but a way of "saying" or "showing" how and that being is. Human language constitutes a response to being's originary saying, but one that belongs to such saying as what is granted or addressed to humans (*Zuspruch*) by language (*Sprache*).[21] But humans of course fail to respond to this address in a correspondingly originary way, instead grasping at language as a mere "medium" of communication in contrived systems of signs, codes, words, and expressions. What we find in poetry is the unfolding of the very momentum of language as an originary opening up and emergence that does not fit neatly into the metaphysical encasements of presence and representation. Poetry's dense and thickened (*dicht*) kind of saying prevents humans from any smooth and effortless appropriation of its language. Instead, poetizing enacts a form of saying that allows us to linger in its density and, in this way, provokes a corresponding possibility of thinking that might attune us to another experience with language than one of signification and representation.

Against the propositional language of statements, poetic language invites us to heed the pauses, the interruptions, and the caesurae that call us to attend to what is not said or can never be said in language. It brings our attention to the fissures of speech that break open a path into the abyssal ground or, rather, non-ground of being. Perhaps no modern poet is as attuned to this intense concentration of language as an abyssal trace as Paul Celan. In his "Meridian" speech, Celan speaks of the abyss that opens onto "the frightful falling silent" of the poem.[22] Nietzsche too speaks of the silent force of language as that which harbors in itself the power of what cannot be said. In *Thus Spoke Zarathustra* he relays the story of Zarathustra's confrontation with the empty speechifying of the marketplace (especially in Zarathustra's own attempts to "say" the truth of the death of God, the transhuman, and of remaining true to the earth). As the story unfolds, Zarathustra becomes more disenchanted with the language of doctrines, teachings, *(Lehre)* and proclamations—and abandons his role as "teacher" (*Lehrer*). In the aftermath of his turn away from the language of the marketplace, he then begins to convalesce from the metaphysics of philosophical assertion and retreats to the silence of a "voiceless" sanctuary where he can listen to the stillness of "the stillest hour." The German term that Nietzsche employs here—*Stille*—needs to be heard as "silent stillness," but also as that which has something secretive attached to it. The language of eternal return—which cannot be "said"—belongs to the language of *Stille*. Hence, in a work that undermines spoken language through the idiom of the written and purports to offer "speeches" of its protagonist, Nietzsche turns to the language of silence for a way to "communicate" the thought of eternal return. It is in this way that the voice of silence "speaks" to Zarathustra at the end of Part Two:

> It is the stillest words that bring the storm. Thoughts that come on dove's feet steer the world.[23]

Nietzsche's *Zarathustra* is part of a long tradition in German thinking going back to Meister Eckhart that privileges silence as the very heart of language. In one of his sermons, Eckhart speaks of the soul's receptivity toward "the word of God," which requires of us a letting go of images, likenesses, words, and things. In this stance of detachment, Eckhart relates, there "in the midst of silence was in-stilled within me a concealed word."[24] In his poem "You be like you" (1967), Celan takes up Eckhart's words concerning silence and stillness and juxtaposes them with texts from the biblical prophet Isaiah and from the Kabbala—precisely in 1967 against the political realities of the Six Day War that shaped his "Andenken" of Jerusalem.[25] In the labyrinthine allusions that proliferate throughout this poem, we find a reference to the first two words from Isaiah 60:1: "kumi ori" (Hebrew), which Eckhart had translated into Latin as "surge illuminare" (Rise up, shine).[26] In his private notebooks Celan offered this link: "kumi ori: it makes itself plain in what is most reticent."[27] For Celan, poetry emerges from the dialogue between language and silence, and in the otherness that binds them together in an impossible separation. So much of Celan's poetry attempts to bring to language the silence that can never be spoken, which remains unsaid—and yet precisely on that account demands that it be said, if only despairingly, in an idiom of silence, withdrawal, voicelessness, and reticence. Hölderlin would express it this way: "This is a law of fate/ . . . That when the silence returns, there shall also be a language."[28]

Heidegger too was attuned to the poetics of silence. In his lectures on Hölderlin, Heidegger points to poetry's power "to leave the unsayable unsaid, and to do so in and through its saying."[29] He goes on to add: "If the essence of truth is to be sought in the revelation of beings, then concealment and veiling prove to be a particular way of manifesting that is proper to revelation." We could also say that this same revelatory power of concealment belongs to thinking as well. Heidegger underlines this tension in his essay "Recollection in Metaphysics" (1941), where he writes: "The thinker can never say what is most proper to him. It must remain unsaid, because the sayable word receives its determination from what is unsayable. What is most proper to a thinker is not, however, something that he possesses; rather, it is the property of being."[30] To situate language in silence, as Heidegger does here, means to reflect on language's proper site. But how would we be properly able to situate it in relation to this site? And what might this situating call for in terms of our comportment and openness to the claim that such a site makes upon us? Were we to address these questions in a measured way, we would need to trace them through the absences of silence alluded to in Eckhart, Hölderlin, and Celan. It is in the language of the poets, in their dialogue with the thinkers, that this situating emerges. Again, we find a hint for thinking this relation in Heidegger's encounter with Hölderlin. In ". . . poetically dwells the human being," Heidegger proposes that we conceive of poetizing as a measure-taking, and indeed one "by which the human being first receives the measure for the expanse of its being."[31] Only the measure-taking of the poet "can gauge the essence of the human," Heidegger tells us. But the measure-taking of what the poet can bring to language is never to be reduced to what can be said. Poetic measure, like language itself, "is grounded in silence. Silence is the most concealed form of holding-the-measure."[32] In its attunement to the silence of language and the absence of any ready-made measure that might guide our actions, "poetizing lets us dwell properly."[33] Moreover, "poetizing founds the essence of dwelling. . . . Poetizing and dwelling belong together."[34] It is as poetizing that language grants us a site for dwelling, since poetizing in its essence is nothing other than *ethos*. In his Heraclitus lectures of SS 1944, Heidegger acknowledges: "*Ethos* means dwelling, sojourn (*Aufenthalt*). We say: it is the dwelling of the human being, its sojourn in the midst of beings as a whole."[35]

To think of poetry as *ethos* involves rethinking language as something other than a human possession, which entails understanding it as the site of a dwelling where we come to habituate ourselves to the enigma of what human life means. Poetry so understood would then be something other than metrical verse or the soundings of tercets in cadence and rhyme. Here, poetry would enact a certain kind of attunement that would be attentive to the unique, singular, nonrepeatable event of language that opens itself to us as that which claims us and to which we are bidden to respond. In its responsiveness to this event, poetry opens the human being to a responsibility that is not grounded in rules, directives, laws, or precepts but, rather, entails what Celan calls "a waiting for the appeal (*Zuspruch*) of language (*Sprache*)."[36] Drawing on Heidegger's claim that "correspondence (*Entsprechung*) to the being of beings always remains our abode (*Aufenthalt*),"[37] Celan writes: "Language, above all, in the poem, is *ethos*—*ethos* as fateful projection of truth." The language of the poem offers a site for the dwelling of the human; in this way it helps humans to respond to the depredations of speech that pervade so much of modern communication. Celan writes to Werner Weber in 1960 about what he sees as the assault upon poetic language in the burgeoning complex of technical life:

> We already have a cybernetic form of lyric poetry. Soon we will also have—long live "logical consistency"!—a lyrical cybernetics.
>
> No more language, no more conversation—no, only Informatics, word systems with exact specifications of the wave-lengths for "reception."[38]

In his own time, Hölderlin (like Celan) concerned himself with the fate of language and the inability of humans to hear its word. Reflecting on the being-historical significance of this plight, Heidegger comes to think this whole relation to language through Hölderlin's notion of "homecoming," and "poetic dwelling"—what Celan under a quite different set of concerns would call "ethos." As Heidegger put it, "Hölderlin's poetizing abides in its care for 'Homecoming.' It is the care for founding the site for the poetic dwelling of humans, the patient waiting for rescue in this earthly sojourn (*Aufenthalt*)."[39]

In *Philosophers and Their Poets*, we have sought to bring together a wide range of essays that address the diverse concerns of several German philosophers from Fichte to Gadamer concerning the relation of poetic language to philosophy. In gathering these essays we have sought to explore different possibilities of an ethical relation to language opened up by poets, one that challenges any notion of ethics as residing in subjective volition or the behavior of an autonomous agent. Rather, by pursuing the strange and uncanny conversation between philosophers and their poets, we have attempted to raise the question of the ethicality of language itself. In Celan's understanding of language as *ethos*, in Hölderlin's poetizing of homecoming as a way of safeguarding the mystery, in Heidegger's thinking of *ethos* as poetic dwelling, and in Gadamer's grasp of poetry and hermeneutic philosophy as "both pursuing an interpretation (*Deut*) that points (*deutet*) into the open," we find ways of opening toward the silent, concealed force of language that challenges us to rethink our sense of the ethical.[40]

Yet there is an inevitable tension in the way poetic verse speaks to and from the *ethos* of language and its ethicality. Like an ancient oracle, the poet's riddling, enigmatic inflections come to us as a call and a provocation. Sometimes the call is direct. One thinks here of Rilke's bold, unequivocal entreaty from "Archaic Torso of Apollo" where, from out of its gleaming marble surface, the headless stone

> bursts forth through its confines
> like a star . . .

and announces: "You must change your life."[41] At other times, however, the poetic call itself becomes oracular—sent like a "message in a bottle" (*Flaschenpost*) to a future, nameless addressee "in the—not always greatly hopeful—belief that somewhere and sometime it could wash up on land."[42] Theodor Adorno famously proclaimed: "to write poetry after Auschwitz is barbaric."[43] But he also proposed an ethical response to such a condition:

> A new categorical imperative has been imposed by Hitler on unfree humankind: to arrange their thoughts and actions so

that Auschwitz will not repeat itself, so that nothing similar will happen.[44]

Yet Celan confronted Adorno's challenge by writing poetry ever mindful of the very barbarism that sought to silence it. And he did so through his understanding of language as the *ethos* from which any possible response could be made. In the face of the banality of "ethical" language during the Third Reich and against its tragic inadequacy to address the enormity of its failure, Celan proffered his own verse as a poetic *ethos* of language. He called for a "Breathturn" that would put into question the tradition of aesthetics that he believed had transmogrified poetic language by detaching it from ethical life. Nonetheless, Celan refrained from offering any ethical pronouncements of his own, given how devastatingly inadequate the "ethical" blatherings of postwar German mea culpas had proved to be. And yet his poetry speaks deeply to a hope that might emerge on the other side of history—in what Heidegger called "an other beginning." Such a beginning could only emerge, Celan seems to tell us, if we come to cast our hopes for what is to come in nets that are weighted down by the burden of a remembrance. Only in this way, attuned to the pain of those whose suffering can never be *aufgehoben* in the unfolding of history, can we ever begin to imagine what the future might hold. Addressing this hope in the ethicality of a language tinged with the sense of the uncanniness/*Unheimlichkeit* of speech, Celan sends out his "message in a bottle" that offers its own poetic measure for what cannot be said in the language of the concept:

> Into rivers north of the future
> I cast out the net, which you
> hesitantly weight
> with stone-engraved
> shadows.[45]

The essays in this volume all address the power of poetic language in its conversation with German philosophy.

The collection begins with a focus on contributions made by German philosophers from the turn of the eighteenth to the nineteenth century. Perhaps appropriately, Chapter 1 presents a late-eighteenth-century contribution to what, in Plato's time, was already considered an old "quarrel between philosophy and poetry."[46] In her "On the Poetical Nature of Philosophical Writings: A Controversy over Style between Schiller and Fichte," María del Rosario Acosta López takes up a debate between Friedrich Schiller and Johann Gottlieb Fichte about the character, relation, and difference of poetical and philosophical writing that arose in correspondence between the two when Schiller rejected a piece by Fichte for Schiller's journal, *die Horen*. Fichte, according to Acosta, believed that Schiller's rationale for rejection was simply a matter of the style (*Manier*) of his exposition. While Schiller's criticism of Fichte did, indeed, pertain to style, for Schiller this is no superficial matter. Quite to the contrary, Schiller's criticism turns on a disagreement with Fichte about nothing less than the vocation of the human being (*Mensch*). Whereas Fichte believes that the vocation of the human being culminates in a moral autonomy of reason free of the sensible, Schiller, by contrast, argues that the vocation of the human being, while moral, culminates in the reciprocal action of reason and sensibility. "To Schiller," Acosta explains, "true moral freedom is aesthetic freedom, that is, one in which a reciprocal action between both aspects of human nature has been achieved and secured."[47] Schiller's criticism is, moreover, closely related to the matter of *philosophical* style. For Schiller, as Acosta argues, the vocation of philosophy is not achieved by abstract conceptuality that is purified of all sensible images—work that may be performed by what Schiller calls the "*Brotgelehrte*," academics in it for the pay and, by implication, more so than for the advancement of knowledge. Rather, philosophy is achieved in what he calls *presentative (darstellende) writing*, a form of writing in which concept and image are in reciprocal relation that achieves an organic whole and, thus, is able to address the reader as a whole person.

This volume includes, as a companion to Acosta's contribution, chapter 2, an original translation by Christopher Turner of the very correspondence between Fichte and Schiller at issue. The remarkable correspondence begins with a letter from Fichte to Schiller that enclosed the piece he intended to contribute to Schiller's journal, *die Horen*, from June 21, 1795. The first lines of Schiller's letter to Fichte in response from June 24, 1795, are the ones that set the exchange in motion:

> As much as the sight of your manuscript pleased me, dear friend, and as loathe as am I to do without a contribution that was already entirely and confidently counted on for the next installment of *die Horen*, I nevertheless find myself compelled to send it back.

Fichte, as one might imagine, was not entirely pleased.

Chapter 3 focuses on Hegel's contributions to the relation of poetic language to philosophy. In his "Hegel, Romantic Art, and the Unfinished Task of the Poetic Word," Theodore George challenges the common view of Hegel's so-called end of art thesis. On this common view, Hegel holds that although both art and philosophy share in the speculative vocation to present truth, philosophy supersedes art in European modernity, so that the forms of art achieved in European modernity (Hegel refers to them collectively as "Romantic" art) are left with no real speculative significance. George argues that this common view of Hegel's "end of art" thesis fails to appreciate the nuance and richness of Hegel's approach to Romantic art. Hegel believes that Romantic art comes to present truth in a novel manner, thanks, in particular, to the role played by language in Romantic art. For Hegel, all art, regardless of form, is constituted as a "work of language." Whereas Hegel believes classical art to have been a work of language that founds (*stiftet*) ancient society, Romantic art, by contrast, is a work that provides only a supplement to any possible foundation. As such a supplement, Romantic art presents truth always only incompletely, in deferral. Yet, as George understands Hegel, this limitation is not a deficiency, but, on the contrary, precisely brings into focus the relevance of Romantic art, and, with this, important ethical dimensions of this relevance. George writes that Romantic art, "allows us to examine the possibilities for our inner lives and the dehiscence we experience in this interiority within modern society."[48]

The next two chapters of the volume concern important but still too little understood aspects of Nietzsche's considerations of poetic language and its relation to philosophy. In chapter 4, Babette Babich turns to Nietzsche's treatment of the ancient Greek lyric poet Archilochus. In this chapter, entitled "Who Is Nietzsche's Archilochus? Rhythm and the Problem of the Subject," Babich observes that Nietzsche has often been associated with poetry but that Nietzsche's relation to the tradition of lyric poetry is complex. While Nietzsche has been taken up in reference to poets as diverse as Pindar, Schiller, and Emerson, his considerations of Archilochus has received less attention. In this chapter, Babich focuses on Nietzsche's approach to Archilochus in the *Birth of Tragedy*. Her examination brings into focus the theme of the lyric subject, and, importantly, the relation of word and music as Nietzsche treats it under the auspices of what he calls quantifying rhythm.

In chapter 5, "Untimely Meditations on Nietzsche's Poet-Heroes," Kalliopi Nikolopoulou examines the role played in Nietzsche's philosophy by a poetic motif, which she refers to as a Homeric heroic ideal.[49] Nikolopoulou recognizes that her treatment of Nietzsche's stress on this poetic motif is what Nietzsche himself might have referred to as "untimely." While much of the reception of Nietzsche in postmodernity has been laudatory, his stress on the ideal of heroism has been widely questioned, criticized, and disavowed. Yet, as Nikolopoulou argues, Nietzsche's invocation of this heroic ideal comprises a decisive feature of Nietzsche's efforts to make an untimely intervention against what he perceived as the nihilism of his times. Nikolopoulou begins with an overview of the aesthetics of heroism in Homer and the legacy of this aesthetics in Plato and Aristotle. Here, heroism is a matter of beautiful death, which, as Nikolopoulou argues, may be grasped as an experience of untimeliness. Turning to Nietzsche, Nikolopoulou traces Nietzsche's debts to this Homeric aesthetics of heroism in *The Birth of Tragedy* in his characterization of Apollo (and the art impulse he names for the Greek God). She argues, in turn, that the Homeric aesthetics of heroism also plays a role in Nietzsche's association of poets, such as Aeschylus, Archilochus, and Pindar, with a sense of vocation that joins them to something greater than themselves. Nikolopoulou concludes her considerations of the role played by an aesthetics of heroism in *The Birth of Tragedy* in reference to Nietzsche's portrait of Euripides as an ambivalent figure, and, indeed, one whose ambivalence may be reflected in Nietzsche's own relation to ancient Greek tragedy.

These essays on late-eighteenth- and early-nineteenth-century German philosophers are followed by three chapters on Heidegger's pathbreaking contributions to questions about the relation of poetic language and philosophy. In chapter 6, "Heidegger's *Ister Lectures*: Ethical Dwelling in the (Foreign) Homeland," Charles Bambach explores the relationship between language and ethics in Heidegger by offering a reading of the SS 1942 lecture course "Hölderlin's Hymn 'The Ister.' " Drawing on Hölderlin's Böhlendorff letter from 1801 and its telling distinction between the native/foreign, Heidegger explores the Hölderlinian *topos* of homecoming as "the future of the historical essence of the German *Volk*." For Heidegger, "poetry is the fundamental event of being as such"; it opens human beings to the possibility of a historical homecoming. Bambach explores this Heideggerian *topos* of homecoming by situating it against the work of two poets whom Heidegger privileges above all others—Sophocles and Hölderlin. What Heidegger takes up in the Ister lectures is the question concerning the possibility of authentic poetic dwelling, a question he addresses by examining the tragic tension within Sophocles's *Antigone*. In the uncanny fate of Antigone, Heidegger finds the poetic grammar for embracing the paradox that marks the human sojourn upon the earth. As Bambach argues, in Antigone's decision to expose herself knowingly to the uncanny strangeness at the heart of existence, she risks losing her sense of home. Yet, paradoxically, it is precisely this risk of losing the home that enables a more authentic form of poetic homecoming, one that connects her to hearth and earth. In risking her home in this way, Antigone offers a model for Hölderlin's own sense of poetic homecoming. On Heidegger's reading, it is this opening up to the uncanny/unhomely that offers a possible pathway for a futural German homecoming. Hence, for Heidegger, in her character as that singular figure who becomes homely in becoming unhomely, Antigone poetizes the very possibility of poetry, which decides on "the potential of human beings for being homely" (HHI: 121/ GA 53:151). In exploring the tension between these oppositional forces in Greek tragedy—precisely by way of an interpretation of Hölderlin—Bambach's essay situates such thinking in terms of the foreign/native dyad as one that both shapes and haunts Heidegger's notion of ethical dwelling.

In chapter 7, "Remains: Heidegger and Hölderlin amid the Ruins of Time," William McNeill examines the significance of Heidegger's celebrated encounter with Hölderlin for Heidegger's elucidation of the relation of language and time. McNeill takes his point of departure from the observation that, for Hölderlin, the essence of time is that it tears: time tears us from the present, opening up a relation both to what exceeds the mortal and to a properly mortal relation to the dead in remembrance. Focused first on Heidegger's 1936 "Hölderlin and the Essence of Poetry," McNeill argues that on Heidegger's elucidation of Hölderlin, poetizing is an event of commemorative remembrance that names what remains in the tears of time. Here, however, poetizing does not name something that is already present but, instead, comprises the event that first institutes or founds the world it commemorates. As McNeill argues, Heidegger's engagement with Hölderlin thus points to a shift in his earlier view of the relation of language and time. In the earlier *Being and Time*, Heidegger holds that *Dasein* is the disclosedness, on the basis of which language is possible. Now, with his engagement with Hölderlin, Heidegger suggests that language, as poetizing, is what allows for disclosedness in the first place. McNeill takes up Heidegger's 1941–42 interpretative engagement with Hölderlin's hymn "Remembrance" to argue, in turn, that for Heidegger remembrance is futural. For Heidegger, remembrance is a greeting, a thoughtful turn to what is greeted, that allows it to appear in its own being as what it is. When remembrance accomplishes such a greeting, however, what is greeted is no longer simply something worn out or finished, but comes into focus as a "buried treasure" indexed to the future.[50]

Chapter 8, "The Poietic Momentum of Thought: Heidegger and Poetry," by Krzysztof Ziarek, shifts focus from Heidegger's intensive encounter with Hölderlin's poetry to the significance of Heidegger's encounters with poetic texts and artworks taken on the whole. Ziarek argues that Heidegger's interpretive engagements with poetic texts and artworks are to be grasped as so many attempts to enact a certain experience of language—a more original, nonmetaphysical language of what Heidegger calls "thinking," rather than as readings or interpretations. Ziarek, following Heidegger, argues that this experience of language may be grasped as a matter of the poietic (or, as this translates Heidegger's German, *dichterisch*) word. With this, the word is to be taken not as a sign that refers to or signifies something, but, more originally, as a momentum, a movement of the openness, which first grants being to what the word names, and which thus allows what the word names to appear as what it is. While Heidegger believes this poietic possibility to belong to language as such, he holds that this possibility is epitomized by both poetizing and thinking. Whereas, in poetry, the poietic momentum of language remains bound to an image, however, in thinking this momentum is released without bounds onto the openness that first grants being to what is named. Based on this, as Ziarek argues, the task of thinking requires that we extend beyond the norms of philosophy that focus on calculative rationality—propositions, arguments, proofs—turning our focus, instead, to a textuality of language that opens onto what cannot be conceived in advance. Ziarek recommends, finally, that such thinking is also precisely what is called for in our encounters with Heidegger.

The final three essays of the volume draw attention to important further twentieth-century contributions to questions of the relation of poetic language and philosophy. In chapter 9, "Learning from Poetry: On Philosophy, Poetry, and T. S. Eliot's *Burnt Norton*," Günter Figal returns to the "old quarrel between philosophy and poetry" that opens the volume in reference to a close reading of the first poem in T. S. Eliot's *Four Quartets* mentioned in Figal's title. Figal reminds us that, beginning with Plato, philosophers in the Western tradition have held that only philosophers, and not poets, seek to learn how things truly are. If this pretense has been brought into doubt since Nietzsche, Figal argues that philosophers such as Heidegger and Gadamer uphold (in different ways) the validity of the philosophical claim to truth but concede that the pursuit of this claim must be "delegated to poetry."[51] Figal, for his part, proposes to inquire whether poetry is true,[52] not through a conceptual elucidation of truth, but, instead, through an attentive reading of a specific poem, *Burnt Norton*, to see whether and, if so, how truth is thereby disclosed. Figal contends that although Eliot's poem appears to refer to something (a manor house in Southwest England), the poem rather seeks to give voice to a world—Eliot calls it a "first world"—that is present through the "grace of sense" alone, freed from our practical interests. Figal argues that the poem allows the world to appear as it would if the tension between past and future that animates practical life were suspended. From this, Figal concludes that the poem is not deceiving, as Plato claims, but is nevertheless beyond truth—if truth is taken, either theoretically or practically, to refer to a factual or possible world as it were outside the poem. Instead, the poem stands as an "objectification" of sense itself, one whose order is discernable but always indeterminate, always allowing (and requiring) further interpretation to be brought, each time only partially, into focus.

In chapter 10, "An 'Almost Imperceptible Breathturn': Gadamer on Celan," Gert-Jan van der Heiden takes up Hans-Georg Gadamer's celebrated (and also sometimes criticized) interpretive engagement with the poet Paul Celan. Van der Heiden maintains that Gadamer's encounter with Celan may be grasped as a "dialogue between philosophy and poetry," in which our understanding of basic tenets of philosophical hermeneutics is brought into question and even transformed by Celan. As van der Heiden argues, the lines of this transformation may be drawn in reference to three keywords of Gadamer's approach to Celan: moment, reserve, and hope. Van der Heiden observes that Gadamer, in his philosophical hermeneutics, introduces the keyword *moment* to describe the completion of the enactment of an interpretation, the moment as the moment when our efforts allow the text to speak to us as a "you." Yet, Celan suggests that his poetry remains marked by a radical incapacity that brings Gadamer's conception into question: for Celan, the possibility that interpretation will lead a poem to speak as a "you" is not a given; it remains possible that such a possibility is not possible after all. Accordingly, as van der Heiden argues, the aim of Celan's poetry is not to illuminate such a "you" in the light of the public sphere, but, instead, to hold back in reserve, to speak with discretion so that this other remains in secret, retains privacy and the possibility of intimacy. And, in turn, Celan's poetry is oriented not so much by the trust that an interpretation will or even can allow this other to become familiar, but, much more tentatively, by the mere hope that the other can take place there at all. For Celan, as van der Heiden concludes, poetry is thus a breathturn, grasped as an inspiration that breaths into this other and, at the same time, depends on this other for its breath.

Chapter 11, the final chapter of volume, is comprised of an original translation of Max Kommerell, "Hölderlin's Empedocles Poems," by Margot Wieglus and Christopher Merwin. Perhaps more widely recognized in German scholarly quarters than in the Anglophone context, Max Kommerell (1902–1944) was a German poet, essayist, and critic. The reception of Kommerell is made complicated, first, by his participation in the circle of Stefan George in the 1920s, with which he broke in 1930; and, second, by dubious political commitments during the National Socialist period. Yet, Kommerell is an influential figure of the interwar period, known not only for his early association with the George circle, but also in connection with Walter Benjamin's critique of his *Der Dichter als Führer in der deutschen Klassik* [*The Poet as Leader in the German Classical Age*] and, later, Celan's interest in Benjamin's critique of this work. Finally, Kommerell is also remembered for his opposition to Heidegger's approach to Hölderlin. Presented here is Kommerell's important essay on Hölderlin's fragments of a drama, *The Death of Empedocles*, published as the final chapter in Kommerell's *Geist und Buschstabe der Dichtung* [The Spirit and Letter of Poetry] (1939).

Notes

1. Plato, *Theatetus*, 155D.
2. Heidegger, GA, 11:22.
3. Heidegger, GA, 11:25–26. This phrase—to "dwell on mountains farthest apart"—comes from Hölderlin's hymn "Patmos," vv. 11–2.
4. Heidegger, GA, 8:21–22.
5. Heidegger, PM: 249/GA, 9:326.
6. Heidegger, GA, 5:56.
7. Heidegger, HGR: 24/GA 39:23.
8. Heidegger, EHP: 58/GA 4:40.
9. Heidegger, BW: 198/GA 5:61.
10. Heidegger, GA, 38:170.
11. Friedrich Wilhelm von Herrmann, *Heideggers Philosophie der Kunst* (Frankfurt: Klostermann, 1994), 334.
12. Heidegger, HGR: 69/GA 39:76.
13. Heidegger, HGR: 29/GA 39:29.
14. Heidegger, E: 285/GA 71:328.
15. Heidegger, GA, 52:5.
16. Friedrich Hölderlin, *Essays and Letters* trans. Jeremy Adler and Charlie Louth (London: Penguin, 2009), 290–93/*Sämtliche Werke*, II, ed. Jochen Schmidt (Frankfurt: Deutscher Klassiker Verlag, 1994), 543–45.

17. Friedrich Hölderlin, *Selected Poems and Fragments*, trans. Michael Hamburger (London: Penguin, 1998), 49–50.
18. Heidegger, HGR: 31/GA 39:32.
19. Heidegger, HGR: 114/GA 39:127.
20. Heidegger, HGR: 114/GA 39:127–28.
21. On the language of event, as *Ereignis*, see Krzysztof Ziarek, *Language after Heidegger* (Bloomington: Indiana University Press, 2013), esp. ch. 1.
22. Paul Celan, *Gesammelte Werke*, III (Frankfurt: Suhrkamp, 1986), 195, 197.
23. Friedrich Nietzsche, *Thus Spoke Zarathustra* (London: Penguin, 1969), 168/*Also Sprach Zarathustra* (Leipzig: Kröner, 1930), 162.
24. Meister Eckhart, *Deutsche Predigten und Traktate*, ed. Joesef Quint (Munich: Hanser, 1985), 416.
25. Paul Celan, *Selected Poems and Prose*, trans. John Felsteiner (New York: Norton, 2001), 322–23. In the condensed language of this poem we find allusions to Hölderlin's *Andenken* via Eckhart's Middle High German word *Gehugnis* (v.7), which denotes "memory."
26. Meister Eckhart, *Werke*, I (Frankfurt: Deutscher Klassiker Verlag, 2008), 165.
27. Paul Celan, *Mikrolithen sinds, Steinchen* (Frankfurt: Suhrkamp, 2005), 125.
28. Hölderlin, *Selected Poems and Fragments*, 212–13.
29. Heidegger, HGR: 108/GA 39:119.
30. Heidegger, GA, 6.2:442–43.
31. Heidegger, PLT: 222–23/GA 7: 200–202.
32. Heidegger, CP: 401/GA 65:510.
33. Heidegger, PLT: 215/GA 7:193.
34. Heidegger, PLT: 227/GA 7:206.
35. Heidegger, GA, 55:214.
36. Paul Celan, "Brief an Werner Weber," in *"Fremde Nähe": Celan als Übersetzer*, ed. Axel Gellhaus (Marbach: Schillergesellschaft, 1997), 398.
37. Heidegger, GA 11:20.
38. Celan, *"Fremde Nähe,"* 398–99.
39. Heidegger, GA, 13:219.
40. Hans-Georg Gadamer, *The Relevance of the Beautiful* (Cambridge: Cambridge University Press, 1985), 72/*Gesammelte Werke* 8 (Tübingen: Mohr-Siebeck, 1993), 23–24.
41. Rainer Maria Rilke, *Selected Poems*, trans. Susan Ranson and Marielle Sutherland (Oxford: Oxford University Press, 2011), 82–83.
42. Paul Celan, *Selected Poems and Prose*, 396/ *Gesammelte Werke* III, 186.
43. Theodor Adorno, *Prisms* (Cambridge: MIT Press, 1983), 34/ *Gesammelte Schriften* 20 volumes (Frankfurt: Suhrkamp, 1986), vol. 10 (1), 30.
44. Theodor Adorno, *Negative Dialectics* (New York: Seabury Press, 1979), 365/ *Gesammelte Schriften* 20 volumes (Frankfurt: Suhrkamp, 1986), vol. 6, 358.

45. Paul Celan, *A Voice . . .* , trans. Muska Nagel (Orono, ME: Puckerbush Press, 1998), 82–83.
46. Plato, *Republic*, 607b.
47. Bambach and George, eds., *Philosophers and their Poets*, 27.
48. Ibid., 80.
49. Ibid., 116.
50. Ibid., 177.
51. Ibid., 203.
52. Ibid., 204.

References

Adorno, Theodor. *Gesammelte Schriften*. Vols. 6, 10. Frankfurt: Suhrkamp, 1986.
———. *Negative Dialectics*. New York: Seabury Press, 1979.
———. *Prisms*. Cambridge: MIT Press, 1983.
Celan, Paul. "Brief an Werner Weber." In *"Fremde Nähe": Celan als Übersetzer*, edited by Axel Gellhaus. Marbach: Schillergesellschaft, 1997.
———. *Gesammelte Werke*, III. Frankfurt: Suhrkamp, 1986.
———. *Mikrolithen sinds, Steinchen*. Frankfurt: Suhrkamp, 2005.
———. *Selected Poems and Prose*, trans. John Felsteiner. New York: Norton, 2001.
———. *A Voice . . .* Translated by Muska Nagel. Orono, ME: Puckerbush Press, 1998.
Eckhart, Meister. *Deutsche Predigten und Traktate*. Edited by Josef Quint. Munich: Hanser, 1985.
———. *Werke*, I Frankfurt: Deutscher Klassiker Verlag, 2008.
Gadamer, Hans-Georg. *The Relevance of the Beautiful*. Cambridge: Cambridge University Press, 1985.
———. *Gesammelte Werke* 8. Tübingen: Mohr-Siebeck, 1993.
Heidegger, Martin. *Basic Writings*. New York: Harper Perennial, 2008.
———. *Contributions to Philosophy*. Translated by Richard Rojcewicz and Daniela Vallega-Neu. Bloomington: Indiana University Press, 2012.
———. *Elucidations of Hölderlin's Poetry*. Translated by Keith Hoeller. New York: Humanity Books, 2000.
———. *The Event*. Bloomington: Indiana University Press, 2012.
———. GA 5; *Holzwege*. Frankfurt: Klostermann, 1977.
———. GA 7; *Vörtrage und Aufsätze*. Frankfurt: Klostermann, 2000.
———. GA 8; *Was heisst Denken?* Frankfurt: Klostermann, 2002.
———. GA 11; *Identität und Differenz*. Frankfurt: Klostermann, 2006.
———. GA 13; *Aus der Erfahrung des Denkens*. Frankfurt: Klostermann, 2002.
———. GA 38; *Logik als die Frage nach dem Wesen der Sprache*. Frankfurt: Klostermann, 1998.

---. GA 39; *Hölderlins Hymne "Germanien" und "Der Rhein."* Frankfurt: Klostermann, 1989.

---. GA 52; *Hölderlins Hymne "Andenken."* Frankfurt: Klostermann, 1992.

---. GA 55; *Heraklit.1. Der Anfang des abendländischen Denkens; 2. Logik. Heraklits Lehre des Logos.* Frankfurt: Klostermann, 1994.

---. GA 71; *Das Ereignis.* Frankfurt: Klostermann, 2009.

---. *Hölderlin's Hymns "Germania" and "The Rhine."* Translated by William McNeill and Julia Ireland. Bloomington: Indiana University Press, 2014.

---. *Pathmarks.* Translated by William McNeill. Cambridge: Cambridge University Press, 1998.

---. *Poetry, Language, Thought.* Translated by Albert Hofstadter. New York: Harper and Row, 1971.

Herrmann, Friedrich Wilhelm von. *Heideggers Philosophie der Kunst.* Frankfurt: Klostermann, 1994.

Hölderlin, Friedrich. *Selected Poems and Fragments.* Translated by Michael Hamburger. London: Penguin, 1998.

Nietzsche, Friedrich. *Also Sprach Zarathustra.* Leipzig: Kröner, 1930.

---. *Thus Spoke Zarathustra.* London: Penguin, 1969.

Plato. *Republic.* In *The Collected Dialogues.* New York: Pantheon Books, 1966.

---. *Theatetus.* In *The Collected Dialogues.* New York: Pantheon Books, 1966.

Rilke, Rainer Maria. *Selected Poems.* Translated by Susan Ranson and Marielle Sutherland. Oxford: Oxford University Press, 2011.

Ziarek, Krzysztof. *Language after Heidegger.* Bloomington: Indiana University Press, 2013.

1

On the Poetical Nature of Philosophical Writing

A Controversy over Style between Schiller and Fichte

María del Rosario Acosta López

"Only a matter of style"

On June 24, 1795, Fichte received a letter from Schiller informing him that his essay "Concerning the Spirit and the Letter within Philosophy in a Series of Letters [*Über Geist und Buchstabe in der Philosophie in einer Reihe von Briefen*]" had been rejected for publication in *Die Horen*.[1] *Die Horen* was a monthly journal for literary and philosophical writings that Schiller had co-founded with the publisher Cotta in Tübingen a few months earlier. Explaining the reasons behind his decision, Schiller wrote in his letter:

> I was hoping to enrich the philosophical section of the journal with your essay on spirit and letter, and the subject that you chose led me to expect a piece of work that would be understandable and interesting to a general audience. What have I received instead, and what do you expect me to present to the public? Old material that does not even seem entirely finished to me, even in the antiquated epistolary style I had already chosen, and all of this according to such an eccentric plan that it is impossible to bring the parts of your essay together into a

whole. I regret to say this but as it stands I am satisfied with neither how it is decked out nor with the content, and I find precision and clarity lacking in this essay, two qualities that usually characterize your work.[2]

If one follows the correspondence that resulted from this initial communication, it becomes clear that for Fichte the reasons behind this harsh rejection came—to say the least—entirely as a surprise. At the time both authors were already aware of their significant philosophical differences. This had not become yet an obstacle for their intellectual exchange. Quite the opposite, Schiller had very recently published an article by Fichte in *Die Horen*, "On Stimulating and Increasing the Pure Interest in Truth [*Über Belebung und Erhöhung des reinen Interesses an Wahrheit*]," which contained a critical response to some of Schiller's latest philosophical reflections. Schiller's only reaction at the time had been to suggest a few changes in the paper's "style." After Fichte insisted that the article be published in its original version, the argument had not gone any further.[3]

Now, in this following essay, there were again indications of a confrontation between Fichte and Schiller's philosophical project. As the former stated in the paper he submitted, the idea of "raising human beings towards the dignity of freedom and, along with it, towards freedom itself by means of aesthetic education, falls into a vicious circle."[4] Fichte was most certainly referring to Schiller's *Letters on the Aesthetic Education of Humanity*, which had just appeared in three parts in *Die Horen*.[5] And indeed, as Schiller himself would explicitly recognize, there is a kind of unavoidable circularity surrounding the project of an "aesthetic education towards freedom." However, such a circularity was for Schiller the only way to achieve an "aesthetic overcoming of duty."[6] If the purpose, as it appeared in the *Aesthetic Letters* (but also in previous essays such as "On Grace and Dignity," which Fichte might also have had in mind when developing his criticisms), is to avoid the risk of turning freedom into a violent subordination of sensibility to reason (something that, according to Schiller, may have been in the letter, but not necessarily in the "spirit" of Kantian practical philosophy), the highest good must be not only moral *but also* aesthetic.[7] To go beyond mere moral duty, the aesthetic dimension of our humanity must serve both as means *and* as end. There is indeed circularity in such a way of arguing, but a necessary one, according to Schiller, since the aesthetic character is both a condition for and the final result of a truly moral character.[8]

These philosophical differences were therefore part of an ongoing discussion between Fichte and Schiller. One could even say that they were part of an ongoing discussion within Schiller's own project, which was in fact also permanently under revision.⁹ Moreover, Fichte's objections and reflections were essential for Schiller, as he recognized in various occasions throughout the *Aesthetic Letters*. Thus, there were no motives to think that such a philosophical disagreement would be the cause for Schiller's rejection of Fichte's paper. Fichte had no way to understand the decision other than as a matter of a difference in *style*. The question was for Fichte how to interpret Schiller's invitation in the "Announcement of *Die Horen*" to "liberate philosophy from its scholastic forms" and to present it "in a more attractive, or at least in an easier wrapping [*einfacher Hülle*], to try to render it understandable for the common sense."¹⁰ This is the context of his initial response to Schiller. Fichte writes:

> This is not the first time that I discovered that we have very different principles concerning the popular philosophical presentation. I already saw it from your own philosophical writings. . . . your popularity is established by your overflowing use of images, which you employ nearly everywhere *in place* of the abstract concept. My popularity is particularly established by the approach [*Gang*] that I take—which misled you into too quickly considering my first letter to be shallow and superficial. . . . In my case, the image does not take the *place of* the concept, but rather *precedes* or *follows* it, as a simile [*Gleichniß*]. . . . If I am not mistaken, all ancient and modern authors who are famous for their excellent presentation have considered it as I endeavor to. But your kind is completely novel. . . . You bind the imagination, which can only be free, and wish to compel it to think. That it cannot do.¹¹

Instead of supplementing abstract concepts with helpful similes, Schiller's writings substitute the former with the latter. He uses *images in the place of*, and not only in addition to, concepts. In doing so, Fichte argues, he forces imagination to *think*, something imagination cannot do. These are the accusations Fichte uses to respond to Schiller's criticisms. Both are clearly for Fichte erroneous ways of making philosophy accessible to a wider audience. Both are also direct responses to some of Schiller's statements in his first letter:

> We must have very different conceptions of what constitutes an appropriate presentation, since I must confess that I am not at all pleased with yours. Above all, I expect a consistent tone from a good presentation, and, if it is to have aesthetic value, *reciprocal action* [*Wechselwirkung*] between imagery and concept, not *alternation* between the two, as is often the case in your letters.[12]

For Schiller, the issue at hand is not a *substitution* of concepts with images, as Fichte suggests in his reply. As he will also insist in his next letter to Fichte, the ideal is rather to be able "to extend what I presented to the understanding [by means of a concept] to the imagination as well [by means of an image]" without losing sight of "the *strictest connection* [*strengster Verbindung*]" between one and the other.[13] Such a connection is expressed by Schiller in terms of a "reciprocal action" in *opposition* to what Schiller describes as a *mere alternation* between images and concepts in Fichte's text.

For anyone relatively familiar with Fichte's philosophical writings, Schiller's description of the problem does not come as a purely *stylistic* one. Schiller is here purposely making use of his opponent's tools: "reciprocal action" is indeed a concept taken from Fichte's *Wissenschaftslehre*, and therefore refers not only to a "style" of writing but also to the actual *contents* of Fichte's philosophy. What seems to be a disagreement on the most adequate "style [*Manier*]" for a "philosophical exposition" thus reveals a much deeper philosophical divergence.[14] In what follows, I will briefly discuss the context of this disagreement, before returning to Schiller's discussion with Fichte on the form of a philosophical style of writing. My intention is at least twofold: first, I want to shed light on the relationship between this debate on style and Schiller's views on the relationship between aesthetics and practical philosophy. This will allow me to move to my second and main goal, namely, to show in more depth all that is at stake for Schiller in a discussion on philosophical modes of writing. I will have to leave aside Fichte's side of the debate, and the consequences it will have for his development of aesthetics as part of his philosophical project.[15]

Reciprocal Action and Schiller's Notion of Aesthetic Freedom

Fichte introduces the concept of *reciprocal action* in the second part of his 1794 *Foundation of the entire Wissenschaftslehre*. According to Fichte, the drive to sensibility is essential for helping us understand the limits of our rational capacities. A reciprocal action between sensibility and reason therefore becomes a necessary intermediate stage toward the full development of our moral freedom. In this stage, sensibility is subjugated to reason, but reason must also be subjected to sensibility. A form of "reciprocity" is thus instituted between them.[16] However, this intermediary stage must ultimately be overcome by a unique and essential drive determined exclusively by rational precepts: the drive to self-activity. "The highest good," Fichte writes in his "Lectures Concerning the Scholar's Vocation [*Einige Vorlesungen über die Bestimmung des Gelehrten*]," also from 1794, "is the complete accordance of a rational being with himself."[17] "Man's final end," Fichte continues, "is to subordinate to himself all that is irrational, to master it freely and according to his own laws."[18] Hence, reason must entirely subsume sensibility if humanity is to achieve its vocation. This is, for Fichte, an end that is as unattainable as it is necessary. The overcoming of sensibility by reason must therefore be the ultimate guide for our determination as human beings.

The concept of aesthetic education in the *Aesthetic Letters* is based mainly on Schiller's discomfort with this reading of morality and freedom, which understands them both exclusively in terms of a negation and an overcoming of sensibility. According to Schiller, this interpretation is as present in Kant as it is in Fichte (at least, as mentioned above, in the "letter" and not necessarily in the "spirit" of their practical philosophy).[19] Fichte's concept of reciprocal action, no longer taken only as an intermediary stage, but also, and simultaneously, as an end in itself, becomes for Schiller the point of departure for an alternative interpretation of the best possible state for humankind. Thus, in critical distance to what he describes at the beginning of the *Aesthetic Letters* as the risks of a too "technical" and "analytical" mode of procedure in philosophy,[20] he argues in the thirteenth letter:

> Once one postulates a primary, and therefore necessary, antagonism between these two drives [sensibility and reason], there is of course no other means of maintaining unity in us than by unconditionally *subordinating* the sensuous drive to the rational. From this, however, only uniformity can result, never harmony, and we go forever being divided. Subordination there must, of course, be; but it must be *reciprocal*. . . . Both principles are therefore at once subordinated to each other and coordinated with each other, that is to say, they stand in reciprocal relation

[*Wechselwirkung*] to one another (This concept of reciprocal action and its fundamental importance, is admirably set forth in Fichte's *Fundaments of the Theory of Knowledge*; Leipzig, 1794).[21]

Schiller uses the concept of *reciprocal action* or *reciprocal relation* as a tribute to Fichte, and he connects it to Fichte's ideas on culture and education.[22] The reference to *reciprocal action* as a mode of exposition in his letter to Fichte in June, 1795 is best understood within this context. In a dispute on style and adequate "form" or "clothing" (*Einkleidung*) for a philosophical discourse, Schiller introduces a concept explicitly related for both authors to a philosophical and anthropological debate regarding the ultimate goal or ideal for humanity. For both, the issue at stake is the fulfillment of freedom, but in Fichte's case this is a freedom understood exclusively in relation to reason,[23] whereas for Schiller the question is related to what he describes in the *Aesthetic Letters* as an "aesthetic freedom," namely, a fragile balance resulting from a reciprocal action between our sensuous and our rational drives.[24]

Schiller had already begun to develop his critique of a concept of freedom understood exclusively as rational autonomy in his 1793 essay "On Grace and Dignity [*Über Anmuth und Würde*]." It is important to understand how Schiller describes his disagreement with Kant in this essay, since this is also the point of departure for his criticisms of Fichte. It is not exactly against moral freedom that Schiller orients his criticisms, but rather against what he considers to be a too narrow understanding of morality. He writes in his essay:

> By the fact that nature has made of human being a being both at once rational and sensuous . . . it has prescribed to its humanity . . . not to sacrifice the sensuous being, were it in the most pure manifestations of the divine part; and never to found the triumph of one over the oppression and the ruin of the other. It is only when as human beings we gather, so to speak, our entire humanity together, and *our way of thinking in morals becomes the result of the united action of the two principles*, when morality has become to us a second nature, it is then only that it is *secure*; for, as far as the mind and the duty are obliged to employ violence, it is necessary that the instinct shall have force to resist them.[25]

To Schiller, true moral freedom is aesthetic freedom, that is, one in which a reciprocal action between both aspects of human nature has been achieved. Schiller locates such an ideal, however, in the very notion of morality. What is thus at stake for Schiller is therefore the very conception of such a notion of morality: one in which it is not only the rational drive that has achieved its full development, but also, and precisely thanks to, the full development of the sensuous drive: "The activity of the one [drive] both gives rise to, and sets limits to, the activity of the other . . . [in such a way that] each in itself achieves its highest manifestation precisely by reason of the other being active."[26] Accordance and harmony can only be conceived in terms of a balance or equilibrium, and not as a victory of one drive over the other; since such a victory, Schiller writes, will always be just of one of the forces at play.[27]

The odd thing, however, at least for what concerns us here, is that in both "On Grace and Dignity" and his *Aesthetic Letters*, Schiller seems to closely relate this philosophical debate on the nature of freedom to the discussion about "philosophical style." A too technical notion of freedom—or freedom presented in a "too technical form"—appears in his writings tied together with a *merely moral,* not yet aesthetic, understanding of freedom. Furthermore, "*technical*" in this context does not only qualify the style of the discourse but also the *style of philosophical thinking*. The mode we choose for thinking philosophically, Schiller seems to suggest, bears simultaneously on the process through which we reason and the conclusions that we draw. The divisions resulting from a certain form or style of writing are not only *figuratively* but also *literally* connected to a dual philosophical conception of human nature and to a too "technical" (and hence narrow) idea of human freedom. This is what Schiller seems to have in mind when he describes what happens to the content of one's thought once it must undergo the subjection of a philosophical *analytical* (i.e., merely technical) method:

> Like the analytical chemist, the philosopher can only discover how things are combined by analyzing them, only lay bare the workings of spontaneous nature by subjecting them to the torment of philosophy's own techniques. In order to lay hold of the fleeting phenomenon, the philosopher must first bind it in the fetters of rule, tear its fair body to pieces by reducing it to concepts, and preserve its living spirit in a sorry skeleton of words.[28]

Moreover, under the influence of such a philosophical technical style, Schiller argues, it is easy to *forget* that "human nature forms a whole more united in reality than is permitted to the philosopher, who can only analyze, to allow it to appear."[29] The conception of freedom that results from such an operation has been dissected and disembodied, and one must remember this is the case, if one does not want to get lost in the "letter" and forget the "spirit" of one's own philosophy. This is also the reason why, he argues, "in the account of the analytical thinker," "natural feeling cannot find itself again in such an image" and "truth should appear as paradox."[30] An analytic style of philosophical thinking runs the risk of forgetting that the technical distinctions introduced by this style of writing (and of thinking) do not correspond entirely with the subject matter, but are only the result of a mode of analysis.

Hence, when Schiller writes to Fichte about a reciprocal action between image and concept he is not only speaking about style, but also, and even more so, about the philosophical consequences of a style of writing that dissects truth and tears it to pieces with its distinctions. The analytical procedure used in certain forms of philosophizing—and more specifically, of writing philosophy—is contradictory in itself, since it forgets the difference it seems to be grounded on: the alleged difference between form and content, style and truth. In this difference, however, lies not only the core of the argument between Schiller and Fichte, but also the root of an entire tradition of criticism of Schiller's philosophy (one that, in my opinion, should not be taken lightly).[31] Criticisms of Schiller such as those formulated by Paul de Man, among others, develop what Fichte's original accusation would have initially suggested (thus turning Schiller's argument about the consequences of a style of writing against him): that through a certain form or method in his style, Schiller would have ultimately accomplished a mere indoctrination of reason through the senses, therefore letting poetic form take the place of philosophical content and replacing the unpresentable and paradoxical character of reason with an image much more adequate to the sensible. As De Man puts it in his defense of Kant's *Critique of Judgment* against Schiller's interpretation, Schiller would have (dangerously) sought to reunite what reason cautiously and for practical reasons tried to separate.[32] This is the consequence moreover, according to De Man, of the fact that Schiller was never able to elevate his own discourse to a philosophical one: "It is the difference between a philosopher and Schiller, who is not a philosopher. The type of understanding needed for Schiller is *common understanding*. The kind of understanding you need for philosophers is . . . of a different nature."[33]

The question deserves some attention: Does Schiller ultimately aim, as De Man suggests, to "resolve" dialectically, to "close" and consequently to "aestheticize" what Kant—and perhaps also Fichte—very cautiously tried to leave open and unresolved? And is this connected to the fact that, by giving so much importance to the connection between a poetical and a philosophical style of writing, Schiller ultimately had to give up the latter for the sake of the former? Fichte's accusations, whose spirit is very much behind De Man's reading, inaugurate a reading of Schiller that leads to the charge of an "aestheticization" of truth and, eventually, an "aestheticization" of politics in Schiller's philosophical writings. And this is very much connected to a prejudice about what constitutes a true and responsible mode of philosophical thinking; and whether this requires us to strip truth of its aesthetic obscurity in order to save it from an ultimately dangerous confusion.

I do not have the space here to explore all the consequences of these criticisms, nor to go through all the steps that one needs to take to respond to them.[34] I think, however, that paying attention to what Schiller says about style can also be a first step toward a more appropriate response to such a reading of his work. Perhaps, then, it would be helpful to return to Schiller's nuanced response to this question. This might help at least to clarify that some of these criticisms, in particular those coming directly from Fichte's accusations, presuppose a series of dichotomies and polarities that Schiller was trying to question. And this questioning takes place in Schiller's work not only in thought but precisely in the *exercise of another kind of writing*; and with it, of another *style of philosophizing*.

The Role of Imagination in Philosophical Discourse: The *darstellende Schriftsteller*

What then is the justification for moving from stylistic to philosophical matters, from a discussion about the relationship between image and concepts to the relationship between our sensuous and rational drives in the actualization of our freedom? In his letters to Fichte, Schiller starts to make clear what will later become a much more carefully developed claim. Indeed, the stylistic issue at stake is connected to an aesthetic one, namely, the *experience* that whoever writes wishes to arouse in the reader. To appeal to reciprocal action between images and concepts is not, in this sense, entirely detached from the relationship between drives or faculties that even a philosophical exposition should provoke in its reader. Schiller writes:

> My continual tendency, aside from the inquiry itself, is to employ the ensemble of mental forces [*Gemüthskräfte*] and to the extent that it is possible to have an effect on all of them. I thus do not wish merely to make my thoughts clear to others, but at the same time to transmit my entire soul to them, and to influence both their sensuous and spiritual forces.[35]

Schiller recognizes that a writer whose concerns are only centered on a strictly logical presentation of the argument can certainly gain clarity of exposition, but he or she should know that instead of exploring all the possibilities available to a truly philosophical mind, they are acting exclusively as an "employed scholar [*Brotgelehrte*]." This is an expression Schiller uses in his *Antrittsvorlesung* of 1789 at the university in Jena to refer critically to the kind of "professional" or "bureaucrat" of philosophy who sticks strictly to doing the "job" he or she is being paid to do. Schiller writes:

> In the same cautious way in which the "employed scholar" separates their science from the rest, the philosophical mind tries to broaden their field of work in order to relate it to others. While an employed scholar separates, a philosophical spirit unites. Soon the latter is convinced that in the field of understanding, as in the world of senses, everything is interrelated, and their instinct—eagerly seeking accordance—will not be satisfied with fragments. . . . The philosophical spirit reaches higher instances by means of its always new and more beautiful intellectual forms, while the employed scholar (within the eternal inactivity of spirit) protects the sterile monotony of their scholastic concepts.[36]

A true philosophical spirit "loves truth more than their own philosophical system."[37] It can thus search for higher instances than those merely appropriate for a scientific and logical analysis of concepts, without, however, sacrificing the clarity gained by the latter. And by encountering increasingly "beautiful intellectual forms," it can create a presentation that allows truth to achieve its greatest and most appropriate expression. This is what Schiller has in mind when he insists in his letters to Fichte on the "aesthetic value" of philosophical exposition.[38] It has to be possible to find a "truly beautiful way of writing" where thought and intuition, understanding and imagination, appear in need of each other as they reciprocally strengthen and stimulate one another. Beauty of style is not a simple "beautiful appearance," a mere "clothing" that leaves contents untouched. When images are the "graceful clothing" of concepts, they give form to spirit in ways that the mere use of understanding cannot. *Mere understanding,* Schiller would reply borrowing Fichte's own words, *cannot do such a thing.*

These are all ideas that Schiller will thoroughly explain in his essay "On the Necessary Limitations in the Use of Beautiful Forms [*Über die notwendigen Grenzen beim Gebrauch Schönen Formen*]," an essay he wrote precisely in response to his controversial issue with Fichte.[39] A figure like that of the "employed scholar" seems this time to be personified by Fichte himself. He is (tacitly) referred to in the essay as the kind of narrow-minded, dogmatic thinker that can only "understand by differentiating," and who can therefore, as a reader, become at the most a rather "vulgar critic [*gemeine Beurtheiler*]."[40] That means, according to Schiller, a kind of thinker and writer incapable of appreciating "the triumph of presentation [*Darstellung*]," namely, the capacity to produce in writing a "harmonious unity where the parts are blended in a pure entirety."[41] Let us briefly pause in the first pages of this essay, before proceeding to the figure that should interest us the most in the context of this paper: the *darstellende Schriftsteller* (another name for what Schiller had described in his earlier essays as the "truly philosophical spirit," this time, however, in explicit relation to a certain "style of philosophical writing").

The essay on the use of beautiful forms begins with a description of what, according to Schiller, are the three most common types of philosophical exposition: the *merely* scientific, the popular, and the sensuous or aesthetic.[42] The scientific presentation seeks to show to the understanding, and only to the understanding, the strict logic that governs the relation among concepts in a philosophical argument. Thus, it must if necessary "knock down the effort of imagination" and follow exclusively the needs of the understanding.[43] Due to the restrictions forced upon imagination, these presentations often appear as "mechanical works," their causal and systematic connections only "imparting an *artificial* life to the whole."[44] Schiller relates this kind of exposition to the figure of the "instructor [*der Lehrer*]," tacitly referring to Fichte's own terms in his "Lectures Concerning the Scholar's Vocation." The instructor, Schiller writes, is solely interested in "indoctrinating" his audience, and hence produces at most a "solid but dogmatic address."[45] He "has only in view in his lecture the object of which he is treating," and is not in the least concerned with his listener's state of mind, nor, in this sense, with using a *form* of discourse that may correspond to or evoke any particular state of mind.[46] He is entitled to do so, Schiller continues, as far as he can presuppose an eagerness in his listeners and a patient ability on their part to apprehend through fragments what only later will be united in a systematic whole. The instructor, Schiller explains, "gives us a tree with its roots, though with the condition that we wait patiently for it to blossom and bear fruit."[47] The fullest expression of a concept does not take place, therefore, in the act of communication, but rather relies on a process that must go beyond discourse and take definitive form *after* and not *in* its exposition.

Unlike the instructor's address, both the popular and the aesthetic style of writing give a more predominant role to imagination. However, it is clear that Schiller is not at ease with either of these two modes of exposition. While the popular address uses images only *in the place of* concepts (and here one should recall Fichte's accusations against Schiller as stated above), and hence limits imagination to what Schiller describes as its merely *reproductive* mode, the sensuous or aesthetic presentation offers too quickly an image of the whole, without taking understanding and its contents into consideration.[48] To achieve its goal it must therefore strip the discourse of its universal value. While it offers "a complete picture, an entirety of conditions, an individual" precisely there where otherwise one would only have abstract determinations, it nonetheless also "only confines to a single individual and a single case what ought to be understood of a whole sphere."[49] Hence, its final results are exactly the opposite of those achieved by the instructor. It is "satisfied with gathering its flowers and fruits, but the tree that bore them does not become our property, and once the flowers are faded and the fruit is consumed our riches depart."[50]

In opposition to all these three modes of exposition, Schiller moves on in his essay to what he will describe as a "truly beautiful style of writing." Without giving up the rigor and clarity of exposition proper to the scientific style, this style can make a full use of imagination's productive and "self-creating power," achieving thereby a perfect balance between imagination and understanding.[51] In this form or style lies the *possibility of the highest philosophical discourse*, the "highest possible level of presentation [*Darstellung*]" that Schiller connects to the figure of the *darstellende Schriftsteller*.[52]

The *darstellende Schriftsteller* seeks to "present," "exhibit," and "stage" a *complete image* of a concept (these words all relate to what "Darstellung" means in Schiller's works).[53] This idea of a *sensible presentation* (*Darstellung*) of an otherwise abstract and empty concept evokes Kant's use of the term in both his first and third *Critiques*. Schiller probably had in mind in particular the symbolic sensible exhibition (*hypotyposis*) of a concept that Kant presents in section §59 of the *Critique of Judgment*. However, it is very clear in these passages that, for Kant, an intuitive exhibition of the concept can only render *analogically*, and hence exclusively through its *form*, the contents of the concept it is attempting to present or symbolize.[54] The contents remain therefore entirely alien to their sensible form, since strictly speaking they must remain unpresentable. For Schiller, on the contrary, the possibility of a complete and full expression in an image of a concept is perhaps the *most complete form of the concept itself*, inseparable and entirely interdependent from the sensible matter that gives it its meaning and its fullest expression. To the *darstellende* writer, therefore, style is not only a *means* to better expose an already given content. Writing, or, better yet, a truly beautiful style of writing, becomes rather the place where the contents, by being given their most appropriate form, become entirely what they can be and reach their fullest and most meaningful expression.[55]

At the beginning of his essay, Schiller writes: "Something sensuous lies always and ultimately at the ground of our thought."[56] The type of writing associated with what Schiller presents as the *darstellende Schriftsteller* allows one to grasp fully the meaning of such a statement. A writer who achieves such a form of exposition, does not

> confine the effects of their writing to the communication of *dead ideas* [as it happens with mechanical, abstract and strictly logical expositions]; he [or she] rather grasps the living object with a living energy, and seizes at once the entirety of our humanity—our understanding, our heart, and our will.[57]

Hence, the ultimate goal does not force us to renounce a rigorous philosophical exposition. In a parallel move to what Schiller had done before in relation to Kantian morality, namely, seeking not to "lessen" but rather to broaden Kant's notions of morality and freedom, Schiller now explains how, to allow the imagination to take such an important role in philosophical exposition, the *darstellende Schriftsteller* must also have completely taken in the principles of the understanding.

> It is certain that it is necessary to be quite the master of a truth to abandon without danger the form in which it was originally found; a great strength of understanding is required not to lose sight of your object while giving free play to the imagination.... The writer who *besides* [transmitting their knowledge under a scholastic form] is in a condition to communicate it to

me in a beautiful form shows . . . that they *have assimilated it into their nature* and are able therefore to pass it on into their productions and into their acts.⁵⁸

Only then will the concepts formed by the conjunction of the understanding and imagination be the product of a spontaneous performance that is only made possible by having first secured as their source a certain character or temperament, a sort of "second nature" that Schiller in many of his writings associates with a "beautiful" or "aesthetic" character.

In one of his letters, Fichte suggests that the kind of method or mode of writing that Schiller demands, and of which Schiller's own writings are a very good example, ultimately exerts the worst kind of violence on imagination. Let's recall the exact phrase in Fichte's first letter to Schiller: "You bind the imagination, which can only be free, and wish to compel it to think. That it cannot do."⁵⁹ Schiller's response to this critique appears explicitly now in his essay on the use of beautiful forms, and precisely in relation to his description of the *darstellende Schriftsteller*. If only few of us are "simply capable of thinking, it is infinitely more rare to meet any who can think in the *mode of presentation [darstellend denken]*"—that is, in the mode of *imaginative* thinking.⁶⁰ This is why, he continues, sooner or later the *darstellende Schriftsteller* has to face a certain "narrow minded" critic who, unable to carry out the double task his or her writings require, will have to

> start out by translating if they want to understand—as when pure understanding, left to itself and deprived of every faculty of presentation, must first transpose and set apart in its own language beauty and harmony, either in nature or in art, the same as the pupil who needs to spell before they can read.⁶¹

These comments are implicit references to Fichte's first letter, where he writes:

> I believe this [the fact that imagination is compelled to think] explains the tedious effort that your philosophical writings occasion in me, and which they have occasioned in others. In the first place, I must translate everything of yours before I can understand it; and so it goes with others, too. . . . Just as little am I speaking of your philosophical thoroughness, and your profundity, which I admire; *I am only speaking about your style.*⁶²

These passages bring us back to the heart of the problem. It could very well be that Fichte never truly understood that the disagreement with Schiller was not "only a matter of style." Fichte seems to remain convinced that by seeking in the wrong way a more popular and accessible style, Schiller risks producing in his audience the opposite effect: his writings may not communicate as clearly as he thinks the contents that are therefore more suited to a more rigorous—and perhaps less charming—philosophical style. To Schiller, however, the problem lies elsewhere: "If principles were the only thing standing between us I would try with all my might to have you take my side or to take yours; but we *experience* [*empfinden*] differently, we are indeed highly different natures, and against this I do not know what to advise."[63]

"We *experience* differently," Schiller writes; "we *think* differently," "we are highly different natures." If thinking and sensuous experience (*Empfindung*) don't belong to completely different spheres of discourse; and if a certain form of exposition is not only a means to transfer previously attained results but rather the place where thinking can properly unfold, then to Schiller the argument about style evokes a much deeper issue than Fichte seems to be willing to acknowledge. More than a "new style," as Fichte suggests, Schiller was proposing a *new way of philosophizing*. His insistence on the importance of sensibility in the formation of concepts, and hence, imagination's activity in conceptual and philosophical thought, goes together with a new account of how philosophy should understand itself.

Imagination does not have to be suppressed nor entirely controlled by the understanding since there is a third kind of relationship between images and concepts: a balanced reciprocal action that simultaneously limits and fosters the potentialities lying at the ground of each one of these instances of thought. Such an operation can neither exclusively nor completely take place in purely mental and conceptual activity. Thought and discourse are necessary and interdependent moments. Thought's forms are not complete until expressed, presented in, and given shape by, writing. Exposition is an essential moment of thought, and not only the mere re-presentation of something that has been previously clearly understood.

On the opposite side of this spectrum, there is Fichte. "Philosophy," Fichte writes to Schiller, "originally has no letter, but rather is pure spirit."[64] Hence, the question of exposition in philosophy is *only a matter of style,* since style has no essential role in the formation of philosophical concepts. Fichte is indeed right: when reading Schiller's essays, he is compelled to translate the images *into* concepts. This is only because he does not understand, as Schiller will argue, that concepts are already, and in a certain way, one with images; and thus translation, understood as an exercise of "distillation," destroys what Schiller's writing treats as a living subject matter. "An eloquent writer," Schiller writes, "knows how to extract the most splendid order from the very center of anarchy, and he [or she] succeeds in erecting a solid structure on a constantly moving ground, on the very torrent of imagination."[65] To move constantly on unsteady grounds, and to build over and over again on what never stops flowing, is essential to the challenge of philosophizing. This is what it means, for Schiller, that "something sensuous always lies at the ground of thought."[66] Only such a "ground" can turn writing, the "letter" of philosophy, into something alive, and hence "bring scientific knowledge back again to the state of a living intuition."[67]

A philosopher must consequently learn to communicate with the kind of "poetic energy [*Dichtungskraft*]" Schiller writes about in his *Aesthetic Letters*. Through her writing and force of expression, the philosopher, as is the case with the poet, can use her imagination productively to "intercept the rays of truth's triumphant light" even before they "can penetrate the recesses of the human heart."[68] This is the reason why expressive philosophers, as it often happens also to great artists, always have to face a certain amount of "vulgar criticism"—a reception of their work that in the absence of "the feeling for harmony, only runs after details, and even in the Basilica of St. Peter attends exclusively to the pillars on which the ethereal edifice reposes."[69] That is why the philosopher, like the artist, should be able to rise above her time's taste and judgment—"Work for your contemporaries, but create what they need, not what they praise."[70] She should be able to leave the "sphere of the actual" and raise to the sphere of *appearance,* where truth comes to light in all its might: "not only thought [*Gedanke*] can pay it [truth] homage, but sense, too, can lay loving hold on its appearance."[71]

In the final and revised version of "On the Spirit and the Letter in Philosophy,"[72] Fichte writes: "some coarse observers are tempted to accredit the driving force, that *only the spirit possesses*, to the body's form and structure."[73] To Schiller, however—and this is clear from his first writings for the medical academy—it is the body's driving force that brings spirit entirely and completely into activity. A writer must revive over and over again the same dilemmas of the poet: the search for appropriate, impossible, images (body) that can give a definitive drive and force to thought (spirit). There is no one better fit than Schiller to illustrate this everlasting search for the difficult balance between philosophy and aesthetic force, between the necessary clarity of concepts and the strength of images. The words Schiller uses in his works do not only describe the results of a previous experience of reflection: they *are* the experience itself, an experience that is recreated and put into movement through its own writing.

The contents of his philosophical project go by analogy in this same direction (even though I did not have the space here to explain this in detail). By insisting on a reciprocal action between reason and sensibility, on the tension between these two drives, Schiller is inserting in the heart of human action the elements of contingency, finitude, and a permanent and necessary dialogue with a world that is never entirely in our power to control.[74] This relationship and its effects are also present in the discussion on philosophical style. This discussion reflects on philosophy itself, inviting us to understand the boundaries of thought, and the very rich possibilities that come along the recognition of these boundaries.

Notes

The present version of this paper is a revised version of an article originally published as part of a special issue on Friedrich Schiller, edited by Laura Anna Macor for *Philosophical Readings* (cf. volume 5 [2013], 172–93). I would like to thank Kevin Thompson and Rachel Zuckert for inviting me to discuss this paper in the context of Chicago's 2015 meeting of the German Philosophy Consortium. The comments and questions that came up during that session were essential for my revision and rewriting of this paper. I would also like to thank Christopher Eagle for being such a patient reader of several versions of this paper, and for helping me to produce a more refined account of my philosophical ideas as well as a better translation of this text into English. I also want to thank Colin McQuillan for copyediting the final version of this paper for publication in this volume.

1. This was the first version Fichte wrote of this work. It was written in the epistolary genre and was originally composed of three letters (cf. J. G. Fichte, *Gesamtausgabe der Bayerischen Akademie der Wissenschaften* [Stuttgart, 1962]. From now on GA followed by the volume, issue and pages. In this case: cf. GA I/6, 333–61.

2. Letter from Schiller to Fichte, June 24, 1795, Turner's translation in the present volume, p. 49 (cf. GA III/2, 334).

3. Cf. Fichte GA III/2, 227.

4. Fichte GA I/6, 348; my translation.

5. Letters 1 to 9 appeared in January, Letters 10 to 16 in February, and Letters 17 to 27 in June 1795, *Die Horen* Volume 2. The *Aesthetic Letters* were then published again in a new and revised edition in Volume 3 of *Kleinere prosaische Schriften* (Crucious: Leipzig, 1801), 44–309.

6. "eine ästhetisches Übertreffen der Pflicht," cf. F. Schiller, "Letters on the Aesthetic Education of Man," trans. Wilkinson and Willoughby and repr. in Schiller, *Essays*, ed. Walter Hinderer and Daniel Dahlstrom (New York: Continuum), 86–178. From now on LAE, followed by the letter's number and then the translation's page. For the present quote: LAE XXIII, 155. Wilkinson and Willoughby translate *übertreffen* as "transcending"; I prefer "overcoming."

7. Cf. F. Schiller, LAE XIII, 122.

8. I will examine much more closely Schiller's proposal later in this paper. For my attempt at a more in-depth analysis of the idea of an "aesthetic overcoming of duty," cf. M. R. Acosta, "¿Una superación estética del deber? La crítica de Schiller a Kant," *Episteme N.S.* 28, no. 2 (2008): 3–24; and Laura Macor, "Schiller on Emotions. Problems of (In)Consistency in His Ethics," in *Aesthetic Reason and Imaginative Freedom: Friedrich Schiller and Philosophy*, ed. M. R. Acosta and J. Powell (Albany: State University of New York Press, 2018), 23–37.

9. As a matter of fact, as it was also the case with Fichte's *Wissenschaftslehre*, Schiller's proposal of an aesthetic education was also an ongoing project of which the *Aesthetic Letters* were only a moment. A more accurate approach to his proposal would have to take into account further developments of the argument in Schiller's later essays, particularly those concerning the sublime. I have tried to argue this elsewhere. Cf. M. R. Acosta, "Making Other People's Feelings Our Own: From the Aesthetic to the Political in Schiller's Aesthetic Letters," in *Who Is This Schiller Now?*, ed. J. High, N. Martin, and N. Oellers (London/New York: Camden House, 2014), 187–203.

10. Cf. "Ankündigung der Horen," in Friedrich Schiller, *Werke in Drei Bänden, Band II* (Darmstadt: Wissenschaftliche Buchgesselschaft, 1984): 667–68.

11. Letter from Fichte to Schiller, June 27, 1795, Turner's translation in the present volume, slightly modified, cf. p. 53 (cf. GA III/2, 338–39).

12. Letter from Schiller to Fichte, June 24, 1795, Turner's translation in the present volume, slightly modified, cf. p. 50 (cf. GA III/2, 334–35; my emphasis).

13. Letter from Schiller to Fichte, August 3, 1795, Turner's translation in the present volume, cf. p. 56 (cf. GA III/2, 361).

14. Cf. Letter from Schiller to Fichte, August 3, 1795, Turner's translation in the present volume, cf. p. 56 (cf. GA III/2: 360).

15. Whether aesthetics occupies an important role for Fichte is also a matter of discussion among the interpreters. A rigorous approach to Fichte's side on this matter, and how his debate with Schiller would have led to a development of an aesthetical proposal as part of his own philosophical project, can be seen in Manuel Ramos and Faustino Oncina's introductory study to J. G. Fichte, *Filosofía y estética. La polémica con F. Schiller* (Valencia: Universidad de Valencia, 1998), 13–102. Their edition includes the translation into Spanish of Fichte and Schiller's correspondence on this matter, along with some of what, according to the editors, are Fichte's main essays on aesthetics. This book has been very helpful for my own approach to the

subject, and my dissatisfaction with the absence of a clearer account of Schiller's side of the debate is what actually led me to write this paper in the first place. For another very insightful account of the role of imagination in Fichte's aesthetics, see Elizabeth Millán Brusslan, "Poetry and Imagination in Fichte and the Early German Romantics, a Reassessment," in *The Imagination in German Idealism and Romanticism*, ed. Gerad Gentry and Konstantin Pollock (Cambridge: Cambridge University Press, forthcoming).

16. Cf., for example, the second part of *Grundlage der gesamten Wissenschafstlehre* (*Grundlage des theoretischen Wissens*), at the end of the "Deduktion der Vorstellung," in J. G. Fichte, *Sämtliche Werke*, ed. I. H. Fichte (Berlin: Veit, 1845/1846), I 239.

17. J. G. Fichte in *Early Philosophical Writings*, ed. and trans. D. Breazeale (Ithaca: Cornell University Press, 1988), 152.

18. Ibid., 151.

19. Cf. F. Schiller, LAE XIII, 122.

20. F. Schiller, LAE I.

21. F. Schiller, LAE XIII, 121, translation slightly modified to avoid the use of "man" as referring to humankind in the English version.

22. Cf. again here Fichte's "Lectures Concerning the Scholar's Vocation."

23. Cf. Fichte, *Early Philosophical Writings*, 171ff.

24. Cf. F. Schiller, LAE XX, 146.

25. F. Schiller "On Grace and Dignity," in *The Aesthetical Essays* (Project Gutenberg, 2006), translation slightly modified to avoid the use of "man" as referring to humankind in the English version. Cf. the German edition in *Schillers Werke. Nationalausgabe*, ed. Helmut Koopman y Benno von Wiese (Weimar: Hermann Böhlaus, 1962). From now on NA followed by the volume and page numbers. In this case: NA XX, 284; my emphasis.

26. F. Schiller, LAE XIV, 125.

27. What is suggested here is not a suppression of our dual and essentially conflictive human nature, but rather a different means to assume that duality: one that does not require violence but rather a relationship in tension. One might also say that only by recognizing this tension can violence be avoided. Schiller is attempting to replace the figure of subjugation with the idea of a "happy balance," which he considers to be "the condition of all humanity" (cf. LAE XXVI, 166) and the only way to *secure* morality as a second nature. All these notions will be gathered in Schiller's well-known concept of "play," which along with Fichte's reciprocal action, stems also from Kant's explanation of the free play of the faculties (i.e., imagination and understanding) as the ground of the judgment of taste. Cf. §9 in Immanuel Kant, *Critique of the Power of Judgment*, trans. Paul Guyer and Erik Matthews (New York: Cambridge University Press, 2000), 102–103 (5:217). For an explanation of the free play of the faculties that follows the kind of logic explained in Fichte and Schiller in terms of "reciprocal action," see Rodolphe Gasché, "Transcendentality, in

Play," in *The Idea of Form: Rethinking Kant's Aesthetics* (Stanford: Stanford University Press, 2003), 42–59.

28. F. Schiller, LAE I, 87–88; translation slightly modified. It is also interesting to compare the idea of "technique" in this context with the role it plays in Schiller's descriptions of art and the beautiful object in the *Aesthetic Letters* as well as in the *Kallias Briefe* (his first response to Kant's *Critique of Judgment*). In accordance with and in a parallel argument to the notion of reciprocal action, technique and matter will also have to engage in a reciprocal relation in the production of the work of art. If the technique is too visible, Schiller insists, following Kant and his descriptions of the work of art in the *Critique of Judgment*, then the object cannot be beautiful. Art must appear *as* nature, matter as spontaneously giving form to itself, even though technique is necessary as a means toward such an end (cf. "Kallias or Concerning Beauty," trans. Stefan Brid-Pollan, in *Classic and Romantic German Aesthetics*, ed. J. M. Bernstein (New York: Cambridge University Press, 2003), 145–84. As we will soon see below, the same is the case with the adequate philosophical style: an analytic procedure is very much needed, but it cannot be the ultimate goal of the exposition, which needs to keep in mind the necessary balance between technique and nature, form and matter, or, in the specific case of writing and thinking philosophically, between analytical concepts and sensible images.

29. F. Schiller "On Grace and Dignity"; cf. NA XX, 286.

30. F. Schiller, LAE I, 88.

31. For my more in-depth attempt to analyze contemporary criticism regarding the "dangers" involved in Schillerian philosophy, as well as a possible answer to them on behalf of Schiller's aesthetical-political proposal, cf. Acosta, "Making Other People's Feelings Our Own."

32. Cf. Paul De Man, "Kant and Schiller," in *Aesthetic Ideology* (Minneapolis: University of Minnesota Press, 1996), 129–62; for this specific criticism cf. 148–55.

33. Ibid., 144–45.

34. For my attempts to engage seriously and critically with this interpretation of Schiller, see María del Rosario Acosta, "The Resistance of Beauty. On Schiller's *Kallias Briefe* in Response to Kant's Aesthetics," *Epoche* 21, no. 1 (2016): 235–49, and "On an Aesthetic Dimension of Critique: The Time of the Beautiful in Schiller's *Aesthetic Letters*," in *Critique in German Philosophy*, ed. María del Rosario Acosta and J. Colin McQuillan (Albany: State University of New York Press, forthcoming). What I propose in these more recent papers is to understand Schiller's conception of critique, as developed throughout his own conception of the aesthetic as an ethical and political dimension—a dimension where rather than compliance and a violent and surreptitious triumph of form over matter, resistance and interruption are made possible vis-à-vis the violence of the present.

35. Cf. Letter from Schiller to Fichte, August 3, 1795, Turner's translation in the present volume, slightly modified, cf. p. 56 (cf. GA III/2, 360).

36. Cf. F. Schiller, "Was heisst und zum welchem Ende studiert man Universalgeschichte" (München: Carl Hansen Verlag), 11–12; my translation.

37. Ibid., 11; my translation.

38. Cf. Letter from Schiller to Fichte, June 24, 1795, Turner's translation in the present volume, cf. p. 50 (cf. GA III/2, 334).

39. The English version I am using of "Über die notwendigen Grenzen beim Gebrauch Schönen Formen" (NA XXI, 9–27) can be found in *The Aesthetical Essays*, "On the Necessary Limitations in the Use of Beauty of Form" (New York: Collier and Son, 1920) 230–54. Since the translation will be occasionally modified according to the German version, the German reference in NA will always follow the English one.

40. Ibid., 241; NA XXI, 14.

41. Ibid.

42. Schiller occasionally refers to the "merely scientific" exposition as the "philosophical exposition," and sometimes describes the "sensuous presentation" as "beautiful." Two clarifications are needed here: on the one hand, the scientific, the popular, and the sensuous are *all* types of philosophical exposition, so I will refer to the former only as scientific and not as philosophical. On the other hand, to all these forms of presentation, Schiller wants to add one more, that is, the "truly beautiful presentation" achieved only by the *darstellende Schriftsteller*. For the sake of a clear distinction between the latter and the "sensuous" presentation, I will reserve the adjective "beautiful" to designate only the latter.

43. F. Schiller "On the Necessary Limitations . . .": 233; NA XXI, 6.

44. Ibid.: 235; NA XXI, 9.

45. Ibid.: 238; NA XXI, 11–12.

46. Ibid.: 239; NA XXI, 12.

47. Ibid.: 237; NA XXI, 11.

48. Ibid.: 234; NA XXI, 7.

49. Ibid.: 235; NA XXI, 8.

50. Ibid.; 237; NA XXI, 11.

51. Ibid.: 234; NA XXI, 7.

52. Ibid.: 240; NA XXI, 14. Thus, it is not true, as it has been suggested, that Schiller would be interested in opposing to Fichte's merely scientific style one contained in his descriptions of an "aesthetic style" (the third one described above). If this were the case, Schiller would be doing exactly what Fichte had accused him of doing in his correspondence, namely, opting for a style that entirely replaces concepts with images, thereby erasing universality and sacrificing clarity for the sake of a beautiful form. In this matter I agree with Frederick Beiser's suggestions in the few pages he devotes to this particular question in the Appendix to his book on Schiller (cf. Appendix 1 in Frederick Beiser, *Schiller as Philosopher* [New York: Oxford University Press, 2005], 263–67). Beiser points out that, even though Schiller never

makes explicit which of the three modes of philosophical presentation is the best fit for his own style, if left to choose he would have chosen the scientific and not the sensuous or aesthetic discourse as the one more fitted to describe his own philosophical writings. Beiser's intention is to show how Schiller remains a philosophical thinker, against a long tradition of interpreters who insist he remained always and overall a poet, a dramatist, and a rhetorician. I agree with Beiser that what remains of ultimate importance for Schiller is the possibility of a philosophical and scientific discourse, namely, one that can never give up the rigor and clarity of exposition for the sake of pedagogical or aesthetic needs. However, I would like to suggest, in a nuanced deviation from Beiser's interpretation, that if one is to seek for the most appropriate style of writing according to Schiller, none of the three alternatives outlined in the first part of the essay would entirely serve this purpose. And the *darstellende Schrifsteller* is, following this line of thought, a fourth and different mode of philosophical writing that cannot be subsumed under the first three descriptions.

53. For a detailed study of Schiller's use of the concept of *Darstellung*, cf. F. Heuer, *Darstellung der Freiheit. Schillers Transzendentale Frage nach der Kunst* (Köln: Böhlau Verlag, 1970). The complexities of the use of this term in Schiller's work make him an important part of the tradition of the development of this concept in German Idealism. Many of the ways this notion will be taken up by the Romantics come from Schiller, and not exclusively from Kant and Fichte, as Martha Helfer argues in her otherwise excellent and in-depth study of the history of this concept and its appropriations in German late-eighteenth and early-nineteenth-century philosophy. Cf. Helfer, *The Retreat of Representation. The Concept of Darstellung in German Critical Discourse* (Albany: State University of New York Press, 1996).

54. Cf. Kant, *Critique of the Power of Judgment*, 226–27 (5:352–53).

55. This also goes hand in hand with Schiller's own definition of beauty in his *Kallias Briefe* as "exhibition of freedom [*Darstellung der Freiheit*]" (154). For Schiller, even freedom—that idea that is utterly unpresentable in the case of Kant in its sensuous form—can attain expression in and as sensible presentation when enacted in and through the beautiful object. The beautiful object is, however, for Schiller not "just" an object. It rather behaves as a subject that exhorts us, as subjects, to be free: "[E]very object of natural beauty outside me is a happy citizen which calls to me: be free like me" (Schiller, *Kallias*, 173). There is also an important relation here between Schiller's first theory of beauty and Fichte's conception of subjectivity and freedom conceived as the result of the resistance exercised between the I and the non-I. *Resistance* is a notion that occupies a central role in Schiller's conception of beauty, and gives a very specific meaning to the idea of a reciprocal action in his work. See, for an analysis of this, Acosta, "The Resistance of Beauty."

56. F. Schiller "On the Necessary Limitations . . .": 234; NA XXI, 8.

57. Ibid.: 242; NA XXI, 15.

58. Ibid.: 242; NA XXI, 15–16.

59. Letter from Fichte to Schiller, June 27, 1795, Turner's translation in the present volume, cf. p. 54 (cf. GA III/2, 339).

60. Cf. F. Schiller "On the Necessary Limitations . . .": 241; NA XXI, 14.

61. Ibid.

62. Letter from Fichte to Schiller, June 27, 1795, Turner's translation in the present volume, slightly modified, cf. p. 54 (cf. GA III/2, 339).

63. Letter from Schiller to Fichte, August 3, 1795, Turner's translation in the present volume, translation modified, p. 58 (cf. GA III/2: 364).

64. Letter from Fichte to Schiller, June 27, 1795, Turner's translation in the present volume, cf. p. 51 (cf. GA III/2, 336).

65. F. Schiller "On the Necessary Limitations . . .": 236; NA XXI, 10.

66. Cf. ibid.: 235; NA XXI, 9.

67. Ibid.: 243; NA XXI, 16.

68. Cf. F. Schiller, LAE IX, 109.

69. Cf. F. Schiller "On the Necessary Limitations . . .": 241; NA XXI, 14. Kant also uses the example of the Basilica of St. Peter in his *Critique of Judgment* in relation to imagination's productive activity in the experience of the sublime: when imagination is initially dazzled by what is presented to it, and is unable to grasp in one single glance the entirety of space, it does not renounce the experience and admit failure, but rather transforms it into an aesthetic emotion. There are some experiences that can never be represented adequately by the understanding and Schiller seems to relate this inadequacy to imagination's productive capacity to overcome its initial incapability. Similarly, with the figure of the *darstellende Schriftsteller*, Schiller seems to be thinking of the possibility of a presentation capable of expressing and producing such interdependent relationship between images and concepts (probably, moreover, in connection to what Kant describes in the *Critique of Judgment* as "aesthetic ideas," sensible presentations for which no representation seems entirely adequate). I cannot address here the very complex and fruitful relationship between Schiller's proposal and his reading of Kantian aesthetics. See Acosta, "The Resistance of Beauty," and Acosta, "The Time of the Beautiful."

70. F. Schiller, LAE IX, 110.

71. Ibid., 109 and 110. The notion of appearance as the realm of truth is also a very complex notion in Schiller's writings. Read in a certain light, it situates Schiller's aesthetic project in the tradition of phenomenology, and connects in very interesting ways Schiller's philosophical thought with that of Hegel. Appearance in any case should not be interpreted in Schiller as a merely deceptive state but rather as the realm where, in finding its most adequate sensible expression, truth shows itself. I have tried to develop some of these ideas elsewhere. Cf. M. R. Acosta, "La ampliación de la apariencia: la educación estética de Schiller como configuradora de un espacio compartido," in *Schiller, arte y política*, ed. A. Rivera (Murcia: EDINUM, 2016), 49–90.

72. The essay was finally published in 1800 by Fichte himself in his *Philosophische Journal*. It is not to be confused with "Concerning the Difference between the Spirit and the Letter within Philosophy," which belong to the series of public lectures "Morality for Scholars" that Fichte gave during his first semester at Jena.

The latter has been translated by D. Breazeale in the op. cit. *Early Philosophical Writings*, 185–216.

73. Cf. GA I/6, 359.

74. Unfortunately, I cannot discuss here how Schiller's practical proposal, precisely by presenting itself as an "aesthetics," dialogues with the contingency that characterizes human praxis. This is especially clear in his essay, "Concerning the Sublime," trans. Daniel Dahlstrom, in F. Schiller, *Essays*, 70–85.

References

Acosta López, María del Rosario. "¿Una superación estética del deber? La crítica de Schiller a Kant." *Episteme N.S.* 28, no. 2 (2008): 3–24.

———. "La ampliación de la apariencia: la educación estética de Schiller como configuradora de un espacio compartido." In *Schiller, arte y política*, edited by Antonio Rivera, 49–90. Murcia: EDINUM, 2010.

———. "Making Other People's Feelings Our Own: From the Aesthetic to the Political in Schiller's Aesthetic Letters." In *Who Is This Schiller Now?* edited by J. High, N. Martin, and N. Oellers, 187–203. London/New York: Camden House, 2011.

———. "The Resistance of Beauty. On Schiller's *Kallias Briefe* in Response to Kant's Aesthetics." *Epoché* 21, no. 1 (2016): 235–49.

———. "On an Aesthetic Dimension of Critique: The Time of the Beautiful in Schiller's *Aesthetic Letters*." In *Critique in German Philosophy*, edited by María del Rosario Acosta and J. Colin McQuillan. Albany: State University of New York Press, forthcoming.

Beiser, Frederick. *Schiller as Philosopher*. New York: Oxford University Press, 2005.

De Man, Paul. "Kant and Schiller." In *Aesthetic Ideology*. Minneapolis: University of Minnesota Press, 1996.

Fichte, J. G. *Gesamtausgabe der Bayerischen Akademie der Wissenschaften*. Stuttgart: 1961ff.

———. "On Stimulating and Increasing the Pure Interest in Truth [*Über Belebung und Erhöhung des reinen Interesses an Wahrheit*]." In *Gesamtausgabe der Bayerischen Akademie der Wissenschaften*. Stuttgart: 1961ff.

———. *Foundation of the Entire Doctrine of Scientific Knowledge* (*Grundlage der gesammten Wissenschaftlehre*). In *Sämmtliche Werke*, Band I, edited by I. H. Fichte. Berlin: Veit, 1845/1846.

———. "Lectures Concerning the Scholar's Vocation [*Einige Vorlesungen über die Bestimmung des Gelehrten*]." In *Early Philosophical Writings*, translated and edited by D. Breazeale. Ithaca: Cornell University Press, 1988.

———. "Concerning the Spirit and the Letter within Philosophy in a Series of Letters [*Über Geist und Buchstabe in der Philosophie in einer Reihe von Briefen*]."

In *Gesamtausgabe der Bayerischen Akademie der Wissenschaften*. Stuttgart: 1961ff.

———. Letters between Fichte and Schiller, June 21 to August 4, 1795, in *Gesamtausgabe der Bayerischen Akademie der Wissenschaften*. Stuttgart: 1961ff.

———. *Filosofía y estética. La polémica con F. Schiller*. Translated, edited, and with an introduction by Faustino Oncina and Manuel Ramos. Valencia: Universidad de Valencia, 1998.

Helfer, Martha. *The Retreat of Representation. The Concept of Darstellung in German Critical Discourse*. Albany: State University of New York Press, 1996.

Heuer, F. *Darstellung der Freiheit. Schillers Transzendentale Frage nach der Kunst*. Köln: Böhlau Verlag, 1970.

Macor, Laura. "Schiller on Emotions. Problems of (In)Consistency in His Ethics." In *Aesthetic Reason and Imaginative Freedom: Friedrich Schiller and Philosophy*, edited by M. R. Acosta and J. Powell. Albany: State University of New York Press, 2018.

Millán Brusslan, Elizabeth. "Poetry and Imagination in Fichte and the Early German Romantics, a Reassessment." In *The Imagination in German Idealism and Romanticism*, edited by Gerad Gentry and Konstantin Pollock. Cambridge: Cambridge University Press, forthcoming.

Schiller, Friedrich. "Was heisst und zum welchem Ende studiert Man Universalgeschichte [1789]." In *Werke in Drei Bänden*, Band II. Darmstadt: Wissenschaftliche Buchgesselschaft, 1984.

———. *Nationalausgabe*. Edited by Helmut Koopman and Benno von Wiese. Weimar: Hermann Böhlaus, 1962ff.

———. "On Grace and Dignity [*Über Anmuth und Wurde*]" [1793]. In *Nationalausgabe*, edited by Helmut Koopman and Benno von Wiese. Weimar: Hermann Böhlaus, 1962ff.

———. "Kallias or Concerning Beauty" [1793]. Translated by Stefan Brid-Pollan. In *Classic and Romantic German Aesthetics*, edited by J. M. Bernstein. New York: Cambridge University Press, 2003.

———. "Ankündigung der Horen" [1794]. In *Werke in Drei Bänden, Band II*. Darmstadt: Wissenschaftliche Buchgesselschaft, 1984.

———. "On the Necessary Limitations in the Use of Beautiful Forms" [1795]. In *Nationalausgabe*. XXI. Edited by Helmut Koopman and Benno von Wiese. Weimar: Hermann Böhlaus, 1962ff.

———. "Letters on the Aesthetic Education of Man" [1795]. Translated by Wilkinson and Willoughby. In *Essays*, edited by Walter Hinderer and Daniel Dahlstrom. New York: Continuum, 1993.

———. *The Aesthetical Essays*. Project Gutenberg, 2006.

———. "Concerning the Sublime" [1796]. Translated by Daniel Dahlstrom. In F. Schiller, *Essays*.

2

Fichte and Schiller Correspondence

Translation by Chris Turner

287.2

June (circa the 20th) 1795 Jena

Johann Christoph Friedrich Schiller to Fichte in Osmannstädt.[1]

288 (Sch. 241)

June 21, 1795 Ossmannstädt

Fichte to Johann Christoph Friedrich Schiller in Jena.

Letter.

Oßmannstädt, June 21st, 1795

I thought I promised to send you what I intended[2] for the first part (of *die Horen*) on the 24th, but I can safely count on having it to you by Tuesday.[3] Here is as much as is ready. The rest—the conclusion of the second letter and the third, which, however, will not be long, will be sent on Tuesday.

Page 15 is a strophe[4] from Goethe's *Meister*,[5] which I do not have here, cited from memory. Please check the quality, and update the citation, if it is not correct. Incidentally, I have carefully revised the essay, what here and there seem like difficult constructions are intentional, and I do not believe that it would benefit from the slightest change. With the sequel, I hope to reconcile the reader with the rather weighty disquisition in the middle of the second letter; and an explanation[6] of the passage, which could appear democratic, follows at the beginning of the third letter.

I have had a very hard time with the copyist, and I am quite ashamed to send you such a manuscript. Nevertheless, the bad handwriting is legible, at least I hope that it is, and I have carefully examined it, so that it can safely be relied on. I ask that my punctuation and the *andre*, or *andere* and suchlike,[7] be observed. I first received your letter[8] this evening and immediately wrote this out.

I instructed von Ziegler[9] to go to you tomorrow. My three letters can easily fill more than two pages but I take it to be entirely impracticable to break them up. More on Tuesday or Wednesday. Say hello to those close to me!

Yours,
Fichte.

"Letter" [*Buchstab*] is deliberately in the heading, as, etymologically, "letters" [*Buchstaben*] is too ambiguous. But if it is simply not German enough, then go ahead and improve it.

291c (Sch. 243)

JUNE 24TH, 1795. JENA

JOHANN CHRISTOPH FRIEDRICH SCHILLER TO FICHTE IN OSMANNSTÄDT

3ʳᴰ DRAFT

June 24th

As much as the sight of your manuscript pleased me, dear friend, and as loathe as am I to do without a contribution that was already entirely and confidently counted on for the next installment of *die Horen*, I nevertheless find myself compelled to send it back. In the first place, I must do this on account of its improper length, which can be divined from the way you start out, but I am all the more compelled since the content satisfies me as little as does its treatment.

You entitle the essay "On Spirit and Letter in Philosophy," but the first three pages treat of nothing else than spirit in the fine arts, which as far as I know is something entirely different than the opposite of the letter. Spirit as antithesis of the letter, and spirit as aesthetic quality, seem to me to be worlds apart as concepts, so much so that the latter can be missing entirely from a philosophical work, without it being for that reason less qualified to be established as a paradigm of a pure depiction of *spirit*. Thus indeed I do not see how you can transition from the one to the other without a *salto mortale,* and yet I can even less conceive of how you will find a way from the spirit in the works of Goethe, which one would have hardly expected, given the title of your essay, to the spirit in Kantian and Leibnizian philosophy. From the second installment of your manuscript I indeed see that you believe yourself to have made no such great detour, since after you previously opposed spiritlessness to the aesthetic spirit, you oppose the *letter* to it in a manner that is inconceivable to me and designate as scribblers [*Buchstäbler*] those in whom the capacity for it is lacking.

As counterproductive as I take this introduction to be in regard to the subject to be treated, it is particularly counterproductive for the present needs of *die Horen*. A large portion of my *Letters on the Aesthetic Education of Man* treats the same subject, and in all my efforts I strove to enliven the abstract content by means of the presentation, thus, generally speaking, it would be improper to place such abstract investigations in a journal. I was hoping to enrich the philosophical section of the journal with your essay on spirit and letter, and the subject that you chose led me to expect a piece of work that would be understandable and interesting to a general audience. What have I received instead, and what do you expect me to present to the public? Old material that does not even seem entirely finished to me, even in the antiquated epistolary style I had already chosen, and all of this according to such an eccentric plan that it is impossible to bring the parts of your essay together into a whole. I regret to say this but as it stands I am satisfied with neither how it is decked out nor with the content, and I find precision and clarity lacking in this essay, two qualities that usually characterize your work. Your classification of the drives seems staggeringly arbitrary and bad to me. A basis for the classification is missing, one does not see which sphere has been gone through. The drive for existence or material (the sensuous drive) has no place therein—since it is impossible to bring the drive for multiplicity and the drive for unity together into a single class. It cannot issue from the practical drive, as you define it, without a most violent operation. Since the first two drives are not purely distinct, even the third aesthetic drive, which is supposed to be derived from them, turns out to be nothing but myopic and uncertain. In short, in the discussion of this aesthetic drive there still prevails a confusion that is not to be shaken off, although some specific parts of the discussion are completely satisfactory to me—yet I cannot hope to say what is most necessary of all concerning this material in a short letter. Regarding this, you will hear the judgment of others; this and time will be my justification.

Just one more word on your submission. You write that you worked very diligently on it. However, we must have very different conceptions of what constitutes an appropriate presentation, since I must confess that I am not at all pleased with yours. Above all, I expect a consistent tone from a good presentation, and, if it is to have aesthetic value, interaction between imagery and concept, not alternation between the two, as is often the case in your letters. Hence the unseemly fact that you immediately move from the most abstruse abstractions directly into tirades, an error that is already offensive in your earlier writings, and which recurs here in magnified form. Finally, how *difficulties* can be *necessary* in a good presentation is completely inconceivable to me.

You forbid me from making unauthorized changes to your manuscript, as though I were accustomed to carrying out that sort of thing without the author's own consent. If I changed something in your first essay,[10] you yourself authorized me to do so, and it was urgently needed. That would also particularly be the case here, if the error were not more profound.

Forgive my candor in informing you of my opinion. I would have specified reasons for my decision, so as to avoid an accusation of arbitrariness, but it is not really possible given the heavy demands of *die Horen*. If I have expressed myself in too animated a fashion in a few passages, then the quite natural displeasure over disappointed expectations may be to blame.

Incidentally, this fact will make no difference for your settling of accounts with Cotta. If you let him print the writing on his own he will be happy to publish it. Thus I attach the letter which you sent me for him.[11] Only, you must permit me, if Cotta wants to takes counsel with me regarding the matter, to advise him as his friend, to which he has earned the right.[12]

Yours,
Schiller

Live well! And do not let the friend pay for what the editor could not keep secret.

292 (Sch. 244)

June 27th, 1795 Osmannstädt

Fichte to Johann Christoph Friedrich Schiller in Jena.

Letter.

Osmannstädt, June 27, 1795

The conceptual muddle that you attribute to me is a bit severe. I could not expect that you would conceive the task as I have conceived it, contrary to the ordinary sense of the words, which seems to me to make no sense. But I could expect that you would attribute to a man whose philosophical talent you had until now judged favorably, and to whom you had assigned an honorable place in *die Horen*,[13] that he may perhaps have discovered something in the course of his reflections on a specific subject, which you, without this specific course in your reflections, did not see. Yet I would not have expected that you would suddenly suspect him of having the most muddled of all muddled minds. I was mistaken, as I now see.

The fact is that you did not correctly understand my title or, to just say it directly, you did not understand my idea at all. The meaning you give to it has no meaning. As far as *I* know, spirit in philosophy and spirit in the fine arts are as closely akin as the species of a genus, and I do not think this claim is short on proof. Conversely, I would like to hear from you how one could say spirit *of* philosophy (and not of *Leibnizian*, *Kantian* philosophy, for instance) in the way that one says, for instance, spirit of the Prussian Religious Edict. Philosophy originally has no letter, but rather is pure spirit, and hence it was necessary to grasp and formulate this spirit. Yet how indeed would human beings be inclined to philosophize if philosophy were sharply cut off from all genuine *cognition*? Would there have to be an original predisposition in the human being for it? As though this predisposition were a drive for representation for the sake of representation, which is also the ultimate basis of the fine arts, of taste, and so forth? Had you posed these questions, to which hopefully even the beginning of the first three letters of my essay led, then you would probably have been spared your overhasty verdict.—I have never conceived of the task otherwise than in this sense. I have treated it in this sense in my published lectures, as perhaps Mr. von Humboldt[14] can attest to. I have never believed that it could be understood otherwise by a sound mind, if one but thinks it over. I thought myself, in your good graces, to be working on *this* question for *die Horen*, and it were as though I fell from the clouds when I read: "*Spirit in antithesis to the letter*," and so forth.

You have done me an injustice, and I hope that you will make good on this injustice, as befits any just man. I will finish the essay, and send it to you—not for *die Horen*, of course—and then perhaps you will withdraw the contempt with which you now treat me. If not, then I will certainly send it off to a few recommended referees. Until then, the matter stays between us.

I hope that you will realize what you should have already realized by now, that what was submitted to this point was inseparable from the matter, and that I have not taken as sweeping an approach as you believe. I am startled at the absurdity, and at the same time the base motives, that you must attribute to me since you do not realize this.—That the essay was to fill nine or ten pages is something I told you; and it would have taken up no more than this.

Whoever has no spirit is *spiritless*. Such a person can neither produce something artistic, nor philosophize at all; or he produces one thing, or a philosophical book, which is entirely superficial and has nothing of inner spirit. How would you characterize the latter in distinction from the former? I call him a *scribbler* [*Buchstäbler*]; from the outset I opposed spiritlessness to spirit, and then to the letter [*Buchstaben*]?? Not at all. I have opposed the body, or letter, to the spirit *in a specific product of art*; and distinguished the spirited from scribblers in the case of *those who work in the fine arts*, but not in the case of human beings in general. What a bungler you make me into! You must have read the essay very cursorily.

If my classification of the drives lacks nothing more than the fact that the drive for existence or the material drive is not included, then it is safe and sound. A drive for existence before existence; thus a determination of what does not exist!! All matter emerges from a limitation of what is self-active, not from its activity. (*The presentation of matter* in the mind is something else; this belongs to the conceptual mode under the cognitive drive.) The drive is only a *drive* through limitation; without that it would be an *action* (*That*). The essence of popularity seems to me to lie in the synthetic approach. I had only ascended to the classificatory basis of the drives because I did not wish to descend from it to the individual drives.

Whether my arrangement is capricious will reveal itself in due course; until then I request that you trust that I had good reason for my classification. You find it capricious because you do not surmise the scope of what I have tentatively called the aesthetic drive; and because you define and classify it in another way. We are of a different opinion; and I do not need to remind you that who is right depends on our reasoning. You had not yet heard mine, and to that point the matter between us remained undecided. But with what tone did you render your verdict, and what justified this tone? Admittedly, I have to put up with being treated like a pupil who recites his lesson by people whom I do not esteem; but it is not a matter of indifference from you, because I esteem you highly.

The detrimental consequences of my principle for the doctrine of taste should have already been expressed by now. I would like to know what they are; but how can this happen if it concerns points over which we are not in agreement?

The results of the doctrine of taste could not yet be formulated here due to my approach, since I do not write about them, but rather about the spirit of philosophy; and they should be determined by my synthetic ascension, and the one must be determined by the other. The results will be found. However, I believe that a clarity that is otherwise nowhere to be found is here already diffused over a number of Kant's obscure expressions in the doctrine of taste,[15] with whose results I am largely in agreement. But what am I saying? Your question marks are found in precisely these passages.

This is not the first time that I discovered that we have very different principles concerning the popular philosophical presentation. I already saw it from your own philosophical writings. You mainly proceed analytically, the path of the rigorous system, and your popularity is established by your overflowing use of images, which you employ nearly everywhere in place of the abstract concept. My popularity is particularly established by the approach [*Gang*] that I take—which misled you into too quickly considering my first letter to be shallow and superficial.—After the rigorously philosophical disposition is ready, I make my "approach" according to entirely different principles: I build on a very common experience, and I thus keep the thread going, seemingly according to a mere association of ideas, over which, however, the system invisibly keeps watch. I define nothing more precisely than is necessary beforehand, until ultimately the precise definition emerges of its own accord. In my case, the image does not take the *place of* the concept, but rather *precedes* or *follows* it, as a likeness [*Gleichniß*]: I see afterward that it is suitable; I believe that those in the letters are quite precisely suitable. If I am not mistaken, all ancient and modern authors who are famous for their excellent presentation have considered it as I endeavor to. But your kind is completely novel; and I am aware of none among the ancients or moderns who is comparable to you in this regard. You bind the imagination, which can only be free, and wish to compel it to think. That it cannot do. Hence, I believe, arises the tedious effort that your philosophical writings occasion in me, and which they have occasioned in others. In the first place, I must translate everything of yours before I can understand it; and so it goes with others, too. Whatever my earlier writings are all accused of, and as well-founded as the accusations made against them may be, they are nonetheless often read, and have been noted, and they are recounted here and there, and what is found in them is echoed. Your philosophical writings—I am not speaking here of your poetic writings, nor your historical ones, of which, for example, the history of the siege of Antwerp[16] is a masterpiece that captivates everyone irresistibly and takes them along for a ride. Just as little am I speaking of your philosophical thoroughness, and your profundity, which I admire; I am only speaking about your style—your philosophical writings are bought and marveled at, they hold one spellbound, but they are less often read, and not understood at all, this much I have noticed. Among the wider public, I have not heard any opinion, any passage, any result quoted from them. Everyone commends them as much as he can, but each takes good care to guard against the question: What is actually there?

The appearance of difficulty in the structure of my sentences in great part derives from the fact that my readers cannot read aloud with dramatic intonation. Listen to me read one of my sentences, and I hope that you will not find it difficult anymore. But you are right; our public has never been able to read aloud with dramatic intonation, and one is better served, like Lessing,[17] to adopt measures accordingly.

I do not believe that I deserved the sharp tone that you used in interpreting my statement that the essay would not easily support being changed. You suggested changes for my first essay[18] adversely affecting its meaning, and for this reason I had to request that the first version be restored. Since time was short and the essay could not be sent back to me for revisions, *I made* that request *in all innocence, from the bottom of my heart, and faithfully believing that I was writing to a friend who was not inclined to place statements on the scales.* (I recall with deep embarrassment that immediately afterward I assumed the familiarity of bothering you with an economic imposition.[19] Pardon me for not having been aware of our relationship, but something like that will certainly never happen to me again.) The disclosure, however, that everything which I write has such a pressing need for correction has really gotten my attention, as it should. I will diligently apply myself to discovering the reason for this and will take care of it. At the very least, it is not at all conceivable at present why you marked this or that in the current essay; except that I see that you have not understood it correctly.

I take very seriously and with grateful delight the suggestion at the end of your letter that we still want to remain friends. I hope that the candor with which I replied to your letter will not present a hindrance to the resumption of our friendship. But I believe that I may assume that the friendship between us could only be founded on mutual respect. My respect for you cannot be weakened by an overhasty verdict; only continued injustice would nullify it, and I do not expect this from you. You have failed to respect me, however, and withheld the trust I thought I could expect from you. From this point on I could be nothing to you other than your humble follower, and pupil, and that I will not be. But I expect satisfaction from you in your own good time.

I enclose the letter to which I replied, because it is not to be expected that you have a copy of it. However, I would like it back, for my vindication in case it is necessary.

Fichte

298a (Sch. 249)

AUGUST 3RD/4TH, 1795

JOHANN CHRISTOPH FRIEDRICH SCHILLER TO FICHTE IN OSMANNSTÄDT

OUTLINES OF A LETTER.

Jena August 3rd, 1795

I am immediately replying to your letter,[20] and thus only to those parts of it that allow for such a quick response. Concerning the aesthetic part of our dispute, dear friend, we will never be of one accord, and thus should no longer dispute. Not so much because we differ in principle, since that could ultimately still be respected, but rather because we are different, indeed highly different natures, because we have entirely different sensibilities. Of course, a fitting quotation can be found *about this,* but from a better authority than the public, as it stands, or than an individual belonging to it can be. You would like, so it seems, to appeal to another judge, and it is already the second time[21] that you refer me to public citation. However, I would have to maintain an entirely different idea of the German aesthetic public than I do, to respect such an opinion in a matter concerning which my reason and sensibility have decided, after such a troublesome and serious crisis. There is nothing cruder than the taste of the current German public, and to work on changing this wretched taste, to not take my model from it, is the earnest plan of my life. To be sure, I have not yet brought it about, not because my means were wrongly chosen, but rather because the public is accustomed to make a too frivolous affair of its reading, and is too deeply submerged in aesthetic considerations to be able to be lifted up again so easily.

Regarding the presentation of philosophy, I also cannot admit the validity of a comparison of my manner with that of another, least of all with the manner of a merely didactic writer. My continual tendency, aside from the inquiry itself, is to employ the ensemble of emotional forces and to the extent that it is possible to have an effect on all of them. I thus do not wish merely to make my thoughts clear to others, but at the same time to transmit my entire soul to them, and to influence both their sensuous and intellectual powers. This presentation of my whole nature in even prosaic material, where men are otherwise only accustomed to speak of genre, necessitates a completely different standpoint for the assessment of my manner, and in contrasting Home[22] and his ilk to me you clearly show that you should never have passed judgment on me.

You told me in one of your previous letters[23] that I present my speculations in images, and that one first has to translate me in order to understand me. I am sorry for that but it is really not my fault. Show me a single case in all my philosophical essays where I treated the *inquiry itself* (not mere applications of it) in images. That will and can never be the case for me, since I am quite scrupulous in diligently making my ideas clear. However, if I have conducted the inquiry with precision and logical rigor, I also like and prefer to extend what I presented to the understanding to the imagination as well (yet in the strictest connection with the former). If you would like to verify this remark, I refer you to the Sixth Part of *die Horen*,[24] because just there the application is rather convenient. If you find an unsuitable turn of phrase here in Letters 19, 20, 21, 22, and 23, where the heart of the matter actually is, then I will in fact know that there is no longer any point of agreement in our judgments.

If I protest against every authority, this does not happen because I have nothing to hope for, since if I should ever be condemned then I could still make another attempt afterward, and the authority that *you* propose, namely Goethe, would least of all be to your liking. Goethe, however, cannot do justice to you and his verdict can prove nothing against you. He is much too foreign to the philosophical domain to be able to be reconciled with the aesthetic transgressions with which he would reproach you. It is strange that you have to first hear from me how little Goethe is suited to take your part. It is just as strange that you decline to allow me to judge the taste and entire tone of your writings, and would transfer this office to Goethe, who on this point acknowledges me as a judge in his own manuscripts and writings, and abides by my judgments.

For the rest, I believe that you would do well, if you would explain yourself to him concerning this at some point, since it could still be that you will trust in him what you will never trust in me.

You invoke the fate of our writings ten years from now. Indeed, I will not prognosticate, since who can uncover a rule and consistency in the behavior of the German public? However, this much is certain: if *my* writings could not in substance survive even the single fact that they are simultaneously an aesthetic product, that they present a whole individual, I do not wish to say that another party would assure their permanence. A merely didactic writing, if it is not absolutely decisively and enduringly epoch-making, cannot preserve itself in the face of the rapidity of literature, for when there is progress in knowledge even the pupil already knows what it once took the master much trouble to manage. In contrast, an individual who has vividly lost himself in a book is and eternally remains the only one of his kind, and to be sure can misunderstand something but can never be superseded.

It is sad that such an enormous difference and such an irresolvable quarrel could prevail even among contemporaries, among men who should form a single family in the century in which they live, that what is idiosyncratic always remains isolated, and likewise that this should occur most of all among philosophers, who are supposed to constitute a profession of the true estimation of things.

We have lived in a single era, and posterity will make us, as contemporaries, into neighbors, etc., but how little have we been united.

Whoever wants to regard me as a *teacher* misunderstands me entirely—neither nature nor my educational background has qualified me for that. The teacher must be taught, and there is perhaps no one among all writers that are known, least of all in the philosophical field, who is so little taught as I am, and little to such an enormous degree that if I wanted to tell you what I have read of philosophy and the like over the entirety of my life, you would not know whether you [. . .][25] to change something in particular, but never to turn the course of nature. If principles were the only thing standing between us then I would try with all my might to either draw you to my side or to take yours. But we have different sensibilities, we have entirely different natures, and I do not know what to do about that. The only way in which we could here come to accord with each other is by adopting in common the maxim of sound reason which teaches that things which cannot be compared cannot be contrasted either!

Admittedly, something must also be able to be determined concerning nature and concerning the aesthetical part of the human being, but according to your own principles, not from principles of reason. You admit this yourself in your essay,[26] and your rather frequent appeals for another's judgments in our present dispute demonstrates that you do not recognize reason but rather sensibility (or, better, the whole human being) as aesthetic judge. In this, I am completely of your opinion, only you will have to allow for the fact that I take my aesthetic feeling itself as guide in the choice of this aesthetic middleman.

I would have to arrive at an entirely different idea of the German public than I hold at present if I were to respect its esteem in a matter concerning which my whole nature has finally come to be at one with itself after a protracted and arduous crisis. The general and quite revolting success of mediocrity in our time, the crudeness on the one hand, and the despicable flaccidity on the other, fill me with such a heartfelt disgust for our German public, that in an unhappy hour I could be talked into fighting against this wretched taste but would never forgive myself for making it my model. But, fortunately, I am as far removed from the one kind of folly as I am from the other. Regardless of everything that is thought of and admired in me I merely follow the impulse of my nature or that of my reason, and because it never occurred to me to found a sect or establish a school, this mode of procedure (which, incidentally, I take to be the only decent one for a philosopher) does not require any overcoming. In this state of mind, it admittedly seems strange to me when there is talk of the impression that my writings make on the majority of the public—. Had you had read the most recent ones with a little attentiveness, you would not need to hear from me that a direct opposition to the spirit of the age is their chief characteristic and that including something else would be a quite worrisome piece of evidence against their substance. Nearly all the lines that in recent years have flowed from my pen bear this character and if, for *extrinsic* reasons, I cannot be indifferent as to whether I have a great or small public I have at least put myself out there in a few ways that correspond to my individuality—not to win the public over by cozying up to its idea of art, but rather to surprise, shock, and thrill it with the bold establishment of my own. Given the nature of things, such a writer can never be loved, since one only loves what sets one free, not what compels one, but he obtains satisfaction, hated by wretchedness, by the adopted enthusiastically and from cowardice with[. . .].[27] An individual is always the only one of his kind and can never be superseded or exhausted. As long as you include in your writings nothing other than what a thoughtful person can follow with his mere understanding, you can be sure that another will come after you and say better and in another way what you have said—since, as is well known, the understanding eternally progresses, and is at no point of its course something infinite. But this is not the case with what the imagination portrays. I admit that now and in the future something—perhaps what is best—in my writings is of such a quality that, unfortunately indeed, some will not at all be acquainted with it and thus I will happily concede the reproach that you direct at me.[28] But once the effect they have (no matter whether on few or many) is of an aesthetic kind, then this effect is assured for all subsequent times (in which one understands the author's language). Whether—how—and to what degree of extension and intensity my writings become aesthetically influential, that, note well, is something that cannot be treated here. The minor premise may thus rest on itself, but you as well as I hope to have nothing to oppose to the major one. (Surely I do not need to first tell you that when I interpret the aesthetic alone as immortal this is not supposed to establish any preference over the other, since immortality suits both kinds of works, only with this difference: from the one kind of writing it is the *consequences* that live on forever while from the other it is the *individual* effect. If Aristotle[29] is no longer read, the influence he has had on science and consequently his fame is nevertheless eternal, even should his name be forgotten.) But I must tell you this, because you compare our two writings on a point where to my mind they diverge very startlingly from each other.

In any case, a number of your statements demonstrate to me that you are particularly in error concerning the standpoint from which my person is to be assessed. (Ever since you were ecstatic about a writing such as that of Mr. von Oertel[30] on humanity and made me into its composer I should have no longer had the heart to discuss such a subject with you.)

If you[. . .][31]

JENA, AUGUST 4TH, 1795

I am sorry, dear friend, that I have started a quarrel between us both concerning our manner that can never be ended and should never have been started by me. A misconceived aspiration for fairness led me to this; in rejecting your essay on behalf of *die Horen*, I wanted to head off the accusation of arbitrariness and caprice and hence to justify my procedure. However, I forgot that precisely what led to the essay being rejected by *die Horen* would necessarily prevent all of my reasons from being accessible to you. I had supposed myself to be saying fairly that precisely because you write in such a manner, and because you think in such a manner as a result of this kind of writing, because you are such an individual, no reasons with their source in my individual person would be able to reach you since the aesthetic part of a man is a result of his nature, and perhaps a few kinds of ideas can be changed by means of reasoning, but the course of nature can never be turned. If principles were all that stood between us, then I would have enough trust in our mutual love of truth, and in our capability, to hope that one of us would finally incline to the side of the other. But we have different sensibilities, we have two entirely different natures, and I do not know what to do about that. The only way in which we could here come into agreement with each other would be to adopt in common the maxim of sound reasoning, which teaches that things which cannot be compared cannot be contrasted either.

Of course, something must be able to be ascertained concerning the nature of the human being and what is aesthetical for him, yet according to your own principles [*Grundsätze*], at least not according to principles [*Principien*] that are already on hand. At one point, you admit this in your essay, and your repeated appeals for *another's* judgments in our present dispute shows that in this domain you do not expect the decision to come from reason, but rather from feeling and from the totality of the individual. In this, I am entirely of your opinion, but for just that reason you will likewise allow me to take my own sensibility as guide in the choice of such an aesthetic middleman.

I would have to arrive at an entirely different opinion of the German public than I presently have if I were to respect its esteem in a matter over which my nature has finally come to be at one with itself after an arduous and intractable crisis. The general and revolting success of mediocrity at the present time, the inconceivable inconsistency that with equal satisfaction accepts what is wretched on the same stage where one had just admired what is excellent, the crudity on the one side and the weakness on the other, arouse in me, I must confess, such disgust with what one calls public opinion, that I should perhaps be forgiven if, in an unhappy hour, it occurs to me to want to work against this awful sense of taste, but it would truly be unforgivable were I to make it my guide and paradigm. Fortunately, the one kind of folly is as foreign to me as the other. Regardless of what is thought of me or what is flatteringly said of me, I merely follow the impulse of either my nature or my reason, and since I have never felt the temptation to found a school or to gather youth around me, this mode of procedure (incidentally, the only one I find said to be suitable for a philosopher) does not require any overcoming. In this state of mind, it admittedly seems strange to me when there is talk of the impression that my writings make or do not make on the majority of the public. Had you had read the most recent ones with a little attentiveness, which was to be expected from an impartial seeker of truth, then you would know without my needing to remind you that a direct opposition to the character of the age makes up their spirit and that including anything other than what they explore would be a quite worrisome piece of evidence against their substantive truth. Nearly all the lines that in recent years have flowed from my pen bear this character and if I cannot be indifferent for *extrinsic* reasons, which I still share with other writers, as to whether I acquire a great or small public I have at least put myself out there in a few ways that correspond to my individuality and to my character—not to win the public over by cozying up to the spirit of the times, but rather by my seeking to surprise, shock, and thrill it with the vivid and bold establishment of *my* kind of representation. That a writer who pursues this path cannot be the public's darling lies in the nature of things, since one only loves what sets one free, not what constricts one; but he obtains satisfaction for the fact that he is hated by wretchedness, envied by vanity, seized on enthusiastically by minds that are capable of being swayed, and venerated by base souls with fear and trembling. I have never really sought to make inquiries into the good or bad effect of my writerly existence, but the probing of both has pressed upon me unsought, and still does all the way up to the present moment.

This reminds me of that passage in your letter where you invoke the public's quotation of both of us ten years from now. What will happen in ten years, indeed, I do not know. But I do not in the least doubt that if, as is to be hoped, you are still alive then, still teaching and writing, you will take care to see that your philosophy and your individual person are retained in the memory of listeners and readers. In contrast, as is to be expected, neither teaching nor writing any longer, I will proceed through the public sphere with my philosophy just as tranquilly as I do now. But that in 100 or 200 years, when new revolutions in philosophical thought have happened, your writings will be cited and assessed according to their merits, but will no longer be read, is as much in the nature of things as the fact that mine (understood by those whose hands they fortuitously fall into, since fashion and fortune are decisive here) will then indeed not be read *more* but certainly also not *less* than they are now. And why is this likely to happen? It happens because writings whose worth lies only in the results they contain for the understanding, even if they are quite excellent in this regard, are dispensable to the same degree that the understanding either becomes indifferent to these results or can achieve them in an easier way. In contrast, writings that make an impact independent of their logical content and in which an individual person is vividly expressed can never be dispensed with and contain in themselves an indestructible principle of life, precisely because each individual is unique and therefore also irreplaceable.

Thus, dear friend, so long as you provide no more in your writings than what anyone who knows how to think can appropriate for himself, you can be certain that[. . .][32]

Notes

This is an English translation of J. G. Fichte's correspondence in J. G. Fichte, *Gesamtausgabe: der Bayerischen Akademie der Wissenschaften, Briefe Band II*, Vol. 8, ed. Reinhard Lauth and Hans Jakob (Stuttgart-Bad Cannstatt: Friedrich Frommann Verlag Günther Holzboog, 1970), 325–368. Special thanks to the Glasscock Center for Humanities Research, Texas A&M University, for providing support of this translation.

   1. With his letter from the 21st of June, 1795, Fichte replied to a letter of Schiller's that he had received on the evening of the same day. In this letter, Schiller urged Fichte to send on his promised contribution to *die Horen*.

2. The matter in question concerns three letters of the essay "Ueber Geist und Buchstab in der Philosophie" [On Spirit and Letter in Philosophy], which first appeared, in altered form, in the 3rd issue of the 9th volume of the *Philosophisches Journal einer Gesellschaft Teutscher Gelehrten*, 199 ff.

3. The 23rd of June.

4. This citation is missing in the printed edition. It runs: "I sing as the bird sings in the branches; the song that bursts from the throat is its own abundant reward" (trans. by Richard Stokes). (Cf. L. v. Ulrichs, "Schiller und Fichte," in: "Deutsche Rundschau Herausgegeben von Julius Rodenberg." Volume XXXVI, July/August/September 1883, 252).

5. *Wilhelm Meister's Apprenticeship*, trans. by Erick Blackall (New York: Suhrkamp, 1989).

6. This explanation, too, which forms the beginning of the third letter, is missing in the publication from 1800. It is published in SW VIII, in a postscript after the "Vorrede des Herausgebers" [Editor's Preface]; without page number.

7. [Two variant spellings of the pronoun, both of which mean "other" or "another."]

8. Not extant. Cf. no. 287.2.

9. Further particulars have not been ascertained.

10. "Ueber Belebung und Erhöhung des reinen Interesse für Wahrheit" ["On Stimulating and Increasing the Pure Interest in Truth"], in the first part of the annual volume for 1795 of *die Horen*, 79–93.

11. No. 289.1 from June 22.

12. Already on the 26th of June, Schiller wrote to Cotta: "Should you receive offers from a local author because of the publishing house, I advise you to write me about it first, before you make a decision."

13. Fichte belonged to the board consisting of four persons that was supposed to check article submissions for *die Horen* prior to publication.

14. Friedrich Wilhelm Christian Karl Ferdinand von Humboldt, 1767–1835. Von Humboldt's opinion on this passage in Fichte's letters is found in his letter from July 17, 1795, to Schiller: "I can recognize this much: your admittedly inexcusable wrong consists in the fact that you have posited spirit of philosophy and not in philosophy. That the latter expression is used by the master himself is something I can attest to, and since he refers to me as a disciple, he must allow the validity of my testimony."

15. In the *Critique of Judgment*.

16. "Merkwürdige Belagerung von Antwerpen in den Jahren 1584 und 1585" [Noteworthy Siege of Antwerp in 1584–1585]. In: *die Horen*, 2.4, 68ff. and 2.5, 1ff.

17. Gotthold Ephraim Lessing, 1729–1781.

18. "Ueber Belebung und Erhöhung des reinen Interesse für Wahrheit" ["On Stimulating and Increasing the Pure Interest in Truth"].

19. Cf. Letter 290, from June 22.

20. Not extant. Cf. no. 296.2.

21. See also Letter no. 292 from June 27, 1795.
22. Henry Home, Lord Kames, 1696–1782; advocate, later Scotland's Lord of Justiciary; philosophical writer.
23. Cf. Letter no. 292.
24. "Die Horen Annual Volume for 1795, Part Six," Tübingen 1795.
25. [Lacuna].
26. "Ueber Geist und Buchstab in der Philosophie" ["On Spirit and Letter in Philosophy"].
27. [Lacunae].
28. In Letter no. 292, from June 27.
29. Aristotle, 384–322.
30. Friedrich von Oertel, 1764–1807.
31. [Ends abruptly].
32. [Breaks off abruptly].

References

Fichte, J. G., "Ueber Belebung und Erhöhung des reinen Interesse für Wahrheit" ["On Stimulating and Increasing the Pure Interest in Truth"]. *die Horen* (1795): 79–93.

Goethe, Johann Wolfgang von, *Wilhelm Meister's Apprenticeship*. Trans. Erick Blackall. New York: Suhrkamp, 1989.

Schiller, Friedrich, "Merkwürdige Belagerung von Antwerpen in den Jahren 1584 und 1585" ["Noteworthy Siege of Antwerp in 1584–1585"]. *die Horen*: 2.4.

———. "Ueber Geist und Buchstab in der Philosophie" ["On Spirit and Letter in Philosophy"]. *Philosophisches Journal einer Gesellschaft Teutscher Gelehrten*, Vol 9:3.

Ulrichs, L. v., "Schiller und Fichte." In "Deutsche Rundschau Herausgegeben von Julius Rodenberg," Volume XXXVI (July/Aug./Sept. 1883).

3

Hegel, Romantic Art, and the Unfinished Task of the Poetic Word

THEODORE GEORGE

We are familiar with the question, "What are poets for in a destitute time?" from Martin Heidegger's considerations of the relevance of poetry in modernity, and, of course, from the question as it was first posed at the turn of the nineteenth century by Friedrich Hölderlin in his poem *Bread and Wine*.[1] Much less appreciated, however, is that Hölderlin's contemporary, G. W. F. Hegel, also addresses the relevance of poetry (and the other arts) in modernity. Hegel treats the relevance of art in modernity under the auspices of what he calls "Romantic art," a term he uses to designate the forms and developments of the arts characteristic of Christian and, with this, modern Europe. Until recently, the common scholarly wisdom has been that Hegel sees no relevance of Romantic art so conceived. This common scholarly wisdom is bound up with Hegel's so-called end of art thesis—a misnomer, to be sure, insofar as Hegel himself does not use this turn of phrase. Hegel, we recall, famously thinks that art, religion, and philosophy are forms of "absolute spirit" that share in a speculative impulse to present truth, or, more precisely, to present the defining horizons or contexts of meanings that animate historically unfolding spirit. His "end of art" thesis is supposed to signify that whereas classical art was able to satisfy this impulse in ancient Greece, philosophy alone satisfies the impulse in modernity, and, thus, that there is no real relevance of Romantic art at all. This claim, in turn, is then sometimes said to be driven by Hegel's unjustified prejudice for classical art and thereby to embrace some of the most nostalgic tendencies of the Age of Goethe.[2]

Yet, as I wish to claim, Hegel's treatment of Romantic art is more nuanced than such common scholarly wisdom suggests. Specifically, I argue that while Hegel believes philosophy to be the highest manner in which truth is presented in modernity, he does not hold that art, for that reason, simply abandons its vocation to present truth altogether. Quite to the contrary, Hegel believes that Romantic art continues to present a definitive context of meaning for a historical epoch, in this case, the epoch of modernity, but in a "partial" or one-sided manner.[3] Hegel's position, as I wish to show, turns on his view of the role played by language in classical and Romantic art. For Hegel, all art can be understood as a work of language. Whereas in classical art such a work of language provides a *foundation* of society, however, in Romantic art such a work of language provides only what I shall call a *supplement* to any possible foundation. As such a supplement, in Romantic art the work of language remains incomplete, leaving final meaning always in deferral. Yet, I argue, this limitation of Romantic art's language, far from a deficiency, in fact specifies the relevance of Romantic art. Romantic art is relevant because it poses those who experience it with the infinite task of understanding the interiority of human life and the displacement of this interiority within modern society. In a final section, I will illustrate some of the stakes of Hegel's view of this Romantic sense of language in reference to his treatment of Cervantes's *Don Quixote*.

Art, Truth, and Work of Language

Hegel's elucidation of the relevance of Romantic art builds out from his notion of absolute spirit. Hegel argues that art, religion, and philosophy are distinguished as "absolute" forms of spirit because of their common vocation to present the truth, or, indeed, as Hegel's approach implies, the truth of spirit as such. Philosophers have contested what Hegel means by such a sense of truth for some time. Many in twentieth-century continental European philosophy have asserted a critical or deconstructive position that Hegel's notion of the absolute belongs to the Western tradition of what Heidegger referred to as "ontotheology" and from which we are now called to overcome, overturn, or twist free. In the last decades, proponents of what is sometimes called a "nonmetaphysical" interpretation of Hegel argue that the absolute is not part of some grandiose narrative at all but, instead, simply distinguishes kinds of knowledge claims that satisfy epistemic conditions necessary for the achievement of rigorous science. More recently, scholars from different quarters argue that Hegel's notion of the absolute concerns the character of rationality as such and, in this, the foundations, scope, and limits of normativity.[4]

While these (and other) interpretive frameworks no doubt shed light on Hegel's notion of the absolute, Hegel's approach to absolute spirit—and, in particular, to the form such spirit takes in art—can perhaps best be brought into focus, though, in reference to what Annemarie Gethmann-Siefert calls a "cultural, historical function."[5] By this, Gethmann-Siefert means that "the function of the artwork consists in the fact that, with it, historical truth—in Hegel's words, a historical self-consciousness—is conveyed in a sensible manner that is graspable by any average person."[6] Building on Gethmann-Siefert's approach, we may say Hegel sees art, religion, and philosophy as the results of cultural practices that articulate (and thus allow people to recognize) the defining context of meaning within a "spirit"—that is, a world, a historical moment, or, perhaps, society. For Hegel, the function of art, like that of religion and philosophy, then, is to allow a society as it were to take a good look at itself, to make explicit its deepest context of meaning, the context that otherwise remains merely tacit even as it shapes, orients, and grants legitimacy to all further meanings within that society. Art, religion, and philosophy all concern the absolute in the sense that they aim to present a content that is what Hans-Georg Gadamer, in a somewhat different context, refers to as the immemorial, the irreducible, or as that which cannot be gotten back behind (*das Unhintergehbare*). As Gadamer observes, the term *absolute* "means nothing other than the 'absolved,' and stands in classical Latin as the antonym of the 'relative.' It indicated independence from all restrictive conditions."[7] Art, like religion and philosophy, presents what is absolute for society, the context of meaning that is unconditional within society and that as such also thereby comprises the condition for all further meaning.

If the function of art, religion, and philosophy is the same, they fulfill this function through different forms. Hegel, as we know, thinks that there is a hierarchy among the three based on the respective forms that characterize each. Philosophy, he argues, is highest because the form it relies on—the concept—allows the content at which each of the three aims to be presented in a fullness of universality and determinacy that the other two lack. Religion and art both rely on sensuous images to present their content, and so both present their content with less universality and determinacy than philosophy. Religion is higher than art, however, because what it presents sensuously nevertheless points beyond the sensuous.[8]

Although art is the lowest among philosophy, religion, and art, it is nevertheless characterized by a harmony or balance of form and content. Hegel writes, "The vocation of art is to reveal truth in the form of sensuous artistic shape."[9] With this, Hegel sees the form of art in what can be called hermeneutical terms. His considerations of art focus not on the formal qualities of aesthetic objects and the pleasure or other affects that such objects can induce in us. Rather, for Hegel, art *says* something to us in sensuous form.

> In a work of art we begin with what is immediately presented to us and only then ask what its meaning or content is. The former, the external appearance, has no immediate value for us; we assume behind it something inward, a meaning whereby the external appearance is endowed with spirit.[10]

Art is an articulation of something—for Hegel, the deepest context of meaning within a society—that we, in turn, interpret and can come to understand.

As Gethmann-Siefert observes, Hegel's approach to art may be grasped first in terms of his notion of "work" (*Werk*) and, in particular, in terms of the work of language (*Sprache*). She writes, "He defines the work a unity of labor (*Arbeit*) and language (*Sprache*). . . . Art is 'labor' in the sense of the figuration of pre-given material. At the same time, however, it is 'language,' clarification (*Deutung*), explication (*Auslegung*), because the figuration follows a certain intention."[11]

Building on Gethmann-Siefert's approach, Hegel suggests that artworks are *works,* and, in this, the results of labor. Here, Hegel may be said to remind us that artworks are completions, concrete artifacts, of cultural practices designed to allow society to recognize the contexts of meaning that define it. As such, artworks share in the being of things, and therefore can be experienced communally and can endure over time. Hegel identifies the creation of artworks not foremost as the achievement of a singular genius, as many of his Romantic contemporaries believed, but rather thinks of the efforts of artists simply as one aspect of a larger societal process. Hegel characterizes this larger process in terms of *externalization*. In the "Introduction" to his *Aesthetics or Lectures on Fine Art*, Hegel asserts that the speculative impulse of art derives from "the fact that the human being is a *thinking* consciousness, that is, that the human being draws out of himself and puts *before himself* what he is and whatever else is."[12] For Hegel, our speculative impulse to become aware of ourselves and the world cannot be achieved in an immediate intuition but, rather, is an accomplishment that requires the mediation of what appears external to us. For Hegel, all of our endeavors, all of our efforts, whether in practical or theoretical life, are bound up with our efforts to put ourselves into something that appears external to us in order that we may better see ourselves in it. With this, the cultural practices that lead to the creation of art are like practices that lead to the production of a mirror, a concrete artifact made of natural material, whose materiality nevertheless recedes precisely in order to allow us to reflect on an image of ourselves.

In turn, Hegel maintains that artworks, as works, result from cultural practices of externalization that involve *language* in particular. Hegel's view of art as a work of language follows from his broader conception of language embodied in his celebrated idea that language is "the existence (*Dasein*) of spirit."[13] With this, Hegel eschews representational theories of language; for him, language is not a passive medium, as it were a vessel or container, that shuttles wholly formed ideas from a speaker's mind through the tongue to a listener's mind through the ear. Rather, Hegel conceives of language as a mode of enactment that brings meaning into existence in the first place. Language does not represent thought that has already been formed but, on the contrary, language is a distinctive mode of activity that determines meaning though the process of negations and differentiation. If language is enacted in words, such enactment is not a matter of positing terms that represent what they refer to, as if to say the word *bird* were to posit a term that represents the little animal I see outside the window. Rather, the enactment of language in words is a form of supersession (*Aufhebung*); the word is, first, a negation of what it refers to in its exteriority, which, however, secondly, raises what was referred to as a meaning that wins determinacy through its relation and difference from other meanings.[14] Art, as a work of language, then, is not a matter of representation. Rather, artworks are the artifacts of cultural practices that present meaning in consequence of processes of negation and determination.

It should be stressed that Hegel takes all art, regardless of kind, to be a work of language. This idea seems counterintuitive in view of the many arts that do not expressly involve the word. Hegel, of course, appreciates this fact. Although all art is distinguished as such by the vocation of presenting truth in sensuous form, the arts are many and, in his *Lectures*, Hegel discerns five major species: architecture, sculpture, painting, music, and poetry.

Hegel's claim that all artworks are works of language may initially seem counterintuitive given that of the five kinds of art he examines, only poetry is clearly linguistic. He believes that if only poetry presents truth expressly in the word, though, the ideality afforded by language is operative, by different artistic media and in different degrees of development, in all of the arts. Art, for Hegel, always signifies meaning, regardless of whether the media that signify are words *strictu senso*. Hegel writes, in a related context, that all art, as art, involves "something inward, a content, and something outward which signifies that content."[15] Hegel thinks that poetry is the highest of the species of art because it presents such content with more differentiation, more refinement than any of the other species. Poetry is thus highest, he holds, because the explicit reliance on the ideality of language that defines it allows for a larger range and more nuance of expression than the other, more materially constrained forms of expression found in the other arts.[16] Indeed, Hegel believes that the species of art fall into a hierarchy based on the refinement of presentation that is allowed by the constraints involved in their material forms, with architecture in the lowest position, then sculpture and, in turn, painting, music, and poetry.[17] Yet, regardless of such a hierarchy, all art, as art, is a work of language, even if the language at work is only explicit in poetry and remains differently and less developed in the other species. It is perhaps for this reason that Hegel treats poetry not only as the highest species of art but also, at the same time, an emblem of all species of art. Referring to the "poetical imagination," he writes that "since this element is common to all art forms, poetry runs through all of them and develops itself independently in each of them."[18]

The So-called End of Art and Its "After"

Hegel argues that while the vocation of all art is to present the deepest context of meaning within a society, art undergoes significant developments over the course of historically unfolding spirit. Hegel's description of these developments is, at least in part, oriented by his concern to establish a system of art, and, indeed, a system that will find a coherent place within his larger system of thought. Yet, Hegel's description of these developments also speaks to his concern for what we have called the historical-cultural significance of the arts, and, with this, his view of the relevance of the arts in modernity. Hegel, as we recall, thinks that art develops in three formal stages: symbolic, classical, and Romantic art.[19]

Hegel's account of these three stages unfolds along several dimensions. One of these dimensions that speaks to Hegel's concern to establish a system of art, in particular, may be called historico-geographical. In this, Hegel identifies symbolic art with the earliest history, or even the "threshold," of the history of the arts, as they were first developed in the ancient Parsi, Indian, and Egyptian cultures.[20] While Hegel's account may be said in fact to reflect the rising interest in German philosophy of the period in non-European cultures, it is also true that Hegel suggests peoples of Africa and Asia make little contribution to the history of art as such and he does not give attention to contributions by peoples in America or Australia.[21] Be that as it may, Hegel next identifies classical art with ancient Greece, and, more specifically, with the classical period of Greek civilization in particular. He identifies Romantic art, in turn, with the art of Christian Europe as this period culminates, as he sees it, in the contemporary art of the Romantic Movement.

Another dimension that speaks, in particular, to Hegel's concern to establish a system of art may be called compositional-structural. Hegel believes that although all art is composed of meaning that is presented in sensuous form, the basic relation of meaning to sensuous form shifts over the course of the three phases. He argues that in symbolic art, the meaning presented in a work remains as it were hidden, or at least partially hidden, by the sensuous form of the materials that comprise such works, such as the Egyptian pyramids. Hegel believes that in classical art, in turn, an immediate, perfect harmony is achieved between the meaning of a work and the sensuous form it takes. Although he suggests that this immediate, perfect harmony prevails in all of the forms of the classical period, it is epitomized by the human figure. And, Hegel thinks that in Romantic art, finally, the meaning of a work comes to overshadow the sensuous forms they take, increasingly, in fact, in painting, music, and poetry.[22]

There is, however, a further dimension of Hegel's account that, while it also contributes to his concern to establish a system of art, nevertheless also speaks in particular to the historical, cultural function of art. On this dimension, Hegel considers the spiritual need to which art answers, and, moreover, he focuses above all on the different needs that classical and Romantic art address. Hegel maintains that for the ancient Greeks who achieved classical art, artworks functioned as the highest manners in which the deepest context of meaning within society was presented. Hegel writes,

> [W]hen art is present in its supreme perfection, then precisely in its figurative mode it contains the kind of exposition most

essential to and most in correspondence with the content of truth. Thus, for example, in the case of the Greeks, art was the highest form in which the people represented the gods to themselves and gave themselves some awareness of truth.²³

Accordingly, for the Greeks, artworks also presented the foundation of society, the context of meaning that shaped, oriented, and served to legitimate all other meaning within society. Given Hegel's idea that art is a work of language, as well as the relation of the German word for foundation, *Stiftung*, to writing, it can perhaps further be said of his view that, for the Greeks, art did not simply *present* a foundation of society, but thereby and more originally *founded* society as such. As the Greeks' highest expression of society's deepest context of meaning, art served as a work of language that at once wrote and underwrote the world of the *polis*. In this, Hegel may be understood to agree with contemporaries in the Romantic Movement that, for the Greeks, at least, the art of their classical period served a mythopoetic function.

Yet, in contrast with some of Hegel's same contemporaries associated with the Romantic Movement, Hegel disavows that Romantic art performs such a foundational function in modernity. Hegel believes that the vocation of Romantic art, like that of all art, remains bound up with the presentation of society's deepest context of meaning. He nevertheless rejects that Romantic art is the highest manner in which such meaning is expressed in modern society, however. In modernity, he believes, this function is performed by philosophy and no longer by art. In accord with this, Hegel observes that "the whole spiritual culture" of the modern period has led to a "world of reflection"²⁴ and, in consequence, "the conditions of our present time are not favorable to art."²⁵ Hegel's claim forms a strong statement against his contemporaries within the Romantic Movement who, in different manners, asserted not only the continued relevance but even the priority of art over philosophy.²⁶ Hegel argues, by contrast, that modernity, as an age of reflection in which philosophy has become the highest expression of society's deepest context of meaning, gives no such priority or role to art. Rather, as Hegel puts the point in perhaps the most well-known assertion of his *Lectures*, "considered in its highest vocation," art "is and remains for us a thing of the past (*ein Vergangenes*)."²⁷

It is, of course, precisely this statement that is commonly understood as the definitive expression of Hegel's "end of art" thesis. On the basis of this statement, scholars surmise that because, in modernity, art no longer performs the function it once did in ancient Greece, it is completely relegated to the past, no longer of broader spiritual relevance whatsoever. As this idea is expressed by one commentator:

> [T]he modern artist is so alienated from society, culture, and the state that he has lost irredeemably his role as spokesman for its fundamental beliefs and values. While art will indeed continue, it will do so in a greatly reduced role: it will be nothing more than a form of self-expression.[28]

The art of modernity, because it no longer serves as the highest expression of society's deepest context of meaning, now performs little or no function at all, and, accordingly, artists of modernity are of no use to society, consigned to a life that is of highly circumscribed significance. From here, it is not difficult to reconstruct the further common scholarly wisdom that Hegel's considerations of art are colored by a prejudice toward classicism. In opposition to his contemporaries in the Romantic Movement, and perhaps also in line with the most nostalgic impulses of German intellectual culture in the Age of Goethe, Hegel upholds classical art, the Greeks, as an epitome of Western civilization that modern Europe can neither equal nor revive.

Yet, if the aspects of Hegel's account that concern his desire to establish a system of art may help fan the flames of this common scholarly wisdom, Hegel's focus on the cultural, historical significance of art, may, as Gethmann-Siefert observes,[29] recommend a different perspective. For, although Hegel believes that modernity is an age of reflection in which philosophy supersedes art as the highest expression of society's deepest context of meaning, this does not mean he thinks that modernity admits of little or no function for art at all. Quite to the contrary, even if art is no longer the highest expression of society's deepest context of meaning, its vocation continues to be the expression of such a context. Art, even in modernity, remains art. Displaced from the highest pedestal it enjoyed in ancient Greece, its vocation is still to tell the truth. Now, however, in modernity, art fulfills this vocation in the service of a different, and, to be sure, partial or one-sided function. In this, even once philosophy supersedes art as the highest expression of society's deepest context of meaning, art, in the form of Romantic art, enjoys what Hegel simply calls an "after,"[30] and, therewith, also enjoys a renewed and distinctive relevance.

Romantic Art as Infinite Task

With the term *Romantic,* Hegel refers first and foremost to the achievements of his contemporaries in the Romantic Movement, and he no doubt has in mind F. W. J. Schelling, Friedrich and August Schlegel, Caroline Schlegel-Schelling, Ludwig Tieck, and others. But, building on the usage of intellectuals of his times, Hegel defines the term more widely than this. As Ernst Behler observes, "In the vocabulary of the major European nations toward the end of the eighteenth century, the word could be used in a variety of contexts."[31] As pertains to the use of the term in more confined intellectual circles of the period, Behler asserts:

> Generally speaking, there are two basic meanings of the term in the literary criticism of the late eighteenth century, a chronological and a typological one. The chronological referred to a tradition of literature originating in the Middle Ages and pervading literary writing in modern Europe. . . . The typological referred to exotic traits in literature, including compositional and structural ones.[32]

Hegel, for his part, may be said to expand on and specify this usage of the period. He sees the Romantic art of his times as a fullest expression and also culmination of developments within European art since the end of the classical period. He also uses the term to identify the specific course of that development. In this, Hegel uses the term *Romantic* to categorize even the achievements of contemporaries such as Goethe and Schiller, focal periods of whose respective works are typically contrasted with those of the Romantic Movement. Hegel moreover uses the term *Romantic* to refer to examples of these developments from the medieval period, such as the romance, and from the modern period, such as the novel. In the broadest terms, Hegel associates Romantic art with Christian Europe.

Romantic art may be distinguished as the "after" of art, however, by a new cultural-historical function it performs within society. This new cultural-historical function may be described as a supplement. In the classical period, we recall, Hegel believes that the function of art was to provide a foundation for society. Hegel thinks that in the modern period, by contrast, philosophical science comes to take over this function of providing such a foundation. With this, art—and now, in the modern period, this means Romantic art—retreats from the function it performed in the classical period and comes to play a new role. In this new role, Romantic art continues to present the deepest context of meaning within society, but from only a finite, and, indeed, partial or perhaps even one-sided point of view.

He specifies, in fact, that Romantic art presents society's deepest context of meaning not from the standpoint of the whole but, instead, from the one-sided perspective of the inner life or "interiority" (*Innerlichkeit*) of the individual, and the "dehiscence" (*Entzweiung*) that individuals experience between their own inner lives and the externality of the modern society in which they find themselves. In his consideration of the end of Romantic art, Hegel sums up that

> now romantic art was from the beginning (*von Hause aus*) the deeper dehiscence of the interiority which finds satisfaction in itself and which, since objectivity does not completely correspond with the spirit's inward being, remained broken or indifferent to the objective world.[33]

In the modern period, Romantic art still performs a function, but this function is no longer to provide a foundation. Rather, the function of Romantic art is to supplement the foundation provided by philosophy: to bring into focus and give contour to this foundation from the fractured standpoint of the inner lives of individuals and their relation to society.

Romantic art's performance of this new cultural, historical function as supplement, however, is bound up with a limitation of language. For Hegel, as we have said, all art is a work of language. Classical art performed the function of foundation because the work done by language in classical art was to make explicit the deepest context of meaning that shaped, oriented, and gave all other meaning within society legitimacy. Classical art functioned to found, *stiften,* a society because it wrote and underwrote that society's deepest context of meaning. Romantic art, by contrast, performs only the function of supplement because the work done by language in Romantic art is partial. Indeed, in a claim that anticipates motifs of deconstruction, Hegel argues that the work done by language in Romantic art is partial because oriented by an intention that is, strictly speaking, impossible to fulfill. This is the intention to express something that, per definition, cannot be put in sensuous form: interiority, and the experience of the dehiscence of interiority and the outside world. Hegel writes, "External appearance cannot any longer express interiority, and if it is still called to do so it merely has the task of proving that the external is a dissatisfying experience and must point back to the inner, to the mind and feeling as the essential element."[34]

In Romantic art, ultimately, language presents its subject matter always only in the mode of absence; the difference between what is intended and what is presented remains always open, and, accordingly, the presence of what is intended remains always in deferral.

The fact that Romantic art's function as supplement is bound up with a limitation of language, however, is not a deficiency in that function. Quite to the contrary, the relevance of Romantic art is itself precisely made possible by this limitation. For, after all, modernity is defined by nothing else than individuals' experience of interiority and the divergence they feel between their inner lives and the society around them. Accordingly, Romantic art precisely gives articulation to an ineluctable aspect of the context of meaning that shapes, orients, and gives legitimacy to modern life. Although Romantic art thus provides no foundation for society, it nevertheless performs important functions. In her research, Gethmann-Siefert observes, for example, that because Romantic art captures the spirit of modernity, it is an important source of education (*Bildung*) for modern individuals as they seek to find a provisional home for their interiority within the complexities of modern society. She writes, "Hegel defined the historical function of art in the modern world as 'formal education' "; in this, "art is as before—in the sense of Schiller's conception of the aesthetic education of man—an essential means to the education of reason, above all, one accessible to all."[35]

Perhaps more crucially still, though, Hegel argues that while Romantic art no longer functions as a foundation but only as a supplement, this supplement itself opens onto infinite possibilities of artistic expression. In this, as philosophers such as Hans-Georg Gadamer have stressed,[36] Hegel's so-called thesis on the end of art is at the same time a declaration of the liberation of art, not only *from* the requirement to provide a society's foundation but also *onto* an infinite possibility. Hegel writes that "the form . . . of Romantic art from its beginning on [is] afflicted by the opposition that infinite subjectivity is in itself irreconcilable with the external material and is to remain unreconciled."[37] There is a flip side to the fact that Romantic art is characterized by an intention that it cannot fulfill: Romantic art is thereby also oriented by a task that is infinite because it can thus neither be relinquished nor completed. Hegel argues that this means Romantic art can treat the inner lives of individuals and their dehiscence from every imaginable angle, from "the side of spiritual aims, mundane interests, passions, collisions, sorrows, and joys, hopes and satisfactions" to "the side of the external, that is, nature and its kingdoms and most detailed phenomena."[38] For Hegel, the "scope" of Romantic art is "infinitely extended. It opens out into multiplicity without bounds."[39] Romantic art, no longer a foundation but a supplement, and, indeed, a supplement cut on a limitation of language, is precisely for that reason a source of infinite possible meaning.

Contrary to much common wisdom and scholarly opinion, then, Hegel's philosophy of art provides a response to the question made familiar in our times by Heidegger and posed originally by Hegel's contemporary Hölderlin at the turn of the nineteenth century: What are poets (or, more broadly, artists) for in the destitute time of modernity? Indeed, Hegel's response to this question is as distinctive as it is rich in implication. On the one hand, Hegel rejects some of the claims made by contemporaries in the Romantic Movement that maintain the priority of art, even in modernity. If art is a work of language that provided a foundation in ancient Greece, then such a function is long since a thing of the past. On the other hand, Hegel affirms that art fulfills a new function after its cultural, historical role as foundation has come to an end. In this, art comes to be charged with the impossible, though for this reason also infinite, task of presenting the inner life of individuals in their dehiscence from society.

Don Quixote as Image of the Relevance of the Romantic

Hegel's claim about the relevance of Romantic art may, in a final suggestion, be described in reference to Hegel's brief commentary in the *Aesthetics* on Cervantes's *Don Quixote*. No doubt, Hegel's comments about Cervantes's novel are made in full cognizance of the opinions of his contemporaries in the Romantic Movement about *Don Quixote*. Especially in early phases of German Romanticism, Cervantes's *Don Quixote* was held up by many as an epitome of the Romantic heritage of art and an anticipation of contemporary Romantic art.[40] This celebration of *Don Quixote* found expression, for example, in Tieck's enthusiasm for and important translation of the novel into German in the period. Friedrich Schlegel's review of the Tieck translation gave more attention to the significance of the novel, as did his treatment of Cervantes and Don Quixote in his *Dialogue on Poetry*. There, Schlegel holds up Cervantes and Shakespeare as "so great that everything else in comparison with them appears as merely preparatory, explicatory, and complimentariety circumstance."[41] And, of *Don Quixote*, he adds that "fantastic wit and lavish abundance of daring ideas prevail."[42] Schelling, in speaking of art in the modern Spanish and English heritages in his *Lectures on Art*, sees in the interplay between the characters Sancho and Don Quixote nothing less than the philosophical theme of a "struggle of the real with the ideal."[43] For these and other early German Romantics, Cervantes's *Don Quixote* was more than an amusing tale; it was one of the most important flowerings of Romantic art.

Though Hegel disagrees with Romantic contemporaries about the significance of Romantic art within modernity, he, too, recognizes that *Don Quixote* is a certain acme of Romantic art itself. Hegel takes up *Don Quixote* in his discussion of the third and final stage of the development of Romantic art. He associates this third and final stage with modern, more secular art; it is preceded, in a first stage, by Romantic art from the religious sphere and, in a second stage, by Romantic art that focuses on chivalry.[44] In the third and final stage, as Hegel argues, Romantic art comes to be most fully liberated from constraints on art imposed by the demands of Christian theology and beliefs, allowing the dehiscence of interiority and the external world that characterizes Romantic art to reach its fullest expression. Here, the focus is on "the further material of human existence . . . which becomes explicitly free and, because it does not appear permeated by religion and compression into the unity of the Absolute, stands on its own feet and treads independently in its own sphere."[45] In this third and final stage, as religiosity and chivalry recede, what "gives new satisfaction is the thirst for this present and this reality itself, the delight of the self in what is *there*, contentment with self, with the finitude of man, and, generally, with the finite, the particular."[46]

Hegel turns to *Don Quixote* as an epitome of the form that this new emphasis on individual, finite existence takes in modern, more secular Romantic art. This is the form of *adventure*. Hegel introduces this term to capture the specific form that the depiction of actions and events take in modern, more secular Romantic art in contrast with classical art. In classical art, he argues, the depiction of actions and events is characterized by "necessity." He writes, "Action and event, taken in the stricter sense of . . . classical art, require an inherently true and absolute necessary end; such an end includes in itself what determines both its external shape and also the manner of carrying it out in the real world."[47] In a classical work of art, paradigmatically, in Greek tragedy, action and events are depicted as a matter of hard and fast destiny. In Sophocles's *Antigone*, for example, once Thebes's civil war has ended with one brother declared a patriot and the other a traitor, all further actions and events are ordained: Creon is obligated to honor one brother in burial and cast the other outside the city walls; Antigone is then obligated on behalf of her family to perform burial rites to her outcast brother; the conflict that follows from their actions is as unavoidable as it is disastrous.

In modern, more secular Romantic art, by contrast, "this is not so."[48] Rather, here, the depiction of actions and events are characterized by "contingency." He writes, "for if here too inherently universal and substantial ends are displayed in their realization, still these ends in themselves neither determine the action nor order or articulate its inner course; on the contrary, this aspect of actualization they must let go and therefore yield it to contingency and accident."[49] In more modern, secular Romantic art, there is no longer a question of a protagonist portrayed as part of a necessary fate. Rather, in such Romantic art, the individual is depicted with an interiority, with ends and desires that find no adequate home in the world, and such an individual thus remains never whole but rather always only divided from the world, errant. It is to bring into focus the depiction of just such an individual that Hegel invokes *Don Quixote*. For Hegel, the protagonist of the same name is no Greek tragic hero, bound by the necessity of fate. Rather, Quixote is on an adventure. In this, Hegel writes, Quixote stands only on "mundane ground" where the

> basic causes of actions and events consist of the endlessly varied and adventurousness of ideas and of the external and internal contingencies of love, honor, and fidelity. . . . In most of these things there is no state of affairs, no situation, no conflict which would make the action *necessary*; the heart just wants out and looks for adventures deliberately.[50]

In modern, more secular Romantic art, actions and events are depicted in the full view of the tension between interiority, our intentions and desires, and the externality of a world in which these intentions and desires bear only contingently on actions and events that follow from them.

If Hegel turns to *Don Quixote* as an epitome of the form that actions and events take in modern, more secular Romantic art, then perhaps Don Quixote may himself be taken as an image of the relevance of Romantic art as such. Romantic art is a supplement, a work of language that remains oriented by an intention that, like Don Quixote's quests, may seem to many in the modern world to be nothing short of lunacy—and, indeed, all the more so, given that this intention is itself something that cannot be fulfilled, leaving Romantic artists and their audiences to explore the possibilities of inner life *ad infinitum*, perhaps as Quixote all but endlessly roams the countryside of La Mancha. Romantic art, in short, is itself something of an adventure. But, in this, Romantic art is nevertheless more than merely amusing; it allows us to examine the possibilities for our inner lives and the dehiscence we experience in this interiority within modern society.

Notes

1. Martin Heidegger, "What Are Poets For?" in *Poetry, Language, Thought*, trans. Albert Hofstadter (New York, London, Toronto, Sydney, New Dehli, and Auckland: Harper Perennial Modern Thought, 2013), 89. Friedrich Hölderlin, *Bread and Wine*, in *Hyperion and Selected Poems* (New York: Continuum, 1990), 185; translation modified.

2. See, for example, Peter Szondi. *Poetik und Geschichtsphilosophie I* (Frankfurt am Main: Suhrkamp, 1974); and Jacques Taminiaux, "Nostalgia for Greece at the Dawn of Classical Germany," in P*oetics, Speculation, and Judgement: The Shadow of the Work of Art from Kant to Phenomenology* (Albany: State University of New York Press, 1993), 73–92.

3. G. W. F. Hegel, *Aesthetics: Lectures on Fine Art*, Vol. 1, trans. T. M. Knox (Oxford: Clarendon Press, 1975, reprinted 2010), 609; translation modified.

4. Characteristic of critical and deconstructive approaches to Hegel's notion of the absolute within the continental tradition are, respectively, Theodor Adorno, *Negative Dialectics* (New York: Continuum, 1973), and Jacques Derrida, *Glas*, trans. John P. Leavey and Richard Rand (Lincoln: University of Nebraska Press, 1990). An important impetus for the nonmetaphysical approach to Hegel's notion of the absolute is Robert Pippin, *Hegel's Idealism, The Satisfaction of Self-Consciousness* (Cambridge: Cambridge University Press, 1989). Finally, an important impetus for approaches to Hegel's notion of the absolute that center on rationality and the scope and limits of normativity may be found in the works of Robert Brandom.

5. Annemarie Gethmann-Siefert, *Einführung in Hegels Ästhetik* (München: Fink, 2005), 31; translation mine. While the purpose of my essay differs from Gethmann-Siefert, my overall approach is deeply indebted to and in several regards parallels that of her *Einführung*. Of particular significance for my chapter are, as becomes clear from this chapter, her focus on Hegel's approach to art as a work and her reconsideration of Hegel's so-called end of art thesis.

6. Ibid.; translation mine.

7. Hans-Georg Gadamer, "Wort und Bild, 'so wahr, so seiend,' " in *Gesammelte Werke*, Vol. 8 (Tübingen: Mohr Siebeck, 1991), 375. Cf. Hans-Georg Gadamer, "The Artwork in Word and Image: 'So true! So full of being!' " in *The Gadamer Reader: A Bouquet of Later Writings* (Evanston: Northwestern University Press, 2007), 197.

8. Hegel elucidates his view of the relation of art, religion, and philosophy in a number of texts and lectures over the course of his career. See, for example, "Absolute

Spirit," or, as it is also translated "Absolute Mind," in G. W. F. Hegel, *Philosophy of Mind, Hegel's Encyclopedia of the Philosophical Sciences (Book 3)*, trans. Wallace and A. V. Miller, rvsd. Michael Inwood (Oxford: Oxford University Press, 2010).

9. G. W. F. Hegel, *Aesthetics: Lectures on Fine Art*, Vol. 1, T. M. Knox (Oxford: Clarendon Press, 1975, reprinted 2010), 55; translation modified.

10. Ibid., 19.

11. Gethmann-Siefert, *Einführung*, 31; translation mine.

12. Hegel, *Aesthetics*, 31.

13. G. W. F. Hegel, *Phenomenology of Spirit*, trans. A. V. Miller (Oxford: Oxford University press, 1977), 395. Cf. Hegel, *Phänomenologie des Geistes*, in *Werke in zwanzig Bände*, Vol. 3 (Frankfurt am Main: Suhrkamp, 1986), 478.

14. For a fuller account of Hegel's views of language, see Josef Simon, *Das Problem der Sprache bei Hegel* (Stuttgart: Kohlhammer, 1966). See also Theodore George, "The Worklessness of Literature: Blanchot, Hegel, and the Ambiguity of the Poetic Word," *Philosophy Today, Selected Studies in Phenomenology and Existential Philosophy* 50, supplement (2006).

15. Hegel, *Aesthetics*, 20.

16. Ibid., 89.

17. See Hegel, *Aesthetics*, 83–90.

18. Ibid.

19. Ibid., 75–81, 299–302.

20. Ibid., 314.

21. The Eurocentrism of Hegel's claims about art may be addressed within the context of many of his other, and often troubling, ideas of his about what he calls "world history." While this and related topics concerned with the significance of Hegel's views on racism and colonialism have received extensive attention, recent contributions include Rocio Zambrana, "Hegel, History, and Race," in *The Oxford Handbook of Philosophy and Race*, ed. Naomi Zak (Oxford: Oxford University Press, 2017); and Alison Stone, "Hegel and Colonialism," *Hegel Bulletin* (2017): 1–24. Note that Hegel may omit considerations of art from peoples of the Americas and Australia in connection with his view that the peoples of these continents do not belong to "world history." See Hegel, *Vorlesungen über die Philosophie der Geschichte*, in *Werke* 12, 107.

22. See Hegel, *Aesthetics*, 73–90. Hegel makes reference to pyramids in this vein at ibid., 354.

23. Ibid., 102.

24. Ibid., 11.

25. Ibid., 10.

26. For a concise statement of the point, see Fredrick Beiser, *The Romantic Imperative: The Concept of Early German Romanticism* (Cambridge: Harvard University Press, 2003), 73–87.

27. Ibid., 11.

28. Frederick Beiser, *Hegel* (New York: Routledge, 2005), 300.

29. Gethmann-Siefert, *Einführung*, 31.
30. Ibid., 103.
31. Ernst Behler, *German Romantic Literary Theory* (Cambridge: Cambridge University Press, 1993), 24.
32. Ibid., 25–26.
33. Ibid., 609; translation modified.
34. Ibid., 527; translation modified.
35. Gethmann-Siefert, *Einführung in Hegels Ästhetik*, 352; translation mine. Gethmann-Siefert's approach to art and education is, in fact, more expansive than the quotation suggests. She furthermore considers, notably, for example, that art can provide indirect orientation in action and a basis for critique. See ibid., ff.
36. See, for example, Hans-Georg Gadamer, "Ende der Kunst? Von Hegel's Lehre von Vergangenheitscharakter der Kunst bis zur Anti-Kunst von Heute" in *Werke* 8, 206–20.
37. Hegel, *Aesthetics*, 574.
38. Ibid., 524.
39. Ibid., 525.
40. See, for example, Anthony Close, *The Romantic Approach to 'Don Quixote': A Critical History of the Romantic Tradition in 'Quixote' Criticism* (Cambridge: Cambridge University Press, 1977), 29–67, here 29–30.
41. Friedrich Schlegel, "Dialogue on Poetry," in *the German Library*, Vol. 21, *German Romantic Criticism*, ed. Leslie Willson (New York: Continuum, 1982), 92.
42. Ibid. Note that Schegel's comment pertains to *Don Quixote*, Part I in particular. He adds that Part II augments the greatness of the novel through the inclusion of an element of "critical judgment." Ibid.
43. F. W. J. Schelling, *Philosophie der Kunst*, in *Sämtliche Werke*, Vol. 5 (Stuttgart: Cotta, 1859), 679.
44. Hegel, *Aesthetics*, 528–29. Hegel stresses that the third stage is more secular again in *Aesthetics*, 573.
45. Ibid.
46. Ibid., 573–74.
47. Ibid., 587.
48. Ibid.
49. Ibid.
50. Ibid., 589.

References

Adorno, Theodor. *Negative Dialectics*, New York: Continuum, 1973.
Behler, Ernst. *German Romantic Literary Theory*. Cambridge: Cambridge University Press, 1993.
Beiser, Frederick. *Hegel*. New York: Routledge, 2005.

———. *The Romantic Imperative: The Concept of Early German Romanticism.* Cambridge: Harvard University Press, 2003.
Bowie, Andrew. *Aesthetics and Subjectivity: From Kant to Nietzsche.* Manchester: Manchester University Press, 2003.
Close, Anthony. *The Romantic Approach to 'Don Quixote': A Critical History of the Romantic Tradition in 'Quixote' Criticism.* Cambridge: Cambridge University Press, 1977.
Derrida, Jacques. *Glas*, Lincoln: University of Nebraska Press, 1990.
Gadamer, Hans-Georg. "Wort und Bild, 'so wahr, so seine.'" In *Gesammelte Werke*, Vol. 8, Tübingen: Mohr Siebeck, 1991.
———. "Artwork in Word and Image: 'So True! So Full of Being!" In *The Gadamer Reader: A Bouquet of Later Writings*, edited by Richard E. Palmer, Evanston: Northwestern University Press, 2007.
———. "Ende der Kunst? Von Hegel's Lehre von Vergangenheitscharakter der Kunst bis zur Anti-Kunst von Heute." In *Gesammelte Werke*, Vol. 8, Tübingen: Mohr Siebeck, 1991.
George, Theodore. "The Worklessness of Literature: Blanchot, Hegel, and the Ambiguity of the Poetic Word." *Philosophy Today, Selected Studies in Phenomenology and Existential Philosophy* 50, supplement (2006).
Gethmann-Siefert, Annemarie. *Einführung in Hegels Ästhetik.* München: Fink, 2005.
Heidegger, Martin. "What Are Poets For?" In *Poetry, Language, Thought.* New York: Harper Perennial Modern Thought, 2013.
Hegel, G. W. F. *Aesthetics: Lectures on Fine Art*, Vol. 1. Oxford: Clarendon Press, 1975.
———. *Phänomenologie des Geistes.* In *Werke in zwanzig Bände*, Vol. 3. Frankfurt am Main: Suhrkamp, 1986.
———. *Phenomenology of Spirit.* Oxford: Oxford University Press, 1977.
———. *Vorlesungen über die Philosophie der Geschichte.* In *Werke in zwanzig Bände*, Vol. 12. Frankfurt am Main: Suhrkamp, 1986.
Hölderlin, Friedrich. *Hyperion and Selected Poems*, New York: Continuum, 1990.
Pippin, Robert. *Hegel's Idealism, The Satisfaction of Self-Consciousness*, Cambridge: Cambridge University Press, 1989.
Schelling, F. W. J. *Philosophie der Kunst.* In *Sämtliche Werke*, Vol. 5. Stuttgart: Cotta, 1859.
Schlegel, Friedrich. "Dialogue on Poetry." In *the German Library*, Vol. 21, *German Romantic Criticism*, edited by Leslie Willson. New York: Continuum, 1982.
Simon, Josef. *Das Problem der Sprache bei Hegel.* Stuttgart: Kohlhammer, 1966.
Stone, Alison. "Hegel and Colonialism." *Hegel Bulletin* (2017).
Szondi, Peter. *Poetik und Geschichtsphilosophie I.* Frankfurt am Main: Suhrkamp, 1974.
Taminiaux, Jacques, "Nostalgia for Greece at the Dawn of Classical Germany." In *Poetics, Speculation, and Judgment: The Shadow of the Work of Art from Kant to Phenomenology.* Albany: State University of New York Press, 1993.
Zambrana, Rocio. "Hegel, History, and Race." In *The Oxford Handbook of Philosophy and Race*, edited by Naomi Zak, Oxford: Oxford University Press, 2017.

4

Who Is Nietzsche's Archilochus?

Rhythm and the Problem of the Subject

BABETTE BABICH

Between Poetry and Philosophy

In *Thus Spoke Zarathustra*, Nietzsche's parodic version of a masterwork, self-proclaimed: *for all and none*, he teases, *Only a fool, only a poet—"nur Narr, nur Dichter."* For the most part, Nietzsche has been read as poetry or as highly styled literature, not merely by literary scholars but in philosophy, with Alexander Nehamas's *Life as Literature*,[1] and David Allison's *Reading the New Nietzsche*.[2] Today, we would hardly dismiss Nietzsche by calling him a poet, the way his teacher, Friedrich Ritschl, chided his pupil for the Parisian-novelistic flourishes of his writing. Nevertheless, Nietzsche yearbooks and journals and monographs and book collections feature disparate sensibilities, at times foregrounding Germanist literary studies, and philosophers who read Nietzsche are likewise, if differently, conflicted, where this last grouping is itself further sundered into mainstream readers (the analytic modality that only considers its own voices and values, even titling themselves "continental," the better to ignore those remaining among the still-inspirational continental tradition of the *New Nietzsche*, that is, reading Nietzsche by way of Heidegger and Gadamer, through Deleuze and Derrida, etc.).

To attend to Nietzsche and poetry, we could focus on many poets who claimed Nietzsche's attention, from Homer and Hesiood to Pindar and the tragic poets, Aeschylus and Sophocles, to Schiller and Hölderlin.[3] Other scholars, in the mode of the analytic tradition following George Stack and Stanley Cavell, have highlighted Nietzsche's affinity with Emerson,[4] and Nietzsche himself would claim Leopardi and Hafiz, among others.

Similarly central is Nietzsche's focus on Goethe, from whom he borrows one element of his notion of the *Übermensch,* just as a caution against reading Nietzsche, in today's fashion, as a transhumanist *avant la lettre,* or reading him romantically, with Sloterdijk, as if, a tad ahistorically, he might be linked to newer names such as Rilke and Benn (American scholars do this by conjoining him with Wallace Stevens), or as if he were the Heinse Nietzsche undoubtedly knew.[5] For my part, I am one of the few scholars who would add the second century CE Lucian to the list, as Nietzsche read this parodist, satirist who left prolific writings, and whom today's classicists devalue in favor of Mennipus of Gadara, whose writings are lost to us.[6]

Here I explore Nietzsche's Archilochus.

Archilochus and the "Birth of Tragedy" Out of the Spirit of Lyric Poetry

In their study of Nietzsche's *Birth of Tragedy,* Michael Silk and Joseph Stern are struck by "the importance" Nietzsche gives "Archilochus as the father of Greek lyric."[7] And they might well be struck, for we know nothing about Archilochus, as Nietzsche reminded his students in his lecture courses on *Greek Lyric,* apart from what this expressly autographic poet tells us.[8]

Archilochus is foregrounded in the lecture courses on *Greek Lyric* Nietzsche offered over a period of ten years at the University of Basel.[9] Yet references to Nietzsche's lecture courses do not go without saying: we typically overlook his philological formation, as we overlook the content of his lecture courses,[10] whatever our own formation may be, philologico-literary or philosophical.[11]

There are a number of reasons for this non-notice, but certainly one of the most important of these is that—apart from the published source work (in Latin and in German) on Diogenes Laërtius—all of this happens to be *Nachlaß.*[12] Compounding matters, the scholar would have to dispose over the same philological competences Nietzsche enjoyed, that is, one would have to be able to translate one's native German into Greek or into Latin as Nietzsche did (and as he taught his students to do—this pedagogic strategy he inherited from Ritschl who taught in Latin). Today, we are rather more interested in questions of Nietzsche's "style," be it as Derrida meant this, or as Alexander Nehamas or Tracy Strong intends (the former in a more literary sense, the latter more rhetorically).

I have argued that Nietzsche's book on tragedy advances a multifarious challenge to his own discipline, including the Homer question as a question, including "Pre-Platonic" philosophy by contrast with the Socratic, including the Platonic and the Aristotelian,[13] including the relation between epic and lyric and tragic poetic modalities, as well as ancillary questions of historiographical methodology and chronology.

To this same extent, *The Birth of Tragedy out of the Spirit of Music* was not dedicated to drumming up publicity for Wagner, as is popularly suggested (attributing the work to a Wagner phase).[14] Thus, Nietzsche himself would claim that his first book raised a heretofore unprecedented question: the question of science as such, including a revolution in thinking about antiquity, particularly with respect to ancient Greek lyric poetry. That revolution included thinking tragedy as born from music, qua spirit, as musical performance. But for us, even for the most recent reconstruction of ancient Greek music, music is ancillary, an accompaniment to the poetic composition. Nietzsche argued that this presentist assumption led us astray in the case of ancient Greek poetry. For us, the notion of a

> *necessary* relation between poem and music accordingly makes no sense for the two worlds of tone and image are too remote from each other to enter more than an external relationship. The poem is only a symbol and related to the music like the Egyptian hieroglyph of courage to a courageous soldier.[15]

Given the relation between music and word, particularly with respect to the things that concerned Nietzsche as philologist, including the measures of quantitifying [*quantitierenden*] rhythm, the question of lyric poetry is the key to Nietzsche's reflections on tragedy.[16]

"[T]ragedy," as Nietzsche writes in a lecture on Greek music drama, "was originally only a choral chant."[17] The claim is *literal*: "True Greek music is purely vocal: the natural liaison between the language of word and tone hadn't yet been sundered."[18] The "birth of tragedy" thus concerns the origin of language:[19] music and word, lyric poetry, including oral poetry, and the original function of writing as a means for recording sound or music.

Nietzsche tells us that Greek music is "purely vocal," in other words: the word itself qua *spoken* is musical. Nietzsche took this to be his "discovery."[20] Paul Maas notes this in his 1923 *Griechische Metrik*, translated by Hugh Lloyd-Jones in 1962 as *Greek Metre*.[21] Indeed, Nietzsche's discovery remains the basis of Greek *prosody*, that is to say, the pronunciation of ancient Greek, to the present day.[22]

To this same extent, Nietzsche emphasized the musicality of the Greek word, contra the emphatic stress-accent;[23] arguing that for the ancients the "rhythmical [stress] ictus is unattested, shows no effect, was, rather, completely excluded." Thus Nietzsche differentiates a "*ton-Iktus*" (pitch ictus), elusive for us owing to our modern European linguistic sensibilities.

On Rhythm

Highlighting a "4fold" rhythmic *efficacy,* Nietzsche explains the Greeks as "compelling" their deities; the same kind of "compulsion" survives in certain formulaic prayers as well as magical formulae, *abracadabra*, and so on.[24]

If the first function of rhythm is compulsion, the second function is designed to appease or "purify" the feelings of the gods, with the most persuasive function that of helping the deities "remember" the prayer put to them, in the same way as rhythm serves this function for human beings and, finally, fourthly, rhythm projects the prayer, allowing it to reach the distant heaven, given the greater resonance of song.

The Gay Science reprises these aspects (of rhythm and prayer) and Nietzsche's unpublished notes emphasize, *per analogiam,* that as the "rhythmic resonates with the body,"[25] it also resonates with the gods: the "rhythmic stamping of the feet calls the deities." Simultaneously, as corollary, the more scientific or modern we become, the less we *need* and the less we *understand* rhythm.

As a specialist in the sources of Diogenes Laërtius, Nietzsche reminds us that the "field of shards,"[26] the textual remnants handed down to us, is a preselected array, chosen for "school use."[27] Consequently, the poetry that has been preserved survived by having been filtered through—whether positively or negatively—the same Hellenistic, Latin taste.[28]

This is no less true of Archilochus, negatively speaking, unsuited as he was to Roman taste. Thus, Nietzsche highlights the "*saltus lyrici*," that is, the leaps in sensibility characteristic of lyric poetry. In this way, Nietzsche writes here, as he repeats in *The Birth of Tragedy*: "Greek music perished even before Hellenism."[29]

Nietzsche's quantitifying rhythmic discovery allows us to speak of changing tones, like Hölderlin's famous *Wechsel der Töne*,[30] which Hölderlin borrows from Archilochus. Just so, Nietzsche argued that tragedy derives from the music of the word, specifically lyric poetic form as such.

New Souls

Where Nietzsche's Zarathustra urges us to learn to "hear with our eyes," Nietzsche's efforts encourage us to read with our ears, musing to himself with respect to the "*neue Seele*" or "child" that was his first book—*sie hätte singen sollen*—this soul should have sung.

But how *should* such a new soul have sung? What does this mean? What would it have sounded like? The question is important because it bears on our modern limitations as we have just retraced these with respect to music in singing ancient tragedy and the tonic sensibility of ancient Greek.

The "alien" quality concerns Dionysus, a god not to be understood apart from Archilochus and religious ecstasy. In addition to Dionysus, Nietzsche emphasizes a revision of conventional understandings of Apollo.[31]

Nietzsche further claims that his theory is more scientifically historical than all the others, foregrounding his account as renouncing any single "decision" whilst offering "multiple possibilities."[32] This indeterminacy follows from our lack of ancient "rhythmic taste" together with "ancient *Melos*" as such. Thus, Nietzsche denies the magisterial appeal of "infallibility" and recognizes that his account will likely afford less *enjoyment* than more popular schemes and less *comprehensibility*. Yet he firmly claims the "undying appeal of unqualified *truth*,"[33] underscored "with no exaggeration" for his "main theory."[34]

This alone should compel attention: Nietzsche claims that his theory is no speculation but unvarnished, the plain and simple *truth*. Dissonant indeed, where Nietzsche otherwise insists, with respect to language and texts, world and experience that there is no truth.

Nietzsche's first book failed to inspire academic response or engagement. This is not unique to Nietzsche but corresponds to academic politics as usual. We academics rarely debate views clashing with the received view; we ignore them; we don't tell our students about them; we don't review their books; we don't reference the authors in our articles.

Add to that the issue of complexity surrounding Archilochus, even if we haven't necessarily heard of him (by contrast, say, with Homer); thus Nietzsche's ranking Archilochus alongside Homer surprises Silk and Stern. And yet Archilochus' "many innovations," as recounted in Plutarch's *de Musica* is worth noting:

> the trimeter, the combination of unlike measures, the recitative or rhythmical recitation of poetry to music, and the style of music to which recitative was set. . . . the epode, the tetrameter, the cretic, the prosodiac, and the lengthening of the "heroic" or dactylic hexameter; and some authorities would add the elegiac, and not only that, but the combination of the epibatic paeon with the iambic, and that of the lengthened "heroic" with the prosodiac and the cretic. He is also credited with the device of reciting some of a number of iambic lines to music and singing the others, a device afterwards employed by the tragic poets and introduced by Crexus into the dithyramb. He is also thought to have been the first to set the music of the accompanying instrument an octave higher than the voice, instead of in the same register with it as had been the custom before his day.[35]

To this listing we may add Nietzsche's own discovery concerning quantitifying (*quantitierenden*) rhythm. This is not the Nietzsche we know. This is not the Nietzsche who proposes the death of Zarathustra (did he plan it? as Dave Allison argued, or stage it as others contend), or the Nietzsche who reflects on the epistemological cold of the godless universe breathing down our necks,[36] prophet of nihilism, or ascendant "will to power," or phantom of transhumanism (same as the old Nietzschean fascism, today's instauration of what Nietzsche called the last man: insisting on the right to "immortality" or, at minimum, a lifespan upgrade.)[37]

Yet Nietzsche's discovery of *quantitirenden Rythmik* would remain so present that he was still writing about music (and word) toward the end of his active life as "phrasing," using a musical device to discuss Riemann with the musicologist Carl Fuchs.[38] In these letters from August 1888, Nietzsche recalls, even to the extent of quoting word for word, his earlier writings.[39]

This original discovery articulates *performance practice* in words. Thus, Nietzsche cites "ποὺς θέσις ἄρσις"[40] drawn from "*Orchestik*," from "walking & dancing." Gestural cues for tonality, as we read in *Concerning Music and*

Word, involve movement, first lifting and then lowering the foot (or hand), generating "two lines." ⌒ ⌢

Nietzsche duly draws two little lightly curved lines to illustrate his point: the one arcing upward and the other descending downward, showing the raising and lowering of dynamic expression, or movement and pitch. Here, Nietzsche cites Aristides on *arsis* and *thesis*, be it for the ear or the eye, with the foot (to be heard and seen) or the hand (to be seen and heard).[41] Lacking Greek musical tonality, it is difficult, if not impossible for modern readers to understand either Greek dance or Greek tragedy.

In a related context, I have sought to illustrate this point by way of a certain negative emphasis,[42] using the example of the late Alan Rickman, who was celebrated for his voice in great part owing to negative stress, a very British use of understatement and dispassion, with unexpected affect in his composure as in his voice, including pauses (metrically, these are *caesurae*), as characteristic of his speech. To refer to a film star and his silences is a very modern example, yet the reference may help us to attend to rhythm and what Nietzsche called the *Ton-ictus*. In the older actor's reflections offered to young actors, Rickman highlighted the importance of doing little, underscoring the extra work required to "do less."[43] Nietzsche's expression for this, though this is another essay, is the expression "dancing in chains," arguing that this is the key to what the ancient tragic poets sought to attain: a self-imposed restraint or measure.[44]

Contra modern stress forms, whether negative or positive, whether overstated (American style) or understated (English style, à la Rickman), Nietzsche emphasized measure. The dance "was no gyrating dance but beautiful walking," highlighting the importance of timing,[45] where, as Nietzsche notes, the intervals are never (mathematically) identical.[46] Emphasizing the transmission of the specific tact for the trimeter,[47] as the above citation of metric innovations in Plutarch reminds us, Archilochus was famed for inventing different modes. And yet, thus the understated stress of Rickman's delivery might be helpful: given that there was no stress ictus in ancient Greek, what kind of ictus was there?

The little lines Nietzsche draws as reproduced above show that the answer is a matter of higher (or rising), or lower (or falling) pitch or tone. Thus, if "lyric poesie is not sung it seems to be 'pure prose.' "[48] In the *Supplements* from various lecture courses on Greek lyric delivered from 1868 to 1879, Nietzsche foregrounds "this orig[inal] connection with music and dance,"[49] emphasizing that the lyric poem "has to be *declaimed* [*v o r g e t r a g e n*] rather than read."⁵⁰ Such lyrical declamation corresponds to what Nietzsche names a "middle thing," midway between speaking and singing, *performatively* expressed. Thus, Nietzsche introduces his 1878–79 Winter course on *Greek Lyrists* with a section entitled "Lyric & Music in the most intimate association,"⁵¹ stating that, unlike modern lyric, "Gr[eek] lyric was sung." The Greek hearing and viewing public, "knew the song *only* in the singing."⁵²

Nietzsche is talking about *singing* Greek, the same in antiquity as *declaiming* Greek. But what would singing/declamation sound like?⁵³ To pose this question, as Nietzsche does, we need the "spirit of music" and we are left, hermeneutico-phenomenologically, in dry dock, to repeat a figurative image Nietzsche offers us, an image alluding to the then-popular Chladni soundpatterns:⁵⁴

> For the rhythm is inclined to the ear, the strophe can only be comprehended in the music. It is as in regions where the sea has withdrawn after imprinting its form on the earth's surface. Thus has the sea of music receded from modern poetry.⁵⁵

In addition, there are further problems in *The Birth of Tragedy*: the problem of lyric poetry, the lyric poet, the subjective artist, the problem of the subject. A related set of problems concerns the chorus and, in addition, Nietzsche was also concerned to argue contra Aristotle, especially contra Aristotle's cathartic (which term Nietzsche was very impolite about characterizing in base physiological terms, as necessary here and there) account of pity and fear in tragedy.⁵⁶

On Metrical Necessity and the Military School of Life

Archilochus was a multifarious inventor of lyric in its various modes, iambic, elegiac, dithyrambic. Saying this cannot make any sense simply because most of us read Archilochus in translation. Obviously, we need to read Archilochus, first as he was among the Greek lyricists, *in Greek*. The injunction is as patent as it is impossible, technically, just given the aforementioned: even when we know Greek, even modern classicists, hear with modern ears—and see with modern eyes.

Regarding the necessity of *speaking* (rather than *reading*) lyric poetry, it is urged that we need to "hear" what Archilochus does with his words, incised, as Nietzsche says of lyric poetry, in stone. Thus, "Poetry should be a thoughtstone [*Denkstein*], more luminous than marble."[57] In the case of Archilochus, in the case of lyric, and so too for the tragic poet, every word, every rhythmic phrase, every elision and juxtaposition matters. Nor can anything be otherwise. For the same reason, Archilochus may be set alongside Homer:

> The lyric is the oldest form of poesie: the epos is developed out of a particular kind of song, the divine and heroic hymns. Lyric is everywhere associated with religious cult, where music and dance come together selecting the rhythm in the word, grouping the atoms of the sentence; rhythm in con[nection] ref[erence] to λόγος is called μέτρον.[58]

Archilochus embodies the lyric poet as one who sings "'as the bird sings,' alone, prompted by his inmost necessity, and has to fall silent when a listener confronts him with his demands."[59] With this, we catch sight of what Nietzsche names the problem of the subject.

Here we recall one of the more famous military teachings of Archilochus, mercenary knight-poet, devoted to the celebration of the rites of Dionysus *and* Demeter, unsparing in his estimation of battle companions and generals—*friends on the field are as night and day off the field*[60] or *picturebook soldiers rarely match the scarred strategist*—antithetic to the famed Spartan admonition urging death before dishonor: "with your shield or on it"— Archilochus famously reports abandoning his shield as a (promissory) gift to his Thracian enemy. This hired sword proclaims his escape, not the prowess for which he was commissioned. In fact, Archilochus mocks the standard claims to bravery, pointing out that these have a habit of multiplying wildly: name a famous battle and everyone remotely associated with the battle will claim to have been among the handful of men in the center of the fray.

Beyond its opposition to standard views of Greek valor,[61] Archilochus invites a different reading of Nietzsche's famous "What doesn't kill me makes me stronger," reflecting its title *From the Military School of Life*. To be sure, there is no *military* school *of life*. The school of war (*Kriegschule*) is a school of death. But as Archilochus was a mercenary, as Pindar wrote his poems for money, fighting for the highest bidder, stakes of war do not hold for hired soldiers. So Archilochus tells us, abandoning his shield at his option (summarizing in a phrase what Aristotle takes a chapter to distinguish on the matter of the voluntary), as the getting of another is easy: thus the warrior's school of *life*.

Living by his spear epitomizes Guy Hedreen's description of Archilochus's "swagger portrait"[62]

ἐν δορὶ μέν μοι μᾶζα μεμαγμένη, ἐν δορὶ δ' οἶνος
Ἰσμαρικός· πίνω δ' ἐν δορὶ κεκλιμένος. (2W)

What works here must be heard/seen, an ear for reading, for hearing with one's eyes, in Nietzsche's discussion of metric. We need to read this in Greek, we need to read this out loud.

We might get a sense of this by citing among a range of translated versions, starting in English with Guy Davenport's:

> My ash spear is my barley bread,
> My ash spear is my Ismarian wine.
> I lean on my spear and drink.

In German, Max Treu's rendering skips the leaning support,[63]

> *Hier der Speer gibt mir Brot,*
> *und den Wein von Ismaros gibt mir hier mein Speer,*
> *und ich trink.*

Nietzsche stresses the recline: "'In my spear is my bread baked for me,' i.e., 'it lies in my spear if I have baked bread, if I drink wine, [and] if I can lay myself down [*an meinem Speer liegt es, wenn ich gebacknes Brod habe, wenn ich Wein trincken u. mich lagern kann.*]."[64]

To the question of the sound, the articulation of Greek (prosody in the case of the rhythmic, intonation of ancient Greek) and to the point of Nietzsche's discovery of tone or pitch as opposed to stress ictus, the key to *The Birth of Tragedy* is poetically, lyrically, the "problem of the subject."

Formally, the "problem of the subject" does not differ from the famous "Homer problem," as Nietzsche refers to this in his inaugural lecture in Basel. Yet the question of the subject compels us to ask how we should read what Hedreen calls the "swagger," or, as a concession to our digital age, an ancient 'selfie,' lyric poetry?

A poet by craft, warrior by trade, can we find the person, the "who" of Archilochus, in the work? Ought we say that the poet, the man, is one thing, as Nietzsche remonstrated with respect to himself (here echoing Aristotle) the poem, the writing, another? Here, we are hostage to the aesthetic tastes of our own tradition, as Nietzsche reminds us in *The Birth of Tragedy*. We need nature *natured*, presented to us à la Kant, *naturally*, unforced, *as if* by nature, unaware, innocent. Yet just here, we lack innocence:

> Precisely Archilochus horrifies us, next to Homer, through his cries of hatred and scorn, through his drunken outbursts of desire, is he, named as being the first subjective artist, not thereby actually the non-artist?[65]

The Birth of Tragedy emphasizes desire, orgy, fertility, Dionysus. Thus, the study of the birth of tragedy is about origins or genealogies, reflecting on the same "lyric poetry which, in its highest articulation, is called tragedy and dramatic dithyramb."[66]

And what do we know of Archilochus? Nothing, so Nietzsche tells us apart from what Horace tells us, "*Archiloqus proprio rabies armavit iambo* [Wrath armed Archilochus with her own Iambic]."[67] The point for Nietzsche is that we have no corroboration for this or any other judgment than the words of the poet himself. It is Archilochus who relates his wrath, his invective, as he writes it. Archilochus tells us who he is: simply because he is the source of the account of everything we know about him.

Archilochus tells us the things he accomplishes with words. Archilochus, the subject, is himself the source of the account we have of the subject. This is the problem of the subject.

But who speaks?

Sex and the Lonely Poet

> Wretched I lie,
> dead with desire, pierced through
> my bones with the bitter pains
> the Gods have given me.
> —Archilochus

Da lieg ich, krank im Gedärm,—	There I lie, gut sick,—
Mich fressen die Wanzen,	Devoured by bedbugs,
Und drüben noch Licht und Lärm!	And over there yet light and noise!
Ich hör' es, sie tanzen . . .	I hear it, they're dancing . . .
	—Nietzsche

At the end of his own life, limited as it would be in the wake of his collapse in Turin, reprising some of his earlier studies on ancient metrics and rhythm, Nietzsche reflects on the orgy in antiquity, asserting that he "was the first who . . . took seriously that wonderful phenomenon by the name of Dionysus."[68] As he goes on to say, the Dionysian is "solely to be explained out of an excess of force."[69]

Thus Nietzsche vindicates himself *contra* Wilamowitz's denunciations of Nietzsche's scholarly faintness (for Herr Nietzsche, so we read Wilamowitz's mocking words in "*Zukunftsphilologie*," a self-published fascicule denouncing *The Birth of Tragedy*, "*ein Phallus ist kein Phallus*.")[70] To be sure, Nietzsche's sensibilities may have had their challenges—consider the constellation: Wagner, Nietzsche, sex[71]—but whether or not Wilamowitz was correct, *and it does not seem he was correct*, Wilamowitz's claims were not meant to be accurate but, as invective, to destroy.

Archilochus was no less aggressive, so he proclaims.

A discovery (made by Anton Fackelman in 1974) may illustrate.[72] If Nietzsche did not know the poem in the form we do, he knew it in other versions. The new fragment is sufficiently arresting that the classicist Reinhold Merkelbach was moved to conclude his reading with unusual violence: dismissing Archilochus as an "egregious [*ein schwerer*] psychopath."[73]

Numerous commentators have underscored this last and the fragment is also one of Archilochus's more moving of his deeply insensitive (to the female and not to the male) erotic poems, recounting his revenge seduction of Neobule's (she who had had the temerity to decline his marriage proposal) younger sister, and Archilochus tells the tale of what is and can only be a fairly "scabrous" rape:

> So much I said / And the maiden amid the flowers in their
>   full bloom
> I took and laid her down . . .
> And caressing [all] her beautiful body
> I shot out my [white] force, / Lightly touching her blond [hair][74]

Some scholars (not infrequently, but not only, male scholars) dispute the charge of rape, declaring in tones familiar to us now from "rape culture" that everything would have been perfectly "consensual" between the old man and the maiden. Others denounce it were it not for—and this is the point—the poem's (and thereby the poet's own) undoing: Archilochus relates a precocious and thereby inconsummate, unaccomplished, that is, technically, *impotent* act.

It has been observed, as an observation easy to make, and the strength of the late Martin West's word choice is that he indicates this overdetermined quality ("precipitate," "premature," "showing too much haste"), that this poem offers one of the earliest accounts we have of premature ejaculation.[75] Thus, the "force" of which Archilochus writes is one that cannot be kept, not even in consummation. This lyric poem tells of the poet's own impotence qua expression that, as such, may not be retained. This is a rape that was not a rape, and Plato, he of the branch that was not a branch (but a reed), birds that were not birds (being bats), pelting that was not pelting (missing the mark), would have found this amusing, just because unconsummated. And the law, in many cases, will still agree with this assessment of non-assault.

Merkelbach's "psychopath" judgment of Archilochus does not exceed the account Archilochus gives, and this is Hesiod's source; Archilochus himself declares that his invective drives an entire family to suicide. Archilochus tells us his subjectivity in autographic, 'objective,' details.[76]

If, as Nietzsche tells us in *The Birth of Tragedy*, the lyric artist will not be, because he cannot be, the subject, the lyric poem is not, and cannot be, "about" the subject (the whole point of tragedy, hence Nietzsche's recourse to Schopenhauer, being the dissolution of individuation, the recognition of the self in another, the communication into, the transmigration into, ecstatic communion with another being, in fact: through and into all other beings).

Archilochus recounts his cowardly expedience; thus we remember, he tells us he leaves his shield. Archilochus tells us about Lycambes and his daughters, his erotic heedlessness, his violence, and his lack of measure *re* restraint:

> Archilochus, the first Greek lyrist, proclaims to the daughters of Lycambes both his mad love and his contempt, it is not his passion that dances before us in orgiastic frenzy:[77]

But what is Nietzsche doing as he writes: Who is speaking?

To the extent that Archilochus recounts battle achievements, these are less than exemplary (he tells us that he is a coward, he tells us he leaves a shield to slow his enemy, a leaving present, facilitating his exit). Just so his amorous conquests offer fairly literal accounts of erotic abjection, failures—rejected by one, impotent with another he has in full power, disdainful of some lovers, pathetic with others—what follows for the genre, born of lyric, that is tragedy? Everything concerning this subject, however, so Nietzsche tells us, will turn out to have nothing to do with Archilochus.

Subjective Deception

> The subjectivity of the lyricist is a deception.
>
> —Nietzsche, *The Birth of Tragedy*

The "subject" on the authority of the author corresponds to the modern definition of lyric poetry. This modern definition, unsurprisingly, isn't a theme for the ancients: "The artist had already relinquished his subjectivity in the Dionysian procession."[78] Focusing on Archilochus's love *or* his scorn, we fail to hear Archilochus and thereby miss the tragic work of art.[79]

Nietzsche invokes Schopenhauer's language of will:

> In truth, Archilochus, the passionately inflamed, loving, and hating man, is only a vision of the genius, who by this time is no longer Archilochus, but a world-genius expressing his primordial pain analogically in the symbol of the man Archilochus—while the subjectively willing and desiring man, Archilochus, is and never can be a poet.[80]

Key here to this language of "genius," evocative as it is of romanticism and thus of Goethe, is the reference to the "world-genius," which many commentators who take up this issue address in terms of the *Ur-Eine* (and which must however be discussed beyond Schlegel [and Schelling] in terms of the World Artist that is for Nietzsche a reference to antiquity), as what is apart from illusions, fictions, images, representations:

> It is utterly unnecessary, however, that the lyrist should see nothing but the phenomenon of the man Archilochus before him as a reflected manifestation of eternal being; and tragedy demonstrates how far the visionary world of the lyrist may distance itself from this phenomenon which, to be sure, is the most proximate.[81]

By contrast with the epic poet, the lyric poet exemplifies the problem of the subject as the problem of his poetry and as such. The world artist, as the *Ur-Eine,* leads Nietzsche to invoke Schopenhauer, but the image remains Pre-Platonic, as Nietzsche distinguished these philosophers, remnant of an older age, image of an image, representation of a representation, as if

> of its own accord spoken that little word "I." But this mere appearance will no longer be able to seduce us, as it certainly seduced those who had designated the lyrist as the subjective poet.[82]

What is at stake is illusion, fiction, deception.

Archilochus epitomizes the Apollonian and the Dionysian. And, as Archilochus is the father or innovator of folksong and poetry, Haydn effects the same for music and, so Nietzsche reminds us here, Beethoven:

> Thus we observe that in the poetry of the folk song, language is strained to the utmost to imitate music; therefore with Archilochus there begins a new world of poetry, in its deepest foundation contrary to the Homeric. Herewith we have characterized the only possible relation between poesie and music, word and tone: the word, the image, the concept here seeks an expression analogous to music and now suffers in itself the violence of music. (BT §6)

This identification of Archilochus as the first "recognizable" musician and lyric poet, inaugurating the folk song into poetry, entails that what thereby comes to birth is "a new artistic movement, the gradually artistically measured unfolding of the folksong into tragedy" (KSA 7, 192).

Tragedy is born to the lyrist. That is the spirit of music.

If we had the time, better yet the temper requisite for a necessary *da capo,* could we now begin again, we would be on the way to resolving the gnomic formula of the *becoming-human of dissonance*.[83] Here, we find the key to Nietzsche's later reflections on responsibility, the subject of causation, that is, causality, including reflections on the human (all too human), or else, cosmologically regarded, dawns undawned or else "innocent," "gay" science, musings beyond good and evil, the genealogy of morality, all incipient in this, his first book. Elsewhere, Nietzsche offers this comparative (and programmatic) reflection: "If our acting is appearance, so too, naturally enough, is responsibility similarly an appearance. Good and evil. Pity."[84] Thus, the question of the lyric artist articulates the question of the subjectivity of the subject as the question of consciousness.

To forget the lyrist as we often forget the invention of the subjectivity of the lyrist that is his achievement, is also to forget the music, the metric, rhythmic word. Whenever we do this—which we do quite often as scholars, philosophers *and* philologists alike—we imagine we are talking about concepts, ideas, and deeds as things. To this extent, the project of his tragedy book is all about the lyrist, which is to say that it is all about posing the problematic question of the subject, "to explain the subjective."[85]

Again: "The subjectivity of the lyrist is a deception."[86] At every step, we have found it necessary to retrieve Nietzsche's emphasis on the antique parity of Homer and Archilochus. But this equation gives us Apollo and Dionysus. Thus:

> "Archilochus, the lyric," "*the musical mood (Schiller)* as birthplace, that now speaks itself out in images. The Dionysian mania appears with an analogous simile: love to the daughters, with scorn and contempt inmixt. The "folksong" Dionysian. Not surging passion makes the lyrist here but a tremendously strong Dionysian will that expresses itself in an Apollinian dream. It is Dionysus who, entering into individuation, articulates his dual attunement: the lyrist speaks of himself but he means only Dionysus.[87]

The same holds for Homer as for Apollo and the duality dissolves:

> Just as the epicist, departing from the image he purely wishes to transmit and to this extent he excites feeling and moods, i.e., the dreamer is only himself within the dream as he must stand *close* to the things to be contemplated and must understand them.[88]

If Nietzsche can say that we have no more than "a deception" when it comes to the subjectivity and actual praxis of Archilochus, the same may be said for the tragic work of art:

> The dramatic process is only conceived as a vision. Music, dance, lyric is the Dionysian symbolic born out of the vision. Inspiration of the ground of feeling towards the projection of images: between which is now become a natural relatedness.[89]

Archilochus was a lyrist, a singer: inventor of modes and tones. If the subject of the lyric poet is a fiction, meaning that his lyric poetry is not, despite all appearances, a subjective confession, what is at work in the poem is not necessarily the work of a psychopath any more than its salacious, sexual, provocative content.

Conclusion: Once More: On Doing Things with Words

Nietzsche's reading of tragedy is utterly hermeneutic, thoroughly phenomenological. To this extent, Nietzsche takes a step back—this would be his *epoché*—just to ask how things worked: *performatively, in practice.*

What are we doing when we read Archilochus or Anacreon or Sappho? Or when it comes to tragedy, when we read—it is very hard, given what we said above, to speak of performing—Sophocles' Oedipus trilogy?

Are we reading Archilochus, Anacreon, Sappho for the sweet-bitter erotic?[90]

The very same question may be asked of our reading as such, extending to our performative efforts, declaiming, staging, and experiencing tragedy as such, the tragic artform, as actors enacting, as audience enjoying it.

What do we, today, enjoy in the tragic artwork? What did the Greeks enjoy? Is it that we (or the Greeks) delight in the depiction of painful events, deaths, humiliations, frustrations (and surely to some extent it must be said that we do; the very existence of horror movies or stories underscores this), that is: to vary the rhyme (and the calculations) of, as Edgar Allen Poe's raven voices this: unavoidable disaster after unavoidable disaster?

Maybe we're sadists? Maybe we're masochists who enjoy tragic depictions? Similar questions may be raised regarding to the ribald content of Archilochus's lyric: Is this just a pre-internet version of the oldest subject matter in the world?

Is lyric poetry pornography? Is it more than pornography?

If the pornographic drives what I call the "Hallelujah effect," it may be that we are captivated, fascinated by horror. Thus, we can think of tragedy as akin to our popular absorption with vampires, zombies, and other death cults, including the claim, *all men must die*, set in a gamer's scenario world (*True Blood, The Walking Dead, Game of Thrones*), Miami-based serial killers (*Dexter*), and so on. In Plato's wake, Aristotle could argue that the sheer report of unpleasant things, was edifying, *good for us*. So Nehamas argues with respect to television shows, so Andreas Urs Sommer writes of vampires (I am not complaining; I write here about Alan Rickman's diction, elsewhere I write about his 'person,' as Nietzsche would say, in the figure of *Severus Snape*).

Aristotle's edifying claim was that tragedy, by moving us to pity and fear, functioned to purify us of the pitiful and fearful. Hence, the enjoyment of tragedy is subjectively cathartic. Every teacher teaching drama to this day repeats Aristotle's claim. Nietzsche challenges Aristotle's account by speaking of the "birth" of tragedy out of the spirit of music. In addition to the esoteric question of quantifying metrics (i.e., music), Nietzsche so departs from Aristotle's interpretation that we find it hard to parse his claims. If we are footnotes to Plato, it always turns out, thus the force of the dialectic, that we are greater admirers of Aristotle's "truth."

The same Nietzsche who asks in *On the Genealogy of Morals* a practical question regarding the functioning of reinforcement, whereby we name an altruistic deed "good" for so very long that we forget such reinforcement, taking altruism to be good in itself (Nietzsche contends this cannot be, as by dint of repeating that altruism is good, we would learn the dictum not the sentiment), so too, as Nietzsche observes, punishment cannot induce feelings of regret in criminals, as promulgated both legally and moralistically and, practically, given that punishment follows not upon having committed a particular deed, as one can do this with impunity until caught and convicted.

In *The Birth of Tragedy*, Nietzsche inquires into the plausibility of the Aristotelian convention: Does the sight of Orestes or Prometheus or Oedipus move us to pity (or fear), or, claiming that such a vision on stage elicits such feelings, does being so moved constitute catharsis? And if so, could this function seriatim, given only the known content of tragedy but the performative context of ancient contests, staging vista after vista after vista, day into night, over a course of days and nights? For Nietzsche, the closest thing we have to this today is high mass.

In *The Gay Science*, composed, as I have argued, to reprise (at least some of) the savaged arguments of *The Birth of Tragedy*, the author of quantitative metrics argued summarily, "The Athenians went to the theater in order to hear beautiful speeches! And beautiful speeches were what concerned Sophocles, pardon the heresy!"[91]

For Nietzsche,

> They did not want fear and pity—Aristotle in honor and highest honor! But he certainly did not hit the nail, certainly not the head of the nail, when he spoke of the ultimate aim of Greek Tragedy! Just look at the tragic Greek poets to see what excited their energy, their inventiveness, their competitiveness—certainly not the intention to overpower the spectators through affect![92]

More than the subject of the poem, more than the personage of the poet, tragedy is born out of music, that is, the becoming human of dissonance.[93]

Notes

1. Alexander Nehamas, *Life as Literature* (Cambridge: Harvard University Press, 1985).

2. David Allison, *Reading The New Nietzsche* (Lanham, MD: Rowman and Littlefield, 2001).

3. I take up some of the many complexities associated with this elected affinity, including the stylized practice, which goes back to antiquity, of writing letters in the manner of or *style* of classical authors, in Babich, "Songs of the Sun," in *Words in Blood, Like Flowers*, pp. 117ff, along with Nietzsche's concern with (the question of the death of) Empedocles.

4. See for example, Paul de Man's *Allegories of Reading: Figural Language in Rousseau, Nietzsche, Rilke, and Proust*, as well as, cited above, Nehamas, *Life as Literature*. Wallace Stevens is discussed in B. J. Legget, *Early Stevens: The Nietzschean Intertext* (Durham: Duke University Press, 1992). Such associations are complicated, going a bit farther afield back to Goethe, as echoed by Max Weber, who read Nietzsche to reflect on the origins of Weber's "iron cage." See Stephen A. Kent, "Weber, Goethe, and the Nietzschean Allusion: Capturing the Source of the 'Iron Cage' Metaphor," *Sociological Analysis* 44, no. 4 (Winter 1983): 297–319.

5. Hölderlin's *Die Nacht* (1807), the separately published first strophe of *Brod und Wein*, arguably influenced Nietzsche's fountain-oriented night poetry, as we may read Nietzsche's night song in *Thus Spoke Zarathustra*, "*Das Nachtlied* / Nacht ist es: nun reden lauter alle springenden Brunnen." KSA 4, 136. In several places, I argue for Hölderlin's direct influence, tone and meter, on one of Nietzsche's last (and best) poems. See, cited above, Babich, "Songs of the Sun." For a discussion of Wilhelm Heinse (author of the novel Ardinghello to whom Hölderlin dedicated *Die Nacht*), see Max Bauemer, "Heinse und Nietzsche. Anfang und Ende der dionysischen Ästhetik" in Bauemer, *Heinse-Studien* (Stuttgart: Metzler, 1966), 92–124. See too Hans Werner Bertallot's *Hölderlin—Nietzsche* (Hamburg, 1933) and Bauemer, *Das Dionysische in den Werken Wilhelm Heinses* (Bonn: Bouvier, 1964) and, further, Leonhard Hermann "Begegnung im Kanon?" in: Andreas Urs Sommer, ed., *Nietzsche—Philosoph der Kultur(en)?* (Berlin: Walter de Gruyter, 2008), pp. 103–112 as well as more philologically than philosophically, Silvio Vietta, "Heinse und Nietzsche" in: Gert Theile, ed., *Das Mass des Bacchanten. Wilhelm Heinses Über-Lebenskunst* (München: Fink, 1998), pp. 213–229.

6. See further Babich, "Le Zarathoustra de Nietzsche et le style parodique. A propos de l'hyperanthropos de Lucien et du surhomme de Nietzsche," *Diogène. Revue internationale des sciences humaines* 232 (Oct. 2010): 70–93.

7. M. S. Silk and J. P. Stern, *Nietzsche on Tragedy* (Cambridge: Cambridge University Press, 1983), 151. Thus, Silk and Stern duly note that Nietzsche's emphasis accords "with ancient tradition (which did as Nietzsche says in §5, bracket him with Homer) and with a good deal of modern opinion." Ibid.

8. See, however, David B. Allison, "Nietzsche, Archilochus, and the Question of the Noumenon," in *The Great Year of Zarathustra*, ed. David Goicoechea (Lanham, MD: University Press of America, 1983), 297–315, in addition to, among his other discussions, including several studies of Maurice Emmanuel, Christophe Corbier, "Subjectivité littéraire et chanson populaire: Archiloque et le genre iambique de Friedrich Schlegel à Friedrich Nietzsche," *Etudes Germaniques* 67, nr. 2 (2012): 285–307, and in addition to several readings of the "subject" of the subjective artisan, see Christophe Colera, *Individualité et subjectivité chez Nietzsche* (Paris: L'Harmattan, 2004), along with J. F. Humphrey, "Friedrich Nietzsche's Subjective Artist," *Philosophy and Literature* 38, no. 2 (2014): 380–94, and Renate Reschke, "Künstler sind Advokaten der Leidenschaft . . . ? Zum Bild des Künstlers bei Friedrich Nietzsche," *Denkumbrüche mit Nietzsche: Zur anspornenden Verachtung der Zeit* (Berlin: de Gruyter, 2000), 234f. See too Anne Carson's *Eros, the Bittersweet* (Champaign, IL: Dalkey Press, 1998).

9. See further, the final section of Babich, "On Nietzsche's Judgment of Style and Hume's Quixotic Taste: On the Science of Aesthetics and 'Playing' the Satyr," *Journal of Nietzsche Studies* 43, no. 2 (2012): 240–59.

10. See *Nietzsche's Werke. Nachgelassene Werke. Von Friedrich Nietzsche. Aus den Jahren 1872/73–1875/76*, Vol. 10 (Leipzig: C. G. Naumann, 1903). The text of Nietzsche's *Die vorplatonische Philosophen* was published in the Kroner edition in the third volume of *Philologica* (1913) and was included as well in the Musarion edition, published in 1921: *Friedrich Nietzsche Gesammelte Werke. Vierter Band, Vorträge, Schriften und Vorlesungen 1871–1876* (Munich: Musarion, 1921), 247–366. The complete text of these lectures does not appear until *Nietzsche—Werke Vorlesungsaufzeichnungen (WS 1871/72–WS 1874/75), II4*, Fritz Bornmann and Mario Carpitella, eds. (Berlin: de Gruyter, 1995).

11. See however Marcello Gigante, "Friedrich Nietzsche und Diogenes Laertius" in *'Centauren-Geburten.' Wissenschaft, Kunst, und Philosophie beim jungen Nietzsche*, ed. Tilman Borsche, Federico Gerratana, and Aldo Venturelli (Berlin: de Gruyter, 1994), 3–16, as well as Jonathan Barnes's balanced, "Nietzsche and Diogenes Laertius," *Nietzsche-Studien* 15 (1986): 16–40.

12. Much of the material is unavailable in translation and of the translations that do exist are not always easily accessible. Editors typically distinguish between the philosophical and the philological, in addition to *Nachlass* texts related to texts composed for publication and lecture courses as such.

13. See especially Gherardo Ugolini's outstanding " '*Philologus inter philologos.*' Friedrich Nietzsche, die klassische Philologie und die griechische Tragödie," *Zeitschrift für antike Literatur und ihre Rezeption / A Journal for Ancient Literature and its Reception* 174, no. 2 (2003): 316–42, in addition to Paolo D'Iorio's comprehensive

recitation, "L'image des philosophes préplatoniciens chez le jeune Nietzsche," in Borsche et al., *'Centauren-Geburten,'* 383–417.

14. Babich, *The Hallelujah Effect: Music, Performance Practice, and Technology* (London: Routledge, 2016); see here in particular, chs. 8–10.

15. Nietzsche, "On Music and Word," in Carl Dahlhaus, *Between Romanticism and Modernism: Four Studies in the Music of the Later Nineteenth Century* (Berkeley: University of California Press, 1980), 107.

16. See further Paul Allen Miller, *Lyric Texts and Lyric Consciousness: The Birth of a Genre from Archaic Greece to Augustan Rome* (London: Routledge, 1994). Despite the Nietzschean assonance of his title—and despite dedicating a chapter to Archilochus—Miller does not refer to Nietzsche in his book. Before Nietzsche, similar arguments may be found in Herder and Rousseau, among others.

17. Nietzsche, "Greek Music Drama," 25.

18. Ibid.

19. See Christophe Corbier, "Alogia et Eurythmie chez Nietzsche," *Nietzsche-Studien* 38 (2009): 1–38.

20. See, again, the third part of Babich, *The Hallelujah Effect*.

21. To quote Paul Maas, who although himself a student of Wilamowitz, follows Nietzsche in this emphasis, "We have no means of reading, reciting, or hearing Greek poetry as it actually sounded. It may be possible for us to form a mental notion of it; but such a notion is too shadowy to serve as a basis for the scientific investigation of the subject." Maas, *Greek Metre*, trans. Hugh Lloyd-Jones (Oxford: Oxford University Press, 1962 [1923]), 3–4. Worth reading too is Hugh Lloyd-Jones, *Greek in a Cold Climate* (New York: Barnes and Noble, 1991), 206f. Note here that, while he is inclined to replicate, as an ideal, the ahistoricism Nietzsche condemns, Helmut Müller-Sievers, *The Science of Literature: Essays on an Incalculable Difference* (Berlin: de Gruyter, 2015) shares with Nietzsche the view that we cannot reconstruct ancient musical tragedy, and because we are insensible to them, we cannot "hear" Greco-Roman temporal rhythms. Nietzsche held that modern Europeans heard Latin rhythms. Heidegger, without engaging Nietzsche's lyrical research, mysteriously insists that Nietzsche reproduced these, calling him "more Roman" than Greek.

22. See for references, the beginning of the chapter on *mousike techne* in Babich, *The Hallelujah Effect*.

23. Eliding the distinction Nietzsche seeks to make between stress and pitch accent, Koller names this a "Betönungsakzent" in Koller, *Musik und Dichtung im alten Griechenland.* I am grateful to Anke Bennholdt-Thomsen for bringing Koller to my attention as a useful counterpoint to Dale. There are other traditions, as well, including French, including complete with elaborate articulations of positions and figures, especially on Maurice Emmanuel, on dance, in addition to the Italian.

24. See Babich, "Spirit and Grace, Letters and Voice. Or: Performance Practice and Alchemy in Ivan Illich, Alan Rickman, and Nietzsche," *Journal of the Philosophy of Education* 3 (2018): 1–27.

25. Nietzsche, KGW II$_2$, 380.
26. Ibid., 393.
27. See also Babich, "Nietzsche's *Antichrist*: The Birth of Modern Science out of the Spirit of Religion," in *Jahrbuch für Religionsphilosophie*, ed. Markus Enders and Holger Zaborowski (Freiburg i. Briesgau: Alber, 2014), 134–54.
28. Citing Cicero, Nietzsche argues that the "Alexandrians" have given us our grammar books, handbooks, in sum, our "aesthetic science." And the same Alexandrians have inscribed their judgments into convention itself such that the "immoderate, personal, overflowing, unedifying is for this later culture too ugly or too grotesque." Ibid. (KGW II$_2$, 394).
29. Nietzsche, KGW II$_2$, 394. As he emphasizes in *The Birth of Tragedy*, next to Homer, the ancients esteemed Archilochus "more than any other as an original nature" (ibid., 405). In addition to his other poetic competitive achievements, Nietzsche underlines that the sheer fact of their report entails that these were successful "inventions," already cited above in the epigraph from Plutarch's *De Musica*, Archilochus has verse forms named after him, unifying "different kinds of κῶλα in one verse, currently named the dactyl-trochaic" (ibid., 406). The most "powerful innovation," inspiring ancient esteem, earning Archilochus the title of the "father of the musist art," was the "tact-change (μετα βολἠρυθμοῦ)" (ibid.).
30. See for further references, Babich, "Nietzsches Lyrik. Archilochos, Musik, Metrik," in *Nietzsche und die Lyrik. Ein Kompendium*, ed. Christian Benne and Claus Zittel (Frankfurt am Main: Springer, 2017), 405–29.
31. Cf. Marcel Detienne, *Apollon le couteau à la main. Une approche expérimentale du polythéisme grec* (Paris: Gallimard, 1998) and Peter Kingsley, *In the Dark Places of Wisdom* (London: Duckworth, 2001), as well as his earlier and more conventionally philological *Ancient Philosophy, Mystery and Magic. Empedocles and Pythagorean Tradition* (Oxford: Oxford University Press, 1995). See further Babich, "From Winckelmann's Apollo to Nietzsche's Dionysus," in *Nietzsche Forschung*. ". . . An Winckelmann anzuknüpfen . . ."? *Winckelmanns Antike, Nietzsches Klassizismuskritik und ihre Blicke in die Zukunft*, ed. Renate Reschke (Berlin: de Gruyter, 2017), 167–92.
32. *Zweitens giebt es nach meiner Theorie einzelnen rhythm. Schemata gegenüber keine sichere Entscheidung, sondern viele Möglichkeiten. Es ist aber sehr thöricht, darin einen wissenschaftlichen Rückschritt zu finden (wie dies Schmidt gegen Westphal thut). Uns fehlt der antike rhythm. Geschmack, uns fehlt das antike Melos—wie wollen wir unfehlbar sein!* Nietzsche, *Zur Theorie der quantitiereden Rhythmik*, 234.
33. Ibid.
34. Ibid., 235.
35. Cf. Rudolf Georg Hermann Westphal, *Die musik des griechischen alterhumes: Nach den alten quellen neu bearbeitet* (Leipzig: Veit, 1883), 170, contends that Plutarch draws this observation from Aristoxenus as Archilochus predates Terpander. See too, *Handbuch der Musikgeschichte*, Band 1, von Hugo Riemann, Alfred Einstein

(Leipzig: Breitkopf u. Härtel, 1919), 117. Cf. George Grote, *Griechische Mythologie und Antiquitäten, nebst dem Capitel über Homer und auswählten Abschnitten über die Chronologie, Literatur, Kunst, Musik, &c, Band 3* (Leipzig: Teubner, 1858), 322ff.

36. Max Weber speaks at the conclusion of his lecture "Politics as Vocation" of the "polar night of icy darkness." Weber, *"Politik als Beruf,"* originally presented as a speech at Munich University, 1918, published in 1919 by Duncker u. Humboldt, Munich.

37. See for a discussion, Babich, "Nietzsche's Posthuman Imperative: On the Human, All too Human Dream of Transhumanism," in *Nietzsche and Transhumanism: Precursor or Enemy?* ed. Yunus Tuncel (Cambridge: Cambridge Scholars, 2017), 101–13.

38. I discuss this in my chapter "Nietzsche and Beethoven" in *The Hallelujah Effect*, 215, especially footnote 51.

39. Indeed, and shades of the earlier referenced source scholarship debate on Nietzsche's relation to Hölderlin, some argue, in a fairly presentist mindset, that Nietzsche self-plagiarizes. See, however, Babich, "Between Hölderlin and Heidegger: Nietzsche's Transfiguration of Philosophy," *Nietzsche-Studien* 29 (2000): 267–301.

40. Ibid., 270. Mysteriously, especially inasmuch as it is included in all extant German versions, Halporn drops the little lines in his translation as it appears in Arion, "Nietzsche: On the Theory of Quantitative Rhythm."

41. Thus, Nietzsche notes that there are *"Zwei Methoden zu taktiren: für das Auge oder für das Ohr."* Ibid.

42. See Babich, *The Hallelujah Effect*, 214.

43. This underscoring is part of the charm behind the director Ang Lee's advice in *Sense and Sensibility*, "But Alan, be more subtle. Do more." Cited in an interview where Rickman laughingly recalls: "Ang Lee—it's in print in Emma's book—gave us unforgettable notes because of his English." See Emma Thompson, *Sense and Sensibility: The Screenplay & Diaries: The Screenplay and Diaries (Shooting Script)* (New York: Newmarket Press, 2007), 232.

44. See, for a preliminary discussion, Babich, "Nietzsche's Performative Phenomenology: Philology and Music," in *Nietzsche and Phenomenology: Power, Life, Subjectivity*, ed. Élodie Boubil and Christine Daigle (Bloomington: Indiana University Press, 2013), 117–40.

45. Nietzsche, *Zur Theorie der quantitiereden Rhythmik*, KGW II/3, 272.

46. Ibid., 205.

47. Ibid., 271.

48. Thus, Nietzsche reflects: *"erscheinen die Lyriker als reine Prosa, wenn man den Gesang wegnimmt."* Ibid., 276.

49. Nietzsche, *"Zur Vorlesung: Die griechischen Lyriker,"* in *Frühe Schriften*, 355.

50. Ibid. Heinrich Meier rightly points out (personal communication) that such text set with blocked spaces between letters [*gesperrt*] corresponds to a now

standardized printer's convention for Nietzsche's works: a legacy of forgotten constraints on typesetting and printer's plates.

51. Nietzsche, KGW II$_2$, 375.

52. Ibid.

53. Nietzsche, *Zur Theorie der quantitiereden Rhythmik*, S. 274. In this context, he asks: "Is it possible now that this '*word spirit*' [*anima vocis*] vanishes utterly in the singing?"

54. Ernst Chladni discovered a regular relation between acoustic vibration and visual patterns. See Chladni, *Die Akustik* (Leipzig: Breitkopf u. Härtel, 1802). See too Johann Wilhelm Ritter, *Fragmente aus dem Nachlasse eines jungen Physikers: Ein Taschenbuch fuer Freunde der Natur*. 2 (Heidelberg: Mohr und Zimmer, 1810), as well for a useful contemporary discussion, in addition to Adorno's discussion of records, Theodor W. Adorno, *Klangfiguren: Musikalische Schriften I* (Frankfurt a.M.: Suhrkamp Verlag, 1959). Note that although Nietzsche mentions Chladni elsewhere, it is not the case that Nietzsche does so by name in this locus—a point that may go some way toward underlining some of the problems today's scholars face as they increasingly look for everything digitally by searching for a specific word.

55. *Denn der Rhythmus wendet sich an das Ohr, die Strophe is nur in der Musik begreiflich. Es ist wie bei Gegenden, wo sich das Meer zurückgezogen hat, aber die ganze Bodengestalt von ihm seine Form bekommen hat. So ist das Meer der Musik von der modernen Dichtung zurückgewichen.*

56. Failing to note this, or overlooking this, or disagreeing or what have you, renders Stephen Halliwell's "Nietzsche's 'Daimonic Force' of Tragedy and Its Ancient Traces," *Arion: A Journal of Humanities and the Classics, Third Series*, 11, no. 1 (Spring-Summer 2003): 103–23, a little less useful than it might have been.

57. Nietzsche, GS §345.

58. Ibid.

59. Nietzsche, "On Music and Word," 114.

60. Archilochus's reference is to Glaucus. See for a discussion, Andrea Rotstein, *The Idea of Iambos* (Oxford: Oxford University Press, 2010), including useful references, 30–34, and see, if in passing, on the complexities of dating, Alden A. Mosshammer, "Phainias of Eresos and Chronology," *California Studies in Classical Antiquity* 10 (1977): 105–33.

61. Nietzsche's notes even include a reflection on the Spartan rules for capturing, versus killing, a fleeing enemy where for Nietzsche everything in the parsing would have to turn on the Spartan aversion to flight and enemy comportment toward routed Spartans. KGW II2, 428.

62. See, here, Guy Hedreen, *The Image of the Artist in Archaic and Classical Greece: Art, Poetry, and Subjectivity* (Cambridge: Cambridge University Press, 2015).

63. This is not Treu's emphasis but see, if more focused on the literality of position (her focus is on couch tombs), Elizabeth P. Baughan, *Couched in Death:*

Klinai and Identity in Anatolia and Beyond (Madison: University of Wisconsin Press, 2013).

64. Ibid., KGW II$_2$, 408.
65. Ibid., BT §5.
66. Ibid.
67. Horace, *Ars Poetica*. See, on Horace and Archilochus, Michael Paschalis, *Horace and Greek Lyric Poetry* (Crete: Rethymnon Classical Studies, 2002), 35ff. See again, for some sense of this range if burdened by the conviction that today's neuroscience can solve this problematic range for us and limiting Archilochus to his conventional association with invective, Rotstein, *The Idea of Iambos*.
68. Nietzsche, TI *What I owe the ancients*, §4.
69. Ibid.
70. Wilamowitz, *Future-Philologie*. See also my original editor's footnotes to the English translation of this review of Nietzsche's first book in this translation featured in the 2000 issue of *New Nietzsche Studies*, 18.
71. Babich, "Nietzsche und Wagner: Sexualität," trans. Martin Suhr, in *Wagner und Nietzsche. Kultur—Werk—Wirkung. Ein Handbuch.*, ed. H. J. Brix, N. Knoepffler, S. L. Sorgner (Reinbek b. Hamburg: Rowohlt, 2008), 323–41.
72. *Archilochus in Greek Lyric Poetry.* A New Translation by Martin West (Oxford: Oxford University Press, 1994), 4. Cf. West and Reinhold Merkelbach, "Ein Archilochos-Papyrus," *Zeitschrift für Papyrologie und Epigraphik* 14 (1974): 97–113.
73. "ein schwerer psychopath." See West and Merkelbach, "Ein Archilochos-Papyrus," 113.
74. Archilochus fragment 196a. 42–44, 51–53. FN128.
75. Cf. Hedreen's essay, titled with a quote borrowed from Archilochus, " 'I Let Go My Force Just Touching Her Hair": Male Sexuality in Athenian Vase-Paintings of Silens and Iambic Poetry," *Classical Antiquity* 25, no. 2 (Oct. 2006): 277–325, esp. 297. See too C. Eckerman, "Teasing and Pleasing in Archilochus' First Cologne Epode," *Zeitschrift für Papyrologie und Epigraphik*, 2011 and (in passing), Babich, "On Nietzsche's Judgment of Style and Hume's Quixotic Taste."
76. There are many readings in the interim. See for an early account, Miroslav Marcovich, "A New Poem of Archilochus: 'P. Colon.' inv. 75II," *Greek, Roman and Byzantine Studies* 16, no. 1 (Spring 1975): 5–14.
77. Nietzsche, BT §5.
78. Ibid.
79. See again, if also not inclined to depart from the received misology contemporary philologists attribute to the acousmatic Nietzsche, Corbier, "Subjectivité littéraire et chanson populaire."
80. Nietzsche, BT §5.
81. Ibid.
82. Ibid.

83. As I argue in *The Hallelujah Effect*, there are several solutions that must be reviewed with respect to this formula.
84. Nietzsche, KSA 7, 196.
85. Ibid., 222.
86. Ibid.
87. Ibid.
88. Ibid., 721.
89. Ibid., 222.
90. Thus, and although the erotic is certainly there, if even the orgiastic is involved, not to mention cultic or religious spring festivals, to foreground these elements is also to miss the musical importance of the words themselves: "um schöne Reden war es dem Sophokles zu thun!" (FW §80).
91. Nietzsche, GS §80. Again, see Babich, *The Hallelujah Effect*.
92. Ibid. Cf. *Was ist tragische*, WKG 8 3, 203, and 66.
93. See too on this theme, the late Claude Lévesque, *Dissonance: Nietzsche à la limite du langage* (Montréal: Hurtubise HMH, 1988) in addition to Lévesque, "Dissonance," *Musique et textes* 17, no. 3–4 (1981): 53–66.

References

Adorno, Theodor W. *Klangfiguren: Musikalische Schriften I*. Frankfurt a.M.: Suhrkamp Verlag, 1959.
Allison, David Blair. "Nietzsche, Archilochus and the Question of the Noumenon." In *The Great Year of Zarathustra*, edited by David Goicoechea. Lanham, MD: University Press of America, 1983.
Allison, David. *Reading the New Nietzsche*. Lanham, MD: Rowman and Littlefield, 2001.
Ansell-Pearson, Keith, ed., *Companion to Nietzsche*. Oxford: Blackwell, 2006.
Archilochus in Greek Lyric Poetry. A New Translation by Martin West. Oxford: Oxford University Press, 1994.
Asper, Markus. *Onomata allotria*. Stuttgart: Franz Steiner Verlag, 1997.
Babich, Babette. "Between Hölderlin and Heidegger: Nietzsche's Transfiguration of Philosophy." *Nietzsche-Studien* 29 (2000): 267–301.
———. *Words in Blood, Like Flowers: Philosophy and Poetry, Music and Eros*. Albany: State University of New York Press, 2006.
———. "Nietzsche und Wagner: Sexualität." Translated by Martin Suhr. In *Wagner und Nietzsche. Kultur—Werk—Wirkung. Ein Handbuch*, edited by H. J. Brix, N. Knoepffler, and S. L. Sorgner, 323–41. Reinbek b. Hamburg: Rowohlt, 2008.
———. "Le Zarathoustra de Nietzsche et le style parodique. A propos de l'*hyperanthropos* de Lucien et du surhomme de Nietzsche." *Diogène. Revue internationale des sciences humaines* 232 (October 2010): 70–93.

———. "On Nietzsche's Judgment of Style and Hume's Quixotic Taste: On the Science of Aesthetics and 'Playing' the Satyr." *Journal of Nietzsche Studies* 43, no. 2 (2012): 240–59.

———. *The Hallelujah Effect: Music, Technology, and Performance Practice*. New York: Routledge, 2016 [2013].

———. "Nietzsche's Performative Phenomenology: Philology and Music." In *Nietzsche and Phenomenology: Power, Life, Subjectivity*, edited by Élodie Boubil and Christine Daigle, 117–40. Bloomington: Indiana University Press, 2013.

———. "Nietzsche's *Antichrist*: The Birth of Modern Science out of the Spirit of Religion." In *Jahrbuch für Religionsphilosophie*, edited by Markus Enders and Holger Zaborowski, 134–54. Freiburg i. Briesgau: Alber, 2014.

———. "Nietzsches Lyrik. Archilochos, Musik, Metrik." In *Nietzsche und die Lyrik. Ein Kompendium*, edited by Christian Benne and Claus Zittel, 405–29. Frankfurt am Main: Springer, 2017.

———. "From Winckelmann's Apollo to Nietzsche's Dionysus." In *Nietzsche Forschung. ". . . An Winckelmann anzuknüpfen . . ."? Winckelmanns Antike, Nietzsches Klassizismuskritik und ihre Blicke in die Zukunft*, edited by Renate Reschke, 167–92. Berlin: de Gruyter, 2017.

———. "Nietzsche's Posthuman Imperative: On the Human, All too Human Dream of Transhumanism." In *Nietzsche and Transhumanism: Precursor or Enemy?*, edited by Yunus Tuncel, 101–13. Cambridge: Cambridge Scholars, 2017.

———. "Spirit and Grace, Letters and Voice. Or: Performance Practice and Alchemy in Ivan Illich, Alan Rickman, and Nietzsche." *Journal of the Philosophy of Education* 3 (2018).

Barnes, Jonathan. "Nietzsche and Diogenes Laertius." *Nietzsche-Studien* 15 (1986): 16–40.

Bauemer, Max. *Das Dionysische in den Werken Wilhelm Heinses*. Bonn: Bouvier, 1964.

Baughan, Elizabeth P. *Couched in Death: Klinai and Identity in Anatolia and Beyond*. Madison: University of Wisconsin Press, 2013.

Bertallot, Hans Werner. *Hölderlin–Nietzsche*. Hamburg, 1933.

Carson, Anne. *Eros, The Bittersweet*. Princeton: Princeton University Press, 1985.

Chladni, Ernst. *Die Akustik*. Leipzig: Breitkopf u. Härtel, 1802.

Colera, Christophe. *Individualité et subjectivité chez Nietzsche*. Paris: L'Harmattan, 2004.

Corbier, Christophe. "Subjectivité littéraire et chanson populaire: Archiloque et le genre iambique de Friedrich Schlegel à Friedrich Nietzsche." *Etudes Germaniques* 67, no. 2 (April-June 2012): 285–307.

———. "Alogia et Eurythmie chez Nietzsche." *Nietzsche-Studien* 38 (2009): 1–38.

Davenport, Guy. *Archilochos, Sappho, Alkman: Three Lyric Poets of the Seventh Century B.C.* Berkeley: University of California Press, 1980.

D'Iorio, Paolo. "L'image des philosophes préplatoniciens chez le jeune Nietzsche." In *"Centauren-Geburten." Wissenschaft, Kunst, und Philosophie beim jungen Nietzsche*, edited by Tilman Borsche, Federico Gerratana, and Aldo Venturelli, 383–417. Berlin: de Gruyter, 1994.

de Man, Paul. *Allegories of Reading: Figural Language in Rousseau, Nietzsche, Rilke, and Proust*. New Haven: Yale University Press, 1982.

———. Detienne, Marcel. *Ancient Philosophy, Mystery and Magic. Empedocles and Pythagorean Tradition*. Oxford: Oxford University Press, 1995.

———. *Apollon le couteau à la main. Une approche expérimentale du polythéisme grec*. Paris: Gallimard, 1998.

Eckerman, Christopher. "Teasing and Pleasing in Archilochus' First Cologne Epode." *Zeitschrift für Papyrologie und Epigraphik*, 2011.

Gigante, Marcello. "Friedrich Nietzsche und Diogenes Laertius." In *"Centauren-Geburten." Wissenschaft, Kunst, und Philosophie beim jungen Nietzsche*, edited by Tilman Borsche, Federico Gerratana, and Aldo Venturelli, 3–16. Berlin: de Gruyter, 1994.

Grote, George. *Griechische Mythologie und Antiquitäten, nebst dem Capitel über Homer und auswählten Abschnitten über die Chronologie, Literatur, Kunst, Musik, &c, Band 3*. Leipzig: Teubner, 1858.

Halliwell, Stephen. "Nietzsche's 'Daimonic Force' of Tragedy and Its Ancient Traces." *Arion: A Journal of Humanities and the Classics, Third Series*, 11, no. 1 (Spring-Summer 2003): 103–23.

Hedreen, Guy. "'I Let Go My Force Just Touching Her Hair': Male Sexuality in Athenian Vase-Paintings of Silens and Iambic Poetry." *Classical Antiquity* 25, no. 2 (October 2006): 277–325.

———. *The Image of the Artist in Archaic and Classical Greece: Art, Poetry, and Subjectivity*. Cambridge: Cambridge University Press, 2015.

Hermann, Leonhard. "Begegnung im Kanon?" In *Nietzsche—Philosoph der Kultur(en)?*, edited by Andreas Urs Sommer, 103–12. Berlin: Walter de Gruyter, 2008.

Humphrey, J. F. "Friedrich Nietzsche's Subjective Artist." *Philosophy and Literature* 38, no. 2 (2014): 380–94.

Koller, Hermann. *Musik und Dichtung im alten Griechenland*. Bern: Francke, 1963.

Legget, B. J. *Early Stevens: The Nietzschean Intertext*. Durham: Duke University Press, 1992.

Lévesque, Claude. "Dissonance." *Musique et textes* 17, no. 3–4 (1981): 53–66.

———. *Dissonance: Nietzsche à la limite du langage*. Montréal: Hurtubise HMH, 1988.

Maas, Paul. *Greek Metre*. Oxford: Oxford University Press, 1962.

Marcovich, Miroslav. "A New Poem of Archilochus: 'P. Colon.' inv. 75II." *Greek, Roman and Byzantine Studies* 16, no. 1 (Spring 1975): 5–14.

Miller, Paul Allen. *Lyric Texts and Lyric Consciousness: The Birth of a Genre from Archaic Greece to Augustan Rome*. London: Routledge, 1994.

Mosshammer, Alden A. "Phainias of Eresos and Chronology." *California Studies in Classical Antiquity* 10 (1977): 105–33.

Müller-Sievers, Helmut. *The Science of Literature: Essays on an Incalculable Difference*. Berlin: de Gruyter, 2015.

Nehamas, Alexander. *Life as Literature*. Cambridge: Harvard University Press, 1985.
Nietzsche, Friedrich. *Nietzsche's Werke. Nachgelassene Werke. Von Friedrich Nietzsche. Aus den Jahren 1872/73–1875/76*, Vol. 10. Leipzig: C. G. Naumann, 1903.
———. *Friedrich Nietzsche Gesammelte Werke. Vierter Band, Vorträge, Schriften und Vorlesungen 1871–1876*. Munich: Musarion, 1921.
———. *Nietzsche-Werke Vorlesungsaufzeichnungen (WS 1871/72–WS 1874/75), II/4* Edited by Fritz Bornmann and Mario Carpitella. Berlin: de Gruyter, 1995. KGW.
———. "On Music and Word." In Carl Dahlhaus, *Between Romanticism and Modernism: Four Studies in the Music of the Later Nineteenth Century*. Berkeley: University of California Press, 1980.
———. "On the Theory of Quantitifying Rhythm," William Arrowsmith, trans. *New Nietzsche Studies*, Vol. 10, Nos. 1–2 (2016): 69–78.
———. "Greek Music Drama."
———. KGW II/2. Edited by Fritz Bornmann and Mario Carpitella. Berlin: de Gruyter, 1993.
———. *Sämtliche Werke. Kritische Studienausgabe*. Edited by Giorgio Colli and Mazzino Montinari (Berlin: de Gruyter, 1980), 7. KSA.
———. *Was ist tragisch*, WKG 8.
———. *Zur Theorie der quantitierenden Rhythmik*, in KGW II/3.
———. "Zur Vorlesung: Die griechischen Lyriker" in: *Frühe Schriften*. Edited by Fritz Bornmann and Mario Carpitella. Berlin: de Gruyter, 1993.
———. BT. KSA 1.
———. GS/FW. KSA 3.
———. TI. KSA 6.
Paschalis, Michael. *Horace and Greek Lyric Poetry*. Crete: Rethymnon Classical Studies, 2002.
Reschke, Renate. "Künstler sind Advokaten der Leidenschaft . . . ? Zum Bild des Künstlers bei Friedrich Nietzsche." In *Denkumbrüche mit Nietzsche: Zur anspornenden Verachtung der Zeit*. Berlin: de Gruyter, 2000.
Ritter, Johann Wilhelm. *Fragmente aus dem Nachlasse eines jungen Physikers: Ein Taschenbuch fuer Freunde der Natur*. 2. Heidelberg: Mohr und Zimmer, 1810.
Rotstein, Andrea. *The Idea of Iambos*. Oxford: Oxford University Press, 2010.
Silk, M. S., and Joseph Stern. *Nietzsche on Tragedy*. Cambridge: Cambridge University Press, 1983.
Thompson, Emma. *Sense and Sensibility: The Screenplay and Diaries: The Screenplay and Diaries (Shooting Script)*. New York: Newmarket Press, 2007.
Ugolini, Gherardo. "'*Philologus inter philologos*.' Friedrich Nietzsche, die klassische Philologie und die griechische Tragödie," *Zeitschrift für antike Literatur und ihre Rezeption / A Journal for Ancient Literature and its Reception* 174, no. 2 (2003): 316–42.

Vietta, Silvio. "Heinse und Nietzsche." In *Das Mass des Bacchanten. Wilhelm Heinses Über-Lebenskunst*, edited by: Gert Theile, 213–29. München: Fink, 1998.
Weber, Max. "*Politik als Beruf.*" Munich: Duncker u. Humboldt, 1919.
West, Martin, and Reinhold Merkelbach. "Ein Archilochos-Papyrus." *Zeitschrift für Papyrologie und Epigraphik* 14 (1974): 97–113.
Westphal, Rudolf Georg Hermann. *Die musik des griechischen alterthumes: Nach den alten quellen neu bearbeitet*. Leipzig: Veit, 1883.
———. *Handbuch der Musikgeschichte*, Band 1, von Hugo Riemann, Alfred Einstein. Leipzig: Breitkopf u. Härtel, 1919.
Wilamowitz. *Future-Philologie. New Nietzsche Studies*, 4:1/2 (Summer/Fall 2000).

5

Untimely Meditations on Nietzsche's Poet-Heroes

Kalliopi Nikolopoulou

Introduction

It is said that the three tragedians were connected in the Greek imaginary via the date of 480 BC, which marked the Persians' final defeat in Salamis by this otherwise unruly, internally divided, and outnumbered people: Aeschylus was a veteran of Marathon and Salamis, Sophocles was the youth chosen to lead the paean celebrating the victory, and Euripides—the youngest of the three—was born on the day of the battle.[1] Whatever the empirical accuracy of this chronology may be, the symbolic gathering of the tragedians' lives around this glorious event suggests that the Greeks understood how central to tragedy is the notion of heroism.

Indeed, it is this inextricable connection to heroism—most clearly seen in tragedy's continuous adherence to Homer—that has turned tragedy into an impossible genre for modernity and into an ethically tenuous category for much of contemporary continental thought: heroism now is not only viewed as a thing of the past, a state of being that cannot be properly inhabited by the modern subject; more strongly, the very category of the heroic is questioned for its reliance on the aestheticization of death and suffering—namely, the aestheticization of ethics. However, tragedy's affirmation of Homer's heroic ideal—regardless of its various translations and reimaginings by the playwrights—constitutes arguably the strongest reason behind Nietzsche's interest in tragedy as a cultural antidote to what he perceived as the nihilist, antiheroic tendency of modern culture. That Nietzsche's continental legacy has come to eschew, attenuate, or even openly critique this heroic tenet of his thought is itself a symptom of the untimeliness of heroism as well as the untimeliness of Nietzsche's own philosophical performance—an untimeliness that the philosopher self-consciously noted, and that his readers have been aware of. Yet, noting this untimeliness, and at the same time vindicating it as Nietzsche's astute autobiographical prophecy about his legacy, ironically requires that we, his legatees, forego the force of his insight: we extol untimeliness only after having neutralized it by unfastening its link to the heroic.

While the untimely, for instance, now appears under the rubric of Messianic postponements, or quasi-immanent (non)-arrivals/events that are supposed to effect a futural "cut" into our historical present, the untimely in Nietzsche is scandalously figured not simply as a futural or projective anachronism but as an atavistic return. In biological terms, atavism is a reversion, a return to ancestral traits. In atavism, the past appears as a reassertion of its forgotten virility, not as a diluted reference to historical accumulation à la Hegel. The hero is such an atavistic form of being, and in the fragment "A Kind of Atavism" from *The Gay Science*, Nietzsche identifies with this atavistic temporality while attaching to the atavist heroic traits:

> I prefer to understand the rare human beings of an age as suddenly emerging late ghosts of past cultures and their powers—as atavisms of a people and its mores: that way one really can understand a little about them. Now they seem strange, rare, extraordinary; and whoever feels these powers in himself must nurse, defend, honor, and cultivate them against another world that resists them, until he becomes either a great human being or a mad and eccentric one—or perishes early.
>
> Formerly, these same qualities were common and therefore considered common—not distinguished. Perhaps they were demanded or presupposed; in any case, it was impossible to become great through them, if only because they involved no danger of madness or solitude.
>
> It is preeminently in the generations and castes that conserve a people that we encounter such recrudescences of old

instincts, while such atavisms are improbable wherever races, habits, and valuations change too rapidly. For tempo is as significant for the development of peoples as it is in music: in our case, an andante of development is altogether necessary as the andante of a passionate and slow spirit; and that is after all the value of the spirit of conservative generations.[2]

The persistence of the heroic in tragedy echoes this andante tempo that still characterized Attic society despite the tumultuous cultural changes that were taking place in classical Athens: as the sociopolitical and religious landscape shifted dramatically after the archaic period, the playwrights—much like the philosophers, with Plato leading among them—registered these changes by reworking Homer's material and values; nonetheless, surviving all these cultural translations, the principle of heroism remained a staple of the tragic genre, thus keeping intact the trace of "conservatism."

I must clarify at this point that such conservatism should in no way be viewed pejoratively—in the manner that, for instance, we are accustomed to dismiss today the "cultural conservatives." As Nietzsche's fragment illustrates, his kind of conservatism is responsible for the appearance of rare and extraordinary human beings, capable of effecting profound cultural transformations by virtue of the anachronistic temporality they inhabit. That these persons are so improbable in their epoch is precisely their gift to their epoch, which most likely resists them. In other words, it is as anachronism and conservative throwback that the figure of the atavist brings about a moment of radical change in the present, a change that makes him look as if he were ahead of everyone else. This is why Nietzsche suggests that the cultural significance of the atavist consists precisely in the fact that his values are no longer shared, that his existence and experience appear incongruous to his contemporaries' sense of reality. The atavist looks as if he were coming from the future but he is actually a creature from the forgotten past.

Interestingly, anachronism is not only a constitutive element of heroism, as we will see shortly, but a historical fact of tragedy: the mythological world that tragic theater summoned at the peak of the genre belonged to a distant past for the Athenians. Tragedy brought back the time of gods, kings, and heroes—namely, the domain of nobility and sovereignty—amidst a democratic polity busy with civic matters. Put differently, tragedy could not but be an anachronistic genre because its language and characters recollected the heroic age, an age concerned with the ideal of excellence rather than the reality of ordinariness.³ It is this antirealist strain of tragedy that ultimately accounts for its aesthetic—and even more importantly, aestheticizing—character, which is key for Nietzsche.

Additionally, in regard to our present consideration of Nietzsche, the crucial aspect of heroic anachronism also proves to be its aesthetic quality. I would maintain that untimeliness in its heroic (non-Messianic) dimension offers us an aesthetic—instead of a "purely" moral—conception of time. In other words, in the heroic worldview, time is not simply a medium of moral or even aesthetic contemplation but becomes itself an aesthetic experience. For instance, according to the Homeric outlook, the generic destruction that time brings to mortals—namely, the injury and death that are everyone's common lot—does not warrant an epic sense of mourning. Rather, mourning is all the more devastating, and becomes worthy of a great song, when it involves the loss of something precious and unfulfilled, something rare and extraordinary. Of course, such epithets belong to the aesthetic register, which, on the one hand, offends the "democratic," egalitarian spirit of morality that refuses to hierarchize loss; on the other hand, however, I would argue that this aestheticization of morality enriches morality by lending it the aspects of extraordinariness and exceptionality. Without this sense of the extraordinary, it would be impossible to distinguish an ethical performance from other mundane tasks.⁴

Since Nietzsche insists on the precedence of the aesthetic in his understanding of human activity, it is appropriate to survey his reflections on tragedy through this larger connection between the untimely and the heroic. In a preliminary attempt to underline the heroic dimension in Nietzsche, my essay focuses on the depictions of some of Nietzsche's poets in his *Birth of Tragedy*.⁵ His poets exhibit a special relationship to heroism and untimeliness, one that can be articulated through autobiographical, stylistic, and philosophical terms. I begin with a historical and philosophical outline of this aesthetics of heroism inaugurated by Homer, since he is as crucial a source for Nietzsche's reflections on tragedy as are the tragic and lyric poets. This outline will hopefully contribute to our understanding of two further issues in Nietzsche's early work on tragedy: (1) it will elucidate the opposition between the heroic Apollonian and the intoxicating Dionysian tendencies, and the logic by which they were both later subsumed under the umbrella of the Dionysian; (2) it will give us a suppler context within which to explore, and perhaps (trans)valuate what I regard as the current, antiheroic reception of Nietzsche.

Heroism as Beautiful Death:
The Apollonian Legacy of Homer

It is noteworthy that the temporality of heroism has always belonged to the untimely: Hesiod's Golden Age was a time of legend, and even the Homeric heroes are unfathomably old by the time of Homer. According to Gregory Nagy, one of the defining characteristics of the Greek hero (Homeric or otherwise) is unseasonality—that is, untimeliness. Nagy derives the etymology of "hero" from *hora* (hour, season), which, in turn, associates the hero to Hera, goddess of seasonal fulfillment. However, as Nagy stresses, the hero is anything but fulfilled in this lifetime; he is "on time" only with respect to his death.[6] Nagy illustrates this idea through the figure of the Homeric Achilles, whom he considers the most beloved and the most tragic of the Greek heroes, and who—I would add—furnishes the mortal version of the heroic god par excellence: the beautiful, shining, forever-young Apollo. As Nagy notes, though the Greeks sympathized with Hector, they still granted the lion's share of sympathy to Achilles.[7] Behind such sympathetic treatment lie a host of reasons that conspire to make his untimeliness ever more tragic and ever more untimely, if I may use the pleonasm: Achilles is the most beautiful of the warriors, which makes death's disfiguration of his beauty all the more tragic; he is the strongest and most excellent in battle, yet even such superhuman prowess cannot save him from death; finally, he is younger than Hector and unfulfilled in this life, doomed to die alone in a strange land. Hector too is beautiful and noble, but not on the same caliber as his counterpart; he is a responsible defender of his city, but not as gifted as Achilles; and he is older, a family man, someone already fulfilled.

Regardless of the moral valuations we currently attach to these two epic heroes,[8] the point is that, in Homer, the untimely signals an aesthetic experience of time. On the one hand, the greatest hero dies at the unripe age of youth, when the possibility of more greatness is still ahead of him. In fact, it is precisely because he is already unrivaled in all his qualities that death's sudden interruption of his potential appears all the more tragic. On the other hand, death, which destroys and disfigures, paradoxically also allows the hero to live in epic memory as eternally young and on the verge of further glory. The heroic death emerges in Homer as an agent of conservation, and we should not miss the Nietzschean undertones of "conservatism" in this context. Death conserves youth and beauty by arresting the passage of time. Death also infinitizes the heroic potential by leaving it unrealized, by suspending it as it approaches toward its peak. We mourn not only what is lost, but what could have been, and thus the aestheticization of time entails an idealization of it.

This experience of the beautiful death persists in Plato's and Aristotle's meditations on courage in the *Laches* and the *Nicomachean Ethics*, respectively. While the philosophers "translated" Homer to various degrees, both their accounts continue the references to courage in its heroic/aesthetic framework along with its newer, moral determinations. Seth Benardete's commentary on the *Laches* concludes that, while Socrates updated Homeric heroism (*andreia* qua manliness) to meet the demands of his own time by rendering courage into a human virtue rather than an extraordinary gift, the translation came at a cost: by securing courage for human beings, Socrates risked the aesthetic quality of *andreia* qua extraordinariness.[9] As he extended the scope of courage from noble prerogative to conventional, civic virtue—so that even a man who perseveres illness and poverty with dignity can claim the courage of a legendary hero (*Laches* 191d3–4)—Socrates also blurred the sharpness of its boundaries: the element of nobility (which is also translated as "beauty"—*to kalliston*) must now somehow vanish. Benardete notes further the transformation of archaic values in classical Athens by alerting us to the translation of *agathos* from "brave" to "good" (*kalos*).[10]

In his reflections on courage, Aristotle returns to the Homeric *andreia* arguably more faithfully than the Platonic Socrates. Sidelining the Socratic notions of the *Laches* that the quotidian perseverance of hardship as well as knowledge and prudence are expressions of courage,[11] Aristotle insists on thinking of courage in terms of the nobility (beauty, *to kalliston*)[12] of the death in battle,[13] while using Homeric examples. Death is the greatest (*to megiston*)[14] event in one's life, but not all death is courageous, according to Aristotle: *to megiston* must also be *to kalliston* in order to qualify for courage. In other words, the common event of death obtains an extraordinary ethical weight (courage) only after it has been linked back to the heroic scene, which relies on the aesthetics of untimeliness, as I already mentioned. Of course, it is true that war in our days is not waged in the manner Homer described, nor do contemporary soldiers exhibit Homeric attributes. It may thus appear that Aristotle's philosophy of courage is now obsolete, unless, however, we consider it for something more than its contingent example of the hoplite: its larger importance, I would argue, is its infusion of the ethical with the aesthetic—something that is also a key gesture in Nietzsche's thought.

Despite his other philosophical disagreements with Plato and Aristotle, Nietzsche shares with them a strong Homeric inheritance. Homer features in *BT* as the foremost example of Apollonian art—an art Nietzsche aligns with "monster-slaying" militaristic principles not simply because of its chosen theme of war, but because it is itself, formally speaking, an art of extreme discipline: armed with the Apollonian force of rule and restraint, Homer mastered the titanic chaos that preceded him and gave the Hellenes the Olympian beauty that helped them cope with life's terror.[15] Indeed, it is the scholarly consensus that in *BT*, the heroic ideal is connected with the Apollonian principle of individuation and exemplified in the precise art of Homer, whereas its opposing principle is that of the Dionysian collective intoxication.

The difficult question, then, concerns the fate of Apollo in the later Nietzsche, where the name of this god disappears, but his heroic attributes survive strangely mixed with Dionysus. Moreover, the philosopher gives no clarification as to why and how the conflicting pair of *BT* becomes abbreviated in Dionysus. Robert Luyster's essay, "Nietzsche/Dionysus: Ecstasy, Heroism, and the Monstrous,"[16] attempts to answer this question by engaging the interpretive assumptions that underlie Nietzsche's critical reception. He argues that standard Nietzsche scholarship has read *BT* selectively, emphasizing the Dionysian suffering in need of the Apollonian veil, but eliding the ecstatic Dionysus and the experience of immediacy and fusion with nature that the god offers. This, Luyster maintains, is a longstanding effect of Walter Kaufmann's synthetic interpretation of the Dionysian throughout Nietzsche's work: scholars read the Dionysian in *BT* retroactively from what it becomes later on, or from what Kaufmann understood it to have become. Luyster writes that, for Kaufmann, "the Dionysian (after *BT*) is a univocal, subjective principle denoting an extreme of life-affirmation and self-overcoming."[17] However, insofar as self-overcoming corresponds to the Apollonian martial tendency of self-control and the taming of one's passions, this later, combined version of the Dionysian dilutes the element of ecstatic fusion that was attributed to Dionysus in several passages of *BT*.

Indeed, Luyster insists on the separation between the two conceptions of Dionysus in *BT*, warning against commentators' tendency to espouse exclusively one of them. In the first, privileged conception, Dionysus embodies the suffering at the core of existence. Here, nature is viewed as rending itself and its beings asunder during its own self-contradictory strife of becoming, and as a result, the human being has to resort to the beautiful illusion of art (the Apollonian) in order to endure this primordial terror. Notably, this Dionysian reality is not accessible in itself, but only through Apollonian phenomenality, and Luyster is aware of this.[18] We cannot ever experience what lies behind the veil of appearance. While the struggle of the Apollonian artist to give shape to chaos yields a visible form, the primordial chaos itself cannot be directly apprehended. I argue that, besides the Kaufmann-effect that Luyster cites as the cause of neglect of the ecstatic Dionysus, it is the Kantian epistemology of the suffering Dionysus[19] that appeals to the continental (phenomenological) reception of Nietzsche. In endorsing almost exclusively the inaccessible Dionysus, the continental tradition also insists on privileging the phenomenon over what lies behind it.

The second conception of the Dionysian is more salutary in Luyster's account, albeit it remains disavowed by contemporary reception. This Dionysian is figured not as the suffering and self-contradiction, but as the ecstatic joy and harmony, that make up the core of existence. Luyster writes: "By means of Dionysian art (most particularly music, especially Wagnerian music), we are enabled to gain access to this aboriginal ecstasy of existence; via its rituals we are enabled to go behind phenomena, to have direct access to their—to our own—metaphysical source."[20] Shortly after, he continues: "All too often it is apparent that in Nietzsche's thinking the principle of individuation actually does collapse under the appropriate stimulus, that ecstasy is an authentic revelation of our innermost metaphysical depths. Dionysian ecstasy cannot be dismissed as merely phenomenal; Nietzsche is repeatedly insistent on the point that it reveals primal being as it is in itself, prior to individuation, behind individuation. All too briefly—but as a fact nonetheless, it seems—we become one with the One and are able to participate in its narcissistic, self-absorbed bliss."[21]

I suspect that this very language of primordiality and fusional oneness—which, despite our discomfort, remains operative in Nietzsche, and even serves good purposes, as Luyster rightly insists[22]—is the second reason for the current dismissal of the ecstatic Dionysus. Next to the philosophical objection that a graspable immediacy is an impossible metaphysics after Kant, a political objection is now added: the politics of fusion promised by the Dionysian experience seems dangerously close to fascism's myth of a collective primordial origin. The fact that many of these Nietzschean passages about the primordiality of Dionysian ecstasy come from the second part of *BT*, where Wagner's art is extolled as the continuation of the Greeks' tragic spirit, only adds to this problematic politics.

To return to Luyster's analysis: he observes that while the name of Apollo disappears in *Thus Spake Zarathustra*, merging "by some strange, philosophical alchemy" into Dionysus, the binary tension established in *BT* continues.[23] In fact, Luyster remarks, the contrast is more radicalized in both directions now that both gods share the same name:[24] the all-encompassing, nature-loving Dionysian that pervades many of the speeches of Zarathustra shows that ecstasy is no longer restricted to its place behind the phenomenon, but comes forward into the phenomenal surface.[25] At the same time, however, this joyous Dionysus/Zarathustra emerges through the new concept of the will-to-power as an enhanced version of the earlier Apollonian warrior, with all the attendant vocabulary of the strong/weak hierarchy.[26] It is this bellicose Apollo dressed in the Dionysian disguise of intoxication and love for Mother Earth that Luyster finds unsettling in Nietzsche. It is the same Apollo qua heroic prototype that Luyster also sees as the precursor of the further disintegration of Dionysus into a Napoleonic monster in Nietzsche's even later writings.[27] Tracing the disappearance of the ecstatic Dionysus in Nietzsche and in his critical reception, Luyster presents us with the following genealogy: just as the suffering Dionysus of *BT* (whose terror necessitated Apollo's intervention) was espoused over the joyous one, so the heroic Zarathustra qua last philosopher is preferred over the dancing reveler, eventually begetting the amoral monsters of *Beyond Good and Evil*. Somehow Apollonian heroism stands at the origin of this descent into moral terror.

Although I agree with Luyster regarding the detriments of forgetting the ecstatic Dionysus, this forgetting does not imply the celebration of the counterprinciple of heroism. Most crucially, the very attributes of heroism as developed by Nietzsche might not match up with those of its Greek Apollonian prototype. Indeed, while Luyster thinks that Nietzsche's Dionysus veers away from the Greek original,[28] he does not comment on any similar changes in the philosopher's use of Apollo. In regard to the critical reception of the binary, I think it becomes increasingly clear that the loss of ecstasy did not herald the reign of heroism, at least in the continental reappraisal of Nietzsche. On the contrary, both heroism and ecstatic fusion have been theoretically attenuated, displaced, or even abandoned. Today, the notion of the "virile artist" has been rendered as problematic—not to say preposterous—as that of the mystical visionary. Most importantly, I contend that the displacement of both principles results from the same philosophical and political objections that I cited above in relation to the ecstatic alone.

That both heroism and ecstatic fusion are the targets of the same critique shows, however, the intimate relation between Apollo and Dionysus in Nietzsche, which Luyster overlooks in his exclusively conflictual pairing of them: instead, already from *BT*, Apollo and Dionysus relate chiasmatically to one another, and this is most likely why Nietzsche could afford to conflate them in *Zarathustra*. To schematize this chiasmatic pairing: the attainment of the fusional Dionysus as a peak of joy bespeaks a certain "victory," an overcoming of ordinary experience. Otherwise, if harmonious oneness were the default and permanent state of affairs, this joy would not be as short-lived and precious a moment as Luyster, too, admits. Symmetrically, Apollonian self-overcoming orients itself toward a fusional existence. The great Apollonian artist heightens himself, but in this movement of ascent and self-transcendence, he also dissolves the ego's boundaries into the sublime canvas of the Dionysian All-and-One. The examples of Archilochus and Pindar in *BT* perform exactly this movement from heightened individuation to the dissolution into the collective voice, but more on this in the next section.

A final comment is due regarding this intimacy between Apollo and Dionysus, since it also anticipates my later discussion of Euripides's role in *BT*: whatever changes Nietzsche may have made to the ancient prototype of Dionysus, he is not unfaithful to the Greeks in thinking of this god paradoxically, and thus mixing the martial and ecstatic qualities of Zarathustra, as Luyster maintains. Paradox is the essence of Dionysus in Euripides's *Bacchae*, and Euripides does not play a minor role in *BT*. Slave and liberator, punisher and expiator, prey and predator are the main dichotomies through which the chorus depicts the god in this play. In other words, Dionysus names not only the ecstatic experience of nature's orgiastic abundance, but the force of tearing and dismemberment. Most tellingly, in this tragedy, he enters the stage as a kind of triumphant general returning home from an Asian expedition where he established successfully his rites. Even his rival, Pentheus, describes him as a nocturnal hunter who competes and conquers in the shaded fields of desire (ln. 455–58)—a kind of warrior nonetheless, and one who will prove to be monstrous. But it is Teiresias's description of Dionysus as a god "who usurped even the functions of warlike Ares" that answers best the question of the transformation of the heroic from Apollonian ideality to monstrosity (ln. 302–304).

It is worth recalling here that the Greeks had many war gods. This is not so much because they were a belligerent people, but because they wished to express the various aspects in which strife manifests itself in the cosmos and in human life. Though certainly beautiful, Ares is not commensurate with Apollo. He is a bloodthirsty god, one who incites war for no other reason than the waste of life. Embodying the principle of sheer destruction, Ares was hated by gods and humans alike, from Homer to the tragedians. Teiresias's passing comment is of great significance concerning the facets of heroism and war. Nietzsche's transformation of Dionysus into the monstrous may thus be better understood through this ancient link of Dionysus to Ares than as an occasion to undercut the few Apollonian traces of beauty and logos that have been struggling to survive modernity's critique of reason.

My point in all this is not to critique Luyster's well-drawn Dionysian typology, but to amend his overall perspective, according to which the ecstatic has regrettably been elided, while the heroic (particularly in what ought to be solely the ecstatic) persists problematically. I, instead, think that the heroic has met the same fate as the ecstatic, whether as part of the ecstatic or independently of it. Ironically, having abandoned both heroism and fusion for their potential for "violence," we may have been left only with the monstrous Dionysus of *The Bacchae*. Whereas Luyster places the heroic at the origin of the monstrous, with the ecstatic being their common antipode,[29] I see the notion of self-overcoming as the common term that aligns the heroic to the ecstatic, leaving the monstrous as precisely that which is "detached out of [any] cosmic context and justification."[30] However, the monstrous qua extremity and exaggeration is the trope par excellence of modernity, and Euripides was as much a "modern" critic during his antiquity as was Nietzsche an untimely presence in his modernity—hence, Nietzsche's symptomatically persistent disowning of his predecessor. That heroism is not the senseless shattering of all contexts is abundantly evident in the Apollonian artist, Homer: What is the *Iliad* but the attempt to bring back into context, into community and redemption, the hero who approached the beastly? The sober Achilles of the last book cannot exist without a return of Apollonian ideality.

Nietzsche's Other Poet-Heroes: Poetry as Vocation

From Homeric/Apollonian art, which Nietzsche explicitly associates with the martial heroism of the individual genius, we now pass into the lyrical and tragic space more closely associated with the collective voice of Dionysus. However, as I noted above, we must keep in mind that the Dionysian is not devoid of the heroic moment of self-overcoming, and this will become visible in the manner through which Nietzsche describes some of the tragic and lyric poets.

Nietzsche's widely observed preference for Aeschylus is a case in point: the oldest of the three tragedians, Aeschylus was already considered an untimely figure in his own age. Karl Reinhardt has commented on Aeschylus's adherence to archaic ritual and to an earlier, monumental cosmology in which the human being—no matter how flawed and hunted—was still granted a sense of ultimate belonging.³¹ Though Aeschylus participated in the struggle of ideas of his time, and helped reshape Attic religious thought, there remains in him this conservative trait of which Nietzsche wrote in his fragment on atavism. This trait marks not only Aeschylus's religious worldview, but the very solemnity of his language as well, his stylistic aloofness, which was so outdated that it became soon afterward one of comedy's favorite objects of mockery. Subsequently, the context in which Nietzsche chooses to express his admiration for Aeschylus itself discloses Nietzsche's interest in the heroic and untimely elements of tragedy. Nietzsche turns to Aeschylus's *Prometheus Bound* to elaborate the contrast between tragic-heroic morality qua affirmation of life and what he calls the Semitic, feminized morality of the weak that begets Christianity's denial of life.³² The citation of this tragedy is additionally significant because it underlines Aeschylus's untimeliness on two fronts: dramaturgically, this is the only extant play boasting a fifty-member chorus, thus recalling the origins of tragedy in collective ritual song (as Nietzsche proposed it); thematically, it excavates the origins of Greek religion, since its hero is not even an extraordinary mortal but a titan.

Let us backtrack, however, to start with Nietzsche's elaboration of lyric poetry as the other forerunner of tragedy alongside the epic. Following the discussion of the Doric/Homeric art of discipline and plastic form, sections 5 and 6 of *BT* introduce the art of music. For Nietzsche, music propels language to rhythm, which results in a kind of linguistic unevenness that opposes the "steady flow" of the epic. Music is the disjoining of the image in time, the stretch and the shrinkage of the vivid word: "in the poetry of the folk song, language is strained to its utmost that it may imitate music."³³ Thus, the folk song echoes a people's Dionysian pulse, and Nietzsche associates its rise with historically revolutionary moments.³⁴ The very association of the Dionysian with revolution recalls the militant side of Dionysus.³⁵

In section 6, Nietzsche makes some crucial points about Archilochus's relation to the folk song, and Pindar's grand, hortatory style. The most important of his observations concerns the use of the first-person pronoun, which in their poetry acts as a resonating chamber for the collective voice, while transporting the empirical self of the poet outside its narrow confines. In the name of these two poets, who inaugurate and conclude the history of the Greek lyric, Nietzsche gives us not only a historiography of the Dionysian entry into Greek art, but the key to reading him as a Dionysian thinker. Through his choice of these authors, we get a glimpse of what the

Dionysian means for Nietzsche, and therefore, how the style of these authors resonates in Nietzsche's own style.

In her essay "Nietzsche's Psychology and Rhetoric of World Redemption: Dionysus versus the Crucified," Claudia Crawford writes:

> Archilochus's poems . . . represented the two extreme and persistent pressures upon the lives of the ancient Greek citizen: "that of social duty and that of competitive self-realization." He engaged in politics, war, and poetry. He died in battle. As the first lyric poet, Archilochus was famous for his powers of invective; he was a sarcastic reviler in dithyrambs that reflected his turbulent and fierce character. The word dithyramb first appears in Archilochus. He calls it the song of Dionysus that, when under the influence of wine, he sings and leads others to sing, leading forth the "meters" or "dances" of Dionysus.
>
> Pindar represents for Nietzsche another high point of Greek glory for he combines the highest art of dithyramb and lyric with the grand style. In his victory odes, Pindar reflects the tradition of the older logos where physical actions and words reflect and heighten one another; and this very heightening leads to Dionysian festivity. Pindar was the *exarchon,* the poet who strikes up the lyre and song and leads the dance as Archilochus claimed to have done. The real *komos* (celebration), with its crowning of the victorious athlete with flowers and its procession through the streets, was built up to through the use of futures and vocatives in the ode to heighten expectation. In the odes Pindar's "I" is a "first person indefinite" that is meant to be suitable for adoption both by the chorus that speaks it and the audience that is invited to share in it. Through its hortatory, encouraging tone, the ode actually approximates prophetic language. Nietzsche develops this vocative (future calling) and hortatory tone as early as *The Birth of Tragedy,* and continues it to the very end.[36]

My interest in this passage centers on its alignment of heroism with a particular style of language: prophetic truth. This is important because, as we will see, style here is not limited to the rhetoric of the poetic works, but also refers to an autobiographical performance on the part of the poets themselves: style as their human character. Furthermore, it is as character that it furnishes a model for Nietzsche's own philosophical persona.

Though Apollo is the "official" Delphic god of prophecy, his rival and co-habitant at Delphi—Dionysus—also claims mantic powers. However, Dionysus's prophetic nature, which is attested to by Teiresias in *The Bacchae* along with the god's warlike attitude,[37] appears not in the service of rational ends, but through the communal ecstasy of his worship. Whereas Apollo granted oracles to individual pilgrims—oracles that, despite their mad and ambivalent articulation, were eventually meant to serve intelligible purposes—Dionysus disclosed the truth through enthusiastic sharing in a community of revelers.

Let us then further develop two claims from Crawford's passage to elucidate the linkage of the heroic to the prophetic. Firstly, Crawford connects Dionysian diction with prophecy through their common use of the future and the vocative: the exhortatory and forward-looking tone of the choral ode marks it as a form of communal expression and renders it akin to oracular speech.[38] Secondly, Crawford observes the repetition of this poetic/prophetic style and its attendant hortatory rhetoric in Nietzsche's own philosophical practice.

Regarding the first issue, Nietzsche's definition of the dramatist in *BT* is illustrative: "At bottom, the aesthetic phenomenon is very simple: let anyone have the ability to behold continually a vivid play and to live constantly surrounded by hosts of spirits, and he will be a poet; let anyone feel the urge to transform himself and to speak out of other bodies and souls, and he will be a dramatist."[39] Like the prophet who is filled by the god, the poet-dramatist lives in the presence of spirits, a conveyor of Dionysian enthusiasm and an instrument of the collective voice. But how does this enthusiasm relate to the heroic? To address this question, we must consider the risk-taking and untimely temporality involved in prophetic speech. Risk-taking naturally implies courage, whether it be the prophet's courage to utter unpopular truths or the listener's courage to doubt and incur divine wrath. Furthermore, prophecy's paradoxical reversal of past and future renders it an untimely form of speech.

The truth of prophecy does not lie in a series of future predictions, but rather in the prophet's bemoaning of the present and past inability of people to hear the truth. Truth has been already uttered but remained unheard, and one can only hope that it will be heard in the future. In this latter sense, there is always a forward rhetorical thrust to all prophets. Nevertheless, any good tragedian will disabuse us of the hopeful aspect of the prophetic future. The prophet's appeal to the future in effect emphasizes that truth is not to be heard in any future; that the prophet is and will always remain as untimely as the heroic and mad Cassandra who died voicing the truth. The future may vindicate a prophet, but in doing so, the future hardly redeems itself. Incidentally, I would not invest Nietzsche's call to his yet-unborn readers with anything other than such a rhetorical performativity. The call re-cites eternally the prophetic style. This style has traditionally been used to impress upon us the tragedy of never hearing our prophets. Yet, the alternative—namely, heeding to the prophetic word unquestioningly—presents other risks, such as the derailment of enthusiasm into barbarity that *The Bacchae* abundantly shows.

In this latter case, prophecy does not only warn of danger; in its fanaticism, prophecy itself becomes the site of danger. Prophets are no less charismatic than politicians, and Sophocles had both Oedipus and Creon suspect Teiresias for abusing his powers for sinister ends.[40] That both tyrants were wrong about Teiresias does not undermine the sound reasons why people distrusted prophets. In other words, the untimeliness of prophecy—the fact that no one ever listens to Cassandra—is in part a desideratum. It was indeed Apollo (reason) who gave Cassandra the gift of prophecy with one hand, then took it back with the other, condemning her words to fall into the void. The truth of Cassandra's myth, then, says this: reason requires that we not follow blindly the soothsayers, because they might lead us to disaster at least as often as they might save us. And yet, as reason comes to warn us from the prophet's fanaticism, tragedy also comes to prove the prophet right.

Turning to Crawford's second point, I wish to underline that Nietzsche's adoption of the vocative style is tied to the vocational aspect of his philosophy—namely, to the sense that philosophy is a calling to something higher. What he sees in these ancient poets is this sense of communal vocation. The poetry of Aeschylus, Archilochus, and Pindar appeals to him in its profound desire to transcend the confines of the egotistical self. "Transcendence" here should be understood both as the heroic overcoming of the Apollonian artist who reaches the summit precisely in superseding his ego, and the hierophant who echoes the rhythms of a great chorus and joins equally impersonally the Dionysian stream. It is in this sense that the heroic and the fusional have already intermingled in the dualist tension of *BT*: they are not only opposites that puzzlingly collapse into the later figure of Zarathustra, as Luyster argues.

While a heightened prosodic style distinguishes these poets, two of them share something else—something curiously biographical, yet quite revealing with respect to the notion of vocation: touched all by divine fervor,[41] Archilochus and Aeschylus were also soldiers. Archilochus legendarily died in war (though he famously wrote of abandoning his shield in a poem that satirized epic values),[42] while Aeschylus was a Marathon hero. His tomb in Sicily says nothing of his poetry, but simply records his war deeds: "In Gela, rich in wheat, he died, and lies beneath this stone: / Aeschylus the Athenian, son of Euphorion. / His valour, tried and proved, the mead of Marathon can tell, / The long-haired Persian also who knows it all too well."[43] Let me fast-forward to modernity to illustrate this enduring—if also untimely—presence of the heroic in the modern lyric. In his diary, *Mon Cœur mis à nu*, Charles Baudelaire wrote mournfully of three vocations modernity has eclipsed: the priest, the soldier, and the poet.[44] Affected by modern decline, Baudelaire, much like Nietzsche, looked for inspiration to those outdated forms of vocation. Homer, Aeschylus, Archilochus, Pindar, and we might now add Baudelaire: here we have various modalities of the poet-hero, the poet-universal creator, the poet-priest.

Euripides: Anti-Hero or Last Hero?

That Nietzsche's Apollo/Dionysus dichotomy inspired Thomas Mann's *Death in Venice* is undisputed. Just as undisputed is the fact that Nietzsche criticized Euripides for bringing about the death of tragedy by introducing Socratic dialectics into art. Thus, when Mann borrowed *The Bacchae*'s mountain orgy scene to depict the terror of Aschenbach's final moments,[45] he hinted at a crucial but neglected moment of Nietzsche's *BT*: the central figure, the poet-hero of Nietzsche's book, turns out to be its anti-hero. Euripides, the dramatist responsible for tragedy's decline, is also the one who provides Nietzsche his concept of tragedy: Euripides's final play presents the origin of tragedy in Dionysian cult, while performing tragedy's formal development as the synthesis of two intimate yet irreconcilable principles. In the scholarly milieu, Benardete noted this formative role of Euripides, raising *The Bacchae* to a model for Nietzsche: "Of the four philosophers who have discussed tragedy, two are ancient, two modern. For Plato and Aristotle, *Oedipus Tyrannus* was the paradigmatic tragedy, for Hegel it was *Antigone*, and for Nietzsche, Euripides' *Bacchae*."[46]

On the most evident level, Mann and Benardete's insight refers to the strife that *The Bacchae* rehearses and that is repeated in Nietzsche's binary of the Apollonian and Dionysian: the opposition between rationality (Pentheus), insisting on knowledge over belief, and the sacred (Dionysus), revealing itself in disguise. As I have already mentioned, Euripides stages this antagonism in terms of two kinds of "heroics": Pentheus follows the model of the open competition of the city gymnasia (the Olympian/Apollonian model of athletic contest), while Dionysus achieves his clandestine, erotic conquests under an effeminate, vulnerable mask (ln. 455–58).[47] Desire and war are not unrelated. We need only recall that the Trojan War was instigated by the power of desire ("the face who launched a thousand ships"), and that love has been described by the tragedians as a warring force (the choral ode to Eros in *Antigone* sings of "Love invincible in battle" [ln. 781]).

Beside this strife, however, the play unravels another kind of tension, one internal to Dionysus himself. It is this paradox within Dionysus that accounts for Nietzsche's own ambivalent approach to the Dionysian in *BT* and later. Benardete details this self-contradictory performance of the god in Euripides by elaborating the manifold illusions through which the god appears to the chorus, to Pentheus, and even to his own avatar.[48] *The Bacchae* is not only a play about the mortal inability to grasp the "incontrovertible" relation between belief and knowledge; it is also about a god's "frustration" at compromising his own "being for [his] being believed": on the one hand, Dionysus must keep faithful to his divine concealment; on the other, he must disclose himself to the nonbelievers by assuming phenomenal form, yet such disclosure "does not strip him of his disguise." In fact, Benardete even interprets Pentheus's punishment as the result of the god's frustration at being caught between being and seeming: "Pentheus suffers for Dionysus's frustration of his own plan."[49]

Notwithstanding the god's struggle between his divine aloofness and his phenomenal nearness, the play ends with the gruesome effect of this struggle on humans, who have many fewer resources to resolve the opposition, although they—most of all beings—are fated to think in terms of oppositions. Pentheus's severed head at the hands of his mother is not an aesthetic phenomenon in the sense of a "veil," or a representation of pain. In case we doubt the immediacy of this scene, Euripides makes the passage from illusion to reality explicit in Agave's own changing state of mind and perception: under divine madness, she first thinks that she holds the head of a beast; coming to her senses, she collapses seeing what she really holds. This is an example of a direct experience of the nonphenomenal Dionysus. However, this directness is hardly rendered in the joyful manner that Luyster attached to the ecstatic dimension of the Dionysian in *BT*. Here we confront the immediacy of the Dionysus who tears asunder. The aesthetic enigma of *The Bacchae* is that this barbarous victory nullifies the possibility of Apollonian distance that Nietzsche required for the tragic form. The end thus vindicates Teiresias, who linked Dionysus's martial capacities to Ares, the most bloodthirsty of the gods, and we are left wondering what this means for the larger, metatheatrical question of the nature of tragedy that this play raises. This might well be the reason why it was the last tragedy, since it brought the genre, along with its patron god, to their limits.

In light of all this, Euripides's constitutive role in Nietzsche's *BT* poses for us several questions: What does the philosopher achieve by assuming implicitly as the model for his own work the plot of the tragedian he portrayed explicitly as the killer of tragedy? It is tempting to suggest that perhaps tragedy's slayer bequeaths us the greatest of Apollonian legacies in staging the essence of the Dionysian; to further suggest that this is an Apollonian legacy not only in the rationalist sense that Nietzsche's accusations against the "dialectical" Euripides imply, but in terms of the other Nietzschean version of the Apollonian as the heroic artist, the dragon-slayer who overcomes chaos by imposing meaning via form. What could be more aesthetically heroic than confronting the Dionysian as the Dionysian, in its unmitigated horror (as Euripides did), and presenting the most terrible of forces while bringing a genre to its limit? Yet Nietzsche does not reserve any kind words for Euripides despite his own appropriation of the Dionysian model. The question persists: Why this ambivalent relation to a playwright, who, like Nietzsche, reflected on the meaning of an ambivalent god? Perhaps the way to begin unraveling such a question is to think less of the ambivalent god Nietzsche prized and Euripides staged, and more of the other one.

Apollo's absence from *The Bacchae* is as conspicuous as is Nietzsche's absorption of the Apollonian into the Dionysian in his later work. Of course, as many scholars maintain, this absorption does not necessarily imply the erasure of the Apollonian attributes from Nietzsche's thinking; rather, the Apollonian becomes incorporated into the Dionysian because the Dionysian is already a site of internal contradiction. Furthermore, as I have remarked earlier, *The Bacchae* seems to exemplify the Dionysian principle of internal contradiction at least through the words of the chorus, for whom the god is a giver of joy as well as an avenger. I emphasize the qualifier "at least," however, because in contrast to the chorus's image of Dionysus, the god himself appears exclusively in his savagery. Thus, Nietzsche's later incorporation of Apollo into Dionysus—as much as it is warranted by the intimacy of these two principles—should also not be underplayed as a simple choice of nomenclature. After all, the heroic-turned-monstrous is not identical to Apollonian heroism, even though current theoretical critiques of heroism often assume such an identity in order to refute heroism altogether. Luyster's position on heroism is no different on this point, though admittedly, his positive regard for the ecstatic Dionysian is a scholarly rarity.

To return, then, to the conundrum Euripides presents in *BT*: perhaps the decadence Nietzsche detects and disowns in Euripides's Socratic modernity reflects precisely Nietzsche's own anxiety as a modern trying to reinvent and inhabit untimely worldviews, while yet remaining inevitably entangled in, and even distorted by, his modernity. Nietzsche's revealing blind spot, then, is to read Euripides's "decadence" in terms of exaggerated rationality rather than the irrationality of exaggeration that the tragedian exposed through the stubbornness of both Dionysus and Pentheus. But exaggeration, as I noted earlier, is the extreme possibility couched within the Dionysian, and extremity has meanwhile emerged as modernity's privileged trope—hence, Nietzsche's attraction to this play. In turn, it is this blind spot that enables Nietzsche's postmodern heirs to diminish the importance of classical heroism in his work as the truly "conservative" trait—one that may have served Nietzsche's wish to be a cultural atavist now far more profoundly than the emphasis on his "anti-classicism" does.

Notes

1. Gregory, 252.
2. Nietzsche, *Gay Science*, 84.
3. Seth Benardete and Gregory Nagy both observe that even though heroes were mortal, they were above ordinary caliber. See "Achilles and the *Iliad*," in Benardete (15–33, here 18); Nagy (9–10).
4. Despite the revisions that the notion of courage underwent, the requirement of extraordinariness has been preserved. It is there in Plato and Aristotle, and continues to inform most contemporary views. We call courageous those who go the extra mile, and we are especially moved by the death of those who left behind too great a life, or who departed too early, for their beliefs.
5. Heretofore abbreviated as *BT*.
6. Nagy, 32.
7. Ibid., 21.
8. Nagy remarks that Hector elicited the sympathy of the ancient Greeks as well, but not to the extent that he does from the moderns (21). Modernity vilifies Achilles, whom it does not understand. Hector becomes the proper object of modern pity because of his defeat. This shift of allegiance signals the passage from an aestheticized version of ethics to a "pure" morality.

9. Benardete, 258. See "Plato's *Laches*: A Question of Definition" in Benardete (257–76). For Benardete, Nicias and Laches represent the divine and beastly view of courage, respectively. The former is the fully epistemic notion of courage as knowledge and foreknowledge of hope and fear; the latter comes closer to Homeric, natural power. The human forms the middle point between god and beast, and thus, to tailor courage to this middle point, Socrates foregoes the nobility (and aestheticism) afforded by the Homeric model. To recall Nagy and the Achillean example, the Homeric hero is not commensurate to ordinary humans: Achilles oscillates between the nearly divine (he is half-divine on his mother's side) and the beastly (his treatment of Hector).

10. Benardete, 261.

11. Aristotle, *Nicomachean Ethics* 1115a15–20, 1116b4–5.

12. Explaining the various semantic interrelations between the good, the noble, and the beautiful (*kalos/kallos*), translator C. D. C. Reeve of *The Nicomachean Ethics* observes that what makes acts ethically choiceworthy and praiseworthy is that they lie in the mean (*meson*), thus exhibiting a sense of order and proportionality, which are aesthetic qualities. Reeve concludes: "This brings us full circle, connecting what is ethically *kalon* to what is aesthetically noble, lending the former too an aesthetic tinge" (204n20).

13. Aristotle, *Nicomachean Ethics*, 1115a30–31, 1115b21–22.

14. Ibid., 1115a25.

15. Nietzsche opposes the Romantic reading of Homer as a naive artist: "Where we encounter the 'naïve' in art, we should recognize the highest effect of Apollinian culture—which always must first overcome an empire of Titans and slay monsters" (43). He also describes the severity of Doric art in terms of a "permanent military encampment of the Apollinian" (47).

16. Summarily, Luyster argues that *BT* was written in response to Schopenhauer's pessimism. Nietzsche's own ambivalent relation to this philosophy—he was drawn to it but also wished to affirm life—led him to the Apollonian/Dionysian divide. Tragedy as a reconciliation of the two opposites is, for Luyster, only a Hegelian incidental. On the primary opposition, Luyster writes: "As we consider . . . the implications of these conflicting impulses, it becomes increasingly apparent that at this early point in this thinking Nietzsche was decidedly of two minds about the metaphysical status of nature. As over against naïve, bourgeois 'cheerfulness' and simplistic affirmation of life, he was often in full agreement with his philosophical inspiration, Schopenhauer . . . that being was fundamentally a state of misery, from which art alone could distract—though not deliver—us. On the other hand, through his training as a scholar of antiquity he had come to grasp that in the ancient cult of Dionysus a radically alternative perception of nature prevailed, and that at the heart of it lay an entire metaphysic—the Dionysian worldview—that was in every sense the denial, possibly even the overcoming, of Schopenhauer's pessimism" (8–9). Thus, as a modern and antibourgeois critic of optimism, Nietzsche found in Apollo

an affirmation earned after struggle. You have to fight for your joy is Apollo's motto and, through it, Nietzsche avoids vapid contentment and bourgeois complacency. As a classicist in search of a direct, but still not self-indulgent, experience of joy, he went to Dionysus. Nevertheless, I do not think that the modern/classicist (German/Greek) divide corresponds neatly to Apollo/Dionysus, particularly after the modern and postmodern critique of logos.

17. Luyster, 1.
18. Ibid., 4–5.
19. I mean that what is behind the phenomenon (the unmediated Dionysian truth) corresponds to the structure of the Kantian *noumenon,* which remains unknowable to us.
20. Luyster, 6.
21. Ibid., 7; original emphasis.
22. Luyster cites passages where the fusional principle of the ecstatic Dionysus yields a fraternal politics, respect for nature, and a positive figuration of the feminine (14–15). For a contrary view, see Jean-Luc Nancy's critique of communion and fusion in *The Inoperative Community* (17).
23. Luyster, 5.
24. Ibid., 16.
25. Ibid., 12.
26. Ibid., 13–15.
27. Ibid., 20.
28. "We are thus left at last with the strange spectacle of a philosophy that could scarcely be less Dionysian (at least in the sense of the ancient Greek god) instead presenting itself as the very essence of the Dionysian" (3).
29. Luyster, 23.
30. Ibid., 18.
31. Reinhardt writes: "The Aeschylean hero might fall victim to the clash between gods and men, he might be overthrown, hunted, driven and tortured in the most horrible way, but he could never lose at one stroke his connection with what surrounded him, his sense of belonging. . . . Aeschylus belongs to the end of the late archaic period, but he evokes much older forces which still loomed dimly over his age in the realm of ritual, law and custom more than in that of poetry and fully-formed concepts" (3).
32. Nietzsche, *BT,* 70–72. The actual terms of contrast are "Aryan" and "Semitic," and are already problematized in a rather apologetic footnote by Kaufmann. It is not the purpose of this paper to enter into debate about the significance of Nietzsche's terms.
33. Ibid., 53; original emphasis.
34. Ibid.
35. Nicole Loraux writes of the tragic theater as a space conducive to political upheaval (23–25).

36. Crawford, 278.

37. On Dionysus's mantic powers as being prior to Apollo's, Park McGinty writes: "Nietzsche did not specify what Apollo's taking the weapons from Dionysos entailed, but it seems to parallel [Erwin] Rohde's notion that Apollo took over the mantic (god-inspired) prophecy from Dionysos" (202n21).

38. Homer remains the poet through whom the Greeks first sang their common belonging, and both his epics also began with a grand vocative to the Muse.

39. Nietzsche, *BT*, 64; my emphasis.

40. See *Oedipus Tyrannus* (ln. 345–49); *Antigone* (ln. 1092–1107).

41. Mary Lefkowitz discusses an ancient biography of Archilochus, which reports his heroic status and a visitation by the Muses (32–35). Aaron Poochigian tells the legend of Aeschylus's initiation into poetry: "[A]s a young man, he dozed off while guarding a vineyard. Dionysus then appeared to him in a dream and commanded him to write tragedies. Aeschylus began a play the next morning and 'succeeded very easily'" (Introduction, ix). Pindar's poetics and his religious cosmology are based on the divinization of the hero-athlete.

42. See Lefkowitz, 35.

43. Translated by Alan Sommerstein (9). Contra those who maintain that the epitaph was a Hellenistic composition, Sommerstein analyzes its language and restores its authorship to Aeschylus, or at least to a member of his family. Sommerstein argues that Aeschylus's choice to be memorialized as a soldier rather than a poet testifies to the connection between drama and Athenian citizenship (9), a connection Nietzsche rejected.

44. "Il n'existe que trois êtres respectables: Le prêtre, le guerrier, le poëte"; and, "Il n'y a de grand parmi les hommes que le poëte, le prêtre et le soldat" (*Œuvres completes*, 1271, 1287). The ancient trinity is completed with Sophocles who was also a priest.

45. Mann, *Death in Venice*, 65–67.

46. Benardete, 135.

47. In his essay "On Greek Tragedy," Benardete notes that whereas Plato, Aristotle, and Hegel thought of tragedy in relation to the city, "Nietzsche's account of tragedy does not seem to take its bearings by the sacred city" (99–145, here 135). Underlining the sacred, non-civil aspect of Dionysus, this passage from *The Bacchae* supports Nietzsche's antipolitical thesis on tragedy, and shows why Euripides might be much more for Nietzsche than the villain who killed tragedy.

48. Benardete, 137.

49. Ibid., 137 and 136. This parallels Luyster's first interpretation of Dionysus in *BT*: the Dionysian appears only through the heroics of Apollonian, phenomenal form (as in the god's mortal disguise). But Dionysus does at the end reveal himself as a god through the first-person pronoun, even though he does not change his visual form.

References

Aristotle. *Nicomachean Ethics*. Translated by Martin Ostwald. Indianapolis: Bobbs-Merrill, 1962.

Baudelaire, Charles. *Mon Cœur mis à nu*. In *Œuvres completes*, edited by Y.-G. Le Dantec, 1271–1301. Revised edition by Claude Pichois. Bibliothèque de la Pléiade. Paris: Gallimard, 1961.

Benardete, Seth. *The Argument of the Action: Essays on Greek Poetry and Philosophy*. Edited by Ronna Burger and Michael Davis. Chicago: University of Chicago Press, 2000.

Crawford, Claudia. "Nietzsche's Psychology and Rhetoric of World Redemption: Dionysus versus the Crucified." In *Nietzsche and Depth Psychology*, edited by Jacob Golomb, Weaver Santaniello, and Robert Lehrer, 271–94. Albany: State University of New York Press, 1999.

Euripides. *Bacchae*. Translated by William Arrowsmith. In *Greek Tragedies*, edited by David Grene and Richmond Lattimore, 191–262. Vol. 3. 2nd edition. Chicago: University of Chicago Press, 1991.

Gregory, Justina. "Euripidean Tragedy." In *A Companion to Greek Tragedy*, edited by Justina Gregory, 251–70. Oxford: Blackwell, 2005.

Lefkowitz, Mary. *The Lives of the Greek Poets*. 2nd edition. Baltimore: Johns Hopkins University Press, 2012.

Loraux, Nicole. *The Mourning Voice: An Essay on Greek Tragedy*. Translated by Elizabeth Trapnell Rawlings. Ithaca: Cornell University Press, 2002.

Luyster, Robert. "Nietzsche/Dionysus: Ecstasy, Heroism, and the Monstrous." *Journal of Nietzsche Studies* 21 (Spring 2001): 1–26.

Mann, Thomas. *Death in Venice*. In *Death in Venice and Seven Other Stories*, translated by H. T. Lowe-Porter, 3–73. New York: Vintage, 1989.

McGinty, Park. *Interpretation and Dionysos: Method in the Study of a God*. Religion and Reason 16. The Hague: Mouton/De Gruyter, 1978.

Nagy, Gregory. *The Ancient Greek Hero in 24 Hours*. Cambridge: Belknap-Harvard University Press 2013.

Nancy, Jean-Luc. *The Inoperative Community*. Translated by Peter Connor, Lisa Garbus, Michael Holland, and Simona Sawhney. Edited by Peter Connor. Theory and History of Literature 76. Minneapolis: University of Minnesota Press, 1991.

Nietzsche, Friedrich. *The Birth of Tragedy and The Case of Wagner*. Translated by Walter Kaufmann. New York: Vintage, 1967.

———. *The Gay Science: With a Prelude in Rhymes and an Appendix of Songs*. Translated by Walter Kaufmann. New York: Vintage, 1974.

Plato. *Laches*. Translated by Benjamin Jowett. In *Plato: The Collected Dialogues*, edited by Edith Hamilton and Huntington Cairns, 123–44. Bollingen Series. New York: Pantheon, 1963.

Poochigian, Aaron. "Introduction." In *Aeschylus: Persians, Seven against Thebes, and Suppliants*, translated by Aaron Poochigian, ix–xxi. Baltimore: Johns Hopkins University Press, 2011.

Reeve, C. D. C., trans. *Nicomachean Ethics* by Aristotle. Indianapolis: Hackett, 2014.

Reinhardt, Karl. *Sophocles*. Translated by Hazel and David Harvey. New York: Barnes and Noble, 1979.

Sommerstein, Alan H. *The Tangled Ways of Zeus: And Other Stories In and Around Greek Tragedy*. Oxford: Oxford University Press, 2010.

Sophocles. *Antigone*. Edited and translated by Hugh Lloyd-Jones. In *Antigone, The Women of Trachis, Philoctetes, Oedipus at Colonus*. Cambridge: Loeb-Harvard University Press, 1994. Vol. 2 of *Sophocles*. 2 vols. 1–127.

———. *Oedipus Tyrannus*. Edited and translayed by Hugh Lloyd-Jones. In *Ajax, Electra, Oedipus Tyrannus*. Cambridge: Loeb-Harvard University Press, 1994. Vol. 1 of *Sophocles*. 2 vols. 323–483.

6

Heidegger's Ister Lectures

Ethical Dwelling in the (Foreign) Homeland

Charles Bambach

Hölderlin as the Name of an "Other" Beginning of Thinking

The question about the place of Hölderlin within Heidegger's long and twisting thought path confronts us with nothing less than the very question about the meaning and direction of Heidegger's thought itself. "Hölderlin" is less the name of a poet for Heidegger than it is the name for a way of rethinking in a deeply originary way the meaning and sense of the whole Western tradition. Hölderlin—in this sense—is the name that grants the possibility of an "other" beginning for thinking, a commencement that takes up again, in a language that is something wholly other than "metaphysical," the first beginning of Western thinking in Anaximander, Parmenides, and Heraclitus. Heidegger countenances such an interpretation in his notebook of the late 1930s, *Besinnung*, by claiming that Hölderlin is "the poet of the other beginning of our future history."[1] What this means for Heidegger is that Hölderlin's poetry—through its thoughtful dialogue with the thinkers/poets of the first beginning—is able to enter into the provenance of that history in all its questionability. Through a daring—and at times violent—translation of Greek idioms and forms, Heidegger puts forward a breathtaking vision of a German future that emerges from the power of that initial commencement, even as this possibility depends ever more forcefully on the way the poet traces its decomposition and loss in and through that very history. What emerges here for Hölderlin is a vision of history read through the poetic myth of an auroral consummation of the marriage between gods and mortals, a ἱερὸς γάμος that celebrates the shared bond between divinity and humanity. Yet Hölderlin's work is also marked by an all too self-conscious awareness of the loss of this unity within human history, one where the gods have fled[2] and left a distraught humanity in a state of confounding bereavement. In this condition of "sacred mourning,"[3] the poet seeks a fitting word that might attune his fellow mourners to the gravity of their plight in a "time of destitution."[4] Only then, in bringing the word to the *Volk* and gathering its grief into a welcoming call for the return of the gods to the earth, can the poet begin his proper task, which is to vouchsafe a proper dwelling for human beings upon the earth.

At the heart of this Hölderlinian judgment about the path and trajectory of human history is the poet's own preoccupation with "homecoming" (*Heimkehr*), with both the possibility and necessity of finding our authentic home upon this earth, of dwelling in proximity to the gods, in abiding in the promise of the gods' return. I want to suggest here that this Hölderlinian preoccupation with *Heimkehr*, homecoming, poetic dwelling, and finding one's proper or authentic (*eigen-tlich*) abode upon the earth will come to constitute one of the most essential themes in the late Heidegger's philosophical corpus. Indeed, perhaps no other question will shape this later thoughtpath as powerfully as this one about "poetic dwelling" or what Heidegger will alternately designate as our *Weltaufenthalt* (our sojourn/stay/abode within the world).[5]

This question about poetic dwelling—so poignantly addressed in his 1951 essay ". . . dichterisch wohnet der Mensch auf dieser Erde"—will, however, be rethought by Heidegger precisely in terms of Hölderlin's own formulation in the Böhlendorff letter of 1801[6] concerning the relation between one's own/the proper/*das Eigene* and the foreign/the strange/*das Fremde*. On Hölderlin's telling, the poet can only properly come into what is his "own" or *Eigene* when he undergoes a journey to and through the foreign or *Fremde*. The foreign stands in an enigmatic and perplexing relation to the proper; yet it is not merely something "alien" or "unfamiliar." Rather, the foreign has a preeminent and essential relation to the proper—precisely in its character as what is improper or strange. Hence, Hölderlin can speak of the path to one's ownmost as "the most difficult"[7] since it lies in too great a proximity to our native haunts.[8] To come into our own, Hölderlin contends, requires that we must first "veritably appropriate what is foreign" so that the way into one's own (*das Eigene*) involves an appropriation (*Aneignung*) of that which is not our own. For the German poet, this demands an intimative confrontation with the ancient Greeks that resides less in imitation or mimesis of Greek art on the model of Winckelmann or Weimar classicism than it does in a chiastic reversal of the Greeks' ownmost propensity to seek out their opposites as a path to embracing what is fitting for them.

For Heidegger "the experience of the foreign" (*die Erfahrung des Fremden*) as a way of coming into one's own will come to shape not only his interpretation of Hölderlin, but will serve as a guiding thread for thinking through the proper task of the Germans in the epoch of the world's night.[9] In what follows I want to look at some of the ways in which Heidegger's engagement with Hölderlin—especially on the question of the native and the foreign—will take up the issue of authentic dwelling as a way to think Germany's confrontation with its own identity in the age of the modern. As essential to this identity, Heidegger will frame the question of the German as an encounter with the foreign. Moreover, in the Ister lectures of SS 1942, Heidegger will stage a Native encounter with the Foreign by pointing to the singular bond between Greeks and Germans that will shape his whole presentation. What matters most to Heidegger in his figuration of this binary structure is the question of poetic dwelling, which he defines as the way of "being properly homely" (*das eigentliche Heimischsein*).[10] Drawing on the originary dialogue of Hölderlin with Sophocles and his tragedy *Antigone*, Heidegger finds in this dialogue a way of enunciating "the law of becoming homely for the Germans" that will guide his understanding of poetic dwelling: "Dwelling itself, being homely, is the becoming homely of a being unhomely." What is truly unhomely, Heidegger tells us, is "the uncanny," which points to the most fundamental sense of human being—namely, that the human being is a being whose essence runs counter to itself. Both Sophocles and Hölderlin show the counterturning essence of the human being with exemplary care. Moreover, both show this counterturning essence of human being as the struggle to "be" in this place where we find ourselves, the place where we dwell. Drawing on these poetic ways of showing the counterturning essence of human dwelling, Heidegger lays bare how dwelling is nothing we can ever achieve of our own volition, nothing accomplished or effectuated by human planning but, rather, essentially prevails as an *Ereignis* or "appropriating event" that brings us into our own by grappling with the uncanniest of our historical displacement and its various forms of withdrawal, concealment, expropriation (*Enteignis*), and mystery. Only by confronting this uncanniness as that which belongs to being and as that which "looms forth in the essence of human beings" can we confront the genuine homelessness of the human being as the beginning of a path into authentic dwelling. For Heidegger, then, poetic dwelling depends upon entering into the nullity of our own existence, the abyss or *Abgrund* that un/grounds the ground (*Grund*) of our sojourn upon the earth. It involves recognizing the human being as—in its essence—a καταστροφή, a being that turns (στροφή) against (κατα), away from, its own essence in a backward turning reversal that moves it away from its own home into the uncanny realm of the unhomely. It is this vision of the conflicted, counterturning essence of the human being as that being—solely and incomparably among all other beings—who is not "at home" in being, above all not in its own being, that marks the human being as "tragic."

In the lecture course on Hölderlin from Winter Semester 1934/35, Heidegger indicates that the only way to grasp the poem "Germania," which poetizes the fate of the Fatherland, is to cultivate a fundamental attunement of "sacred mourning," that experiences the departure and flight of the gods.[11] Given the devastating losses of the Great War, it is hardly surprising to find Heidegger thematizing such mourning as a way into "belonging to the homeland."[12] It is within and through this same connection to the homeland that Heidegger will read Hölderlin's river hymn "The Ister." What emerges in these lectures is a poetic-thinkerly reflection on what it means to be "at home" (*zuhause*) in "one's own" (*Eigenes*). But given the logic of Hölderlin's Böhlendorff letter, this possibility of appropriating the native and the proper crucially depends on a passageway through the foreign, strange, alien, and other.[13] Hence, in the middle of this lecture course, in a reflection that constitutes the very core of Heidegger's reading of Hölderlin, we find a long discussion of "The Greek Interpretation of Human Beings in Sophocles' *Antigone*"—which will constitute the focus of my essay.[14] Here in Heidegger's reading of the figure of Antigone we come to confront the singular power of the homeland as the force that animates "the future historical essence of the Germans" in the age of the world's night.

Dwelling in the Intimacy of Truth as Oppositional Harmony

In the Hölderlin lectures from WS 1934/35, Heidegger focuses on the problem facing the German Volk which, through his reading of the Böhlendorff letter, he defines as "the free use of what is one's own (*des Eigenen*)."[15]

This, as Hölderlin taught him, "is the most difficult." Near the end of these lectures he remarks that although in the popular imagination "difficulty" connotes misfortune, distress, and adversity, thought within the language of poetic measure, bearing difficulty serves as the highest kind of good fortune since it attunes us to the "Innigkeit" or conflictual intimacy that expresses the deepest unity "in the middle of beyng."[16] This Hölderlinian notion of *Innigkeit* pervades both the 1934/35 course on "Germania and the Rhine" as well as the 1942 course on "The Ister." In both courses Heidegger associates *Innigkeit* with the mysterious power of rivers and with Hölderlin's reading of Sophocles.[17] Here, *Innigkeit* is understood less as a psychological mood, insight, or feeling than as "the supreme force of *Dasein* . . . a force that establishes itself in withstanding the most extreme conflicts of beyng from the ground up."[18] *Innigkeit* shows itself as an "an attuned, knowing standing within that sustains the essential conflict of that which, in being opposed, possesses an originary unity—the harmoniously opposed' (*das Harmonischentgegengesetzte*)."[19] Amid opposition and strife, *Innigkeit* "holds things apart in conflict and at the same time joins them together."[20] In the primordial conflict that reigns throughout all beings there runs a deeper sense of unity and harmonious wholeness that lies concealed to humans. It is the poet's task to express the mystery of such conflict, but precisely in a way that shelters its mysterious character without reducing it to a mere "solution" in the manner of an unmasking.

What remains most mysterious to Heidegger throughout his Hölderlin lectures, however, is Dasein itself since for him "Dasein has become foreign to its historical essence, its mission (*Sendung*) and its mandate (*Auftrag*)."[21] It is in grappling with the mysterious character of "bearing witness to its own Dasein" that Dasein confronts its ownmost possibilities. Such a confrontation happens authentically, however, only in contentious strife. The human task here demands that we become intimate with such oppositional conflict by letting ourselves be open to what is harmoniously opposed (*das Harmonischentgegengesetzte*).[22] In the mystery of such conflictual intimacy (*Innigkeit*) lies "the highest form of truth," one that holds sway in relations between gods and mortals and manifests itself in both the flight and arrival of the gods. As Heidegger phrases it, "There is mystery only there where conflictual intimacy [*Innigkeit*] holds sway." Moreover, "the mystery is not just any riddle or enigma; the mystery is conflictual intimacy, which is, however, beyng itself."[23] As a poet whose poetry has as its task the poetizing of this mystery as *Innigkeit*, Hölderlin is able to hold things together in a poetic idiom that simultaneously honors their separation and contention. Such a vision of variance as congruity emerges in the mediating role that Hölderlin assigns to both rivers and poets who, as demi-gods, are able to manifest the enigmatic unity of opposing realms without losing the mysterious character of such a unity. In both the Rhine and Ister hymns, Hölderlin poetizes this dynamic between harmony and opposition by taking rivers as the proper site for "the poetic dwelling of human beings upon this earth."[24]

Responding to Hölderlin's hymns, Heidegger thinks their meaning in relation to the task of German history. The question for Heidegger—precisely in SS 1942, as it was in WS 1934/35—is whether we are ready "to receive that which is coming (*das Kommende*) as the truth of the earth and of the homeland."[25] To do so requires of us that we stand in the grounding attunement of sacred mourning and stand within the conflict between hiddenness and unhiddenness, concealment and revelation that reigns throughout all being and manifests the *Innigkeit* of authentic ἀλήθεια. What marks these lectures is a poetic-thinkerly reflection on the simplest, yet most perplexing, question of human existence: How are we to dwell? What does it mean to authentically dwell upon the earth so that, in doing so, we become intimate (*innig*) with the truth of being? Only later in the "Letter on Humanism" will Heidegger take up this question explicitly as a question about an "originary ethics" rooted in an *ethos* of authentic dwelling that sets apart the familiar abode of humans (ἦθος) from the open region of the unfamiliar that enables divine presence (δαίμων).[26] But the traces of a profoundly Hölderlinian ethics of dwelling already begins to show itself in the way Heidegger engages Hölderlin's poetizing of the river hymns. In raising the question of one's own and the foreign in terms of the first and the other beginning, Heidegger thinks the chiastic relation between the ancient Greeks and modern Germans in terms of the course of the Danube River as it leaves its source on a journey homeward.

Here in these lectures I believe that we find a Heidegger who (despite all his German exceptionalism with its fear of other nations, cultures, languages, and lines of descent) takes up a fundamentally *ethical* reflection on the meaning of the homeland as our proper place of dwelling upon the earth. Moreover, in these same reflections we find crucial hints, pointers, and indications of an ethics that, abjuring the metaphysical "ethics" of right and wrong, offers insights into a fitting relation between the proper and the strange, the native and the foreign, one's self and the Other. In this thinking that ponders the proper abode of the human being upon the earth, we are enjoined to take up our responsibility for letting being come into our care—and of responding (which means co[r]-responding in the sense of *Ent-sprechung*) to the claim that being makes upon us.[27] This *ethical* dimension of responding to the claim of being has profound consequences for our own possibilities of dwelling, since in dwelling we take care of and shelter the openness of being in the historical situation into which we are thrown. If the question of ethics has to do with the authentic possibility of dwelling—and if dwelling in its most essential form defines "the fundamental character of being, in keeping with which mortals exist"[28]—then the question of the Ister lectures can be understood as fundamentally ethical, since it is in poetizing that we genuinely confront "the fundamental happening of beyng as such"—"the full essence of being human" which occurs in and as dwelling.[29] For what these lectures take up is the question of "the essence of Western humankind" in all its relations to world, to earth, and to the gods and it is to this question of human essence—Who are we?—that Heidegger turns in these lectures, especially in his discussion of Sophocles's choral ode from the tragedy *Antigone*.

Tragedy and the Definition of the Human Being as "Katastrophe"

The uncanny thing about Heidegger's interpretation of the human being as the most uncanny in Sophocles's *Antigone* ode is that its uncanniness is not something that stands opposed to the human being as something alien, strange, or foreign; rather, uncanniness belongs to it fundamentally in an originary way. Already in his first Hölderlin lectures Heidegger had indicated "that the historical being of the human being is shot through with ambiguity and indeed essentially so."[30] In his Parmenides lectures of WS 1942/43, Heidegger again speaks of an "essential ambiguity" that pervades Greek tragedy and that does so not out of any "dramatic 'effect' but spoken to [the poet] from out of the essence of being."[31] What marks the human being as the uncanniest of all those other creatures on the earth who crawl, swim, canter, burrow, meander, and take flight, is that it is *essentially* so as part of how it comes to dwell upon the earth. For Heidegger, this means that human dwelling is marked by a profound and tragic opposition between the yearning to be at home in one's essence *and* the counterturning pull of a movement that drives the human being out of its home. In the very ambiguity of the Greek word τo δεινόν ("the uncanny")—which connotes both the wonderful and the terrible at the same time, both the awesome and the aw(e)ful—Heidegger finds "the fundamental word of [*Antigone*], indeed of Greek tragedy in general, and thereby the fundamental word of Greek antiquity."[32] Yet we must be clear: not only is the language of tragedy ambiguous, contradictory, and counterturning in its essence, but so too is the human being. Moreover, the uncanniness of the chorus's language, as well as the uncanniness of Antigone herself, bespeak an even deeper and more profound uncanniness, which is that of beyng itself. And yet within all the uncanniest of being's manifestations—thunderstorms, tornadoes, tsunamis, earthquakes—"the most powerful 'catastrophes' we can think of in nature and in the cosmos"—Heidegger tells us—"are nothing in terms of their uncanniness compared to that uncanniness that the human essence in itself is."[33]

What matters here for Heidegger in his dialogue with both Sophocles and Hölderlin is to take up this question about the uncanniness of the human being precisely as a question about how human beings can dwell authentically upon the earth. In other words, this question about our *Aufenthalt, ethos,* sojourn, stay, or abode upon the earth is neither a question about residence, settlement, domestic habitat, nor one concerning our "wandering around" or venturing outward in ever newer endeavors. Rather, what is at stake here is a question of "originary ethics," a question about the proper way to dwell for the human being that involves both tarrying/abiding in a native abode as well as journeying outward into the foreign. It involves an awareness that in order to be able to dwell in the proper, native, and homely, we must first abide in the abode of the unhomely, the uncanny, the improper. This is what distinguishes us as the exception among beings, that we both inhabit and are inhabited by an inescapable uncanniness that pervades our *ethos.*

> This kind of uncanniness (*Unheimlichkeit*), namely unhomeliness (*Unheimischkeit*), is possible for human beings alone, because they comport themselves toward beings as such, and thereby understand being. And because they understand being, human beings alone can forget being.[34]

Such a question involves an awareness that in order to dwell in the proper, native, and homely, we first need to abide in the abode of the unhomely, the uncanny, the improper. This sense of the uncanniness of the unhomely—namely, that we are not at home even in our home—finds its expression in the Greek word "καταστροφή"—literally, a "turning" (στροφή), "down," "against," "away from" (κατα), that is a "reversal" or an "overturning." As

Heidegger succinctly puts it: "Human beings are in their essence a *katastrophe*—a reversal that turns them away from their own essence. Among beings, the human being is the sole catastrophe."[35] Moreover, for Heidegger, the exemplary instance of such catastrophe manifests itself in the figure of Antigone, who risks everything to attain her proper task of becoming homely—even as she everywhere encounters "the fact that the homely refuses itself to [her]."[36] In this, Antigone proves exemplary since her fate manifests the very counterturning strife that is at the heart of the human venture to attain a home within being, to enter into its proper *ethos* or abode.

What Heidegger suggests here is that this abode shows itself as the open site for the unconcealment of beings, an unconcealment that happens only in its continuous struggle with that which remains concealed. In other words, it is not on account of the human being's role as a "subject" that being opens up at this site; rather, it is due to being's own appropriation of the human being as the site of its disclosure that we can be at home at all. But even here we either fail to recognize this open site as open or we "forget" that it essentially prevails (*west*) within and as the very essence (*Wesen*) of the human being as the one who stands in the truth of being as ἀλήθεια, the one who ultimately emerges in and through the counterturning hiddenness/disclosure of our historical abode/*ethos*. Again, Antigone is exemplary in this way since it is she who takes upon herself "the 'drama' of becoming homely." As Heidegger writes, "Antigone's becoming homely first brings to light the essence of being unhomely. Becoming homely makes manifest the essential ambiguity of being unhomely."[37] She does this by pursuing the impossible; that is, she decides "to pursue that against which nothing can avail" and takes this sense of the impossible as her point of departure for all of her undertakings in the play. In so doing, she decides (as she tells Ismene) "to take up into my own essence (*ins eigne Wesen*) the uncanny that here and now appears."[38] Here, Heidegger makes clear that what is uncanny—namely, the unhomely—"is nothing that human beings themselves make, but rather the converse: something that makes them into what they are and who they can be."[39]

On Heidegger's reading, Antigone (far more than Creon) steps out of the site of the unhomely of her own power. And unlike her father Oedipus, she *knowingly* "takes it upon herself to be unhomely."[40] Such a decision, if it is to be authentic, "must spring from a belonging to the hearth and thus stem from a kind of being homely." What matters here above all, for Heidegger, is Antigone's authentic resolve to embrace her fate as the one who embodies "the supreme uncanny."[41] If, like Creon, her uncanny expulsion from the hearth of being (Εστία) were occasioned by a mere presumptuousness or *Vermessenheit* that measured all beings from the horizon of subjective volition and self-assertion, then such a movement would merely result in the forgetting and forfeiture of being. But because her unhomeliness emerges out of "a 'thoughtful remembrance' (*Andenken*) of being" that thinks of this unhomeliness as but a preparatory passageway to a homecoming at the hearth of being, Antigone succeeds in fulfilling the fundamental law of human history as "becoming homely in being unhomely." As Heidegger expresses it: "Antigone *is* the poem of being unhomely in the proper and supreme sense."[42]

With this interpretation of Antigone as the one who knowingly takes upon herself, that is, "suffers" the uncanny and "fittingly accommodates herself" (*sich schickt*) to it "as her all-determinative point of departure against which nothing can avail," Heidegger moves beyond Hölderlin's own grasp of Antigone as acting lawlessly against Creon's law of the *polis*. For Heidegger, Antigone does not fulfill the law of the gods; rather, she becomes conflictually intimate (*innig*) with the Holy in such a way that she fulfills the law of becoming homely out of her being unhomely. This destiny (*Geschick*) is fitting (*schicklich*) since it is self-sent (*sich schickt*); it accommodates itself to the enigmatic contradictions and ambiguities of the human being that manifests itself as a "katastrophe."[43] Within the framework of the choral ode this will be expressed in the contradictory language of the oxymoron.

The Language of Contradiction: Oxymoron and Tragic Manifestation

One of the uncanny paradoxes of Greek tragic language is its ability to reveal the hidden in such a way that this hiddenness becomes manifest even as it shelters its concealment in the very act of showing itself *as* concealed. Here, hiddenness does not suddenly appear as revelation in the sense of an unmasking or laying bare; on the contrary, what is revealed is less a "secret" than the very manifestation of secretiveness as that which remains impenetrable or aporous. In the first choral song of the play, Sophocles manifests the hidden unity of tragic being through the linguistic form of the oxymoron. The language of the ode expresses this hidden unity in what Heidegger calls "the fundamental word" of *Antigone*—namely, δεινόν—but also in two other word pairs from the middle of the second strophe—παντοπόρος/ἄπορος [venturing forth in all directions/experienceless without any way out]—and from the middle of the second antistrophe: ὑψίπολις/ἄπολις [towering high above the site/forfeiting the site].

In all of these various designations, Heidegger attempts to relate each one of them back to his central question about the proper dwelling or home of the human being upon the earth. What he sees above all here is the very counterturning character of the δεινόν set within the counterturning language of the poet. As παντοπόρος, the human being ventures everywhere, pressing beyond all limits, traversing boundaries, reaching in far-flung directions to arrive in places where none has ever gone. Yet, at the same time, in all such undertakings and in every place it ventures, the human being everywhere comes to nothing—that is, remains ἄπορος ("without any way out"). As it seeks to impose its Cartesian mastery over all beings and to contest every assault against its dominion, the human being confronts the fundamental aporia at the heart of its own being—namely, that in its attempts to be at home everywhere upon the earth, the human being has become profoundly unable to abide within any home at all. It is in terms of this paradoxical doubling that our essence as human beings unfolds. Antigone comprehends just such a countermovement as the essence of her own being and, in so doing, reverses the very terms that Creon imposes upon her as the outcast one, the one expelled from the *polis*, forced to leave the home and forfeit her abode among the living. In an uncanny way, Antigone's turn against Creon reverses her status as that one dispossessed of the city (ἄπολις). Through her intimacy with the uncanniness of being, she achieves the highest place in the city (ὑψίπολις), thereby displacing the standing of Creon as the one who stands for the highest sense of the city.

Like her father (brother) Oedipus, whose fate is marked by a double reversal from being ἄπολις (exposed on Mt. Cithaeron) to becoming ὑψίπολις (solving the riddle of the Sphinx and becoming king) and then losing his kingship (ὑψίπολις) and being expelled (ἄπολις) as the μίασμος, Antigone enacts the double movement of "counterturning within the essence of human being."[44] We see these kind of reversals becoming manifest throughout the play. For example, those who belong below the earth, such as the slain Polyneices, are forcefully placed above it; and those who belong above the earth, like the living, breathing Antigone, are violently placed below it. In "forfeiting the site" (ἄπολις) of her home above the earth, Antigone risks becoming unhomely. And yet precisely on account of this uncanny risk, Heidegger claims, she embraces "what is fitting" (*das Schickliche*) as "that which is destined to her" (*zugeschickt*) from a realm beyond the gods, a realm that Sophocles leaves "without a name" and about which, as Antigone confirms, "no one knows."⁴⁵ Heidegger, however, dares to designate this realm beyond the gods, beyond the cult of funerary ritual and consanguineous blood lines. He names this "being itself," which he identifies as "the ground of being homely, the hearth." In this bold reading, Heidegger breaks with Hölderlin, Hegel, Karl Reinhardt, Heinrich Weinstock, and other prominent German interpreters by rejecting any claim that *Antigone* presents the struggle between "religion" and the "state," "family" and the "city," chthonic justice and enlightened law, etc.⁴⁶ Rather, in his interpretation, Heidegger stresses that "the counterplay is played out between being unhomely in the sense of being driven about amid beings without any way out and being unhomely as becoming homely from out of a belonging to being." Against Nietzsche's own interpretation of the Greek tragic chorus out of Archilochus and the dithyrambic music cults and in opposition to any philological account of the chorus in terms of its "developmental history," Heidegger understands the chorus as "the essential middle of the tragedy in terms of the history of its essence."⁴⁷ What the chorus sings, Heidegger emphasizes, is being itself and not any individual being or entity. Here "what essentially prevails as being [*was west als das Sein*] . . . can be said only in poetizing or thought in thinking." Insofar as the last lines of the Antigone ode speak of the hearth as Ἑστία and address the human being's exclusion/expulsion from the hearth, Heidegger takes this as an indication that the hearth is "the site of everything homely." Even more, it is *as* the homely that the hearth comes to manifest "the being of all beings."⁴⁸ In plain terms, "the hearth, the homestead of the homely, is being itself."

Yet the chorus sings of banishing the one who is uncanny (το δεινόν) from the precinct of the hearth, rendering it in Greek as παρέστιος, that is, παρα (outside, away from, far—but also, paradoxically, alongside, near, next to) + Ἑστία (house, hearth, home). Here Heidegger offers an unconventional reading of this stanza within the overall context of the drama. Most commentators have understood these final words of the chorus to mean that that figure who has dared to venture upon every path (πανοπόρος) and has sought to attain the height of the city (ὑψίπολις) is not welcome at the hearth of the *polis* and is condemned to a pathless (ἄπορος), citiless (ἄπολις) fate.⁴⁹ Yet Heidegger does not think of Antigone as the one thrown out of the hearth. On his reading, Antigone readily takes upon herself the loss of the hearth in order to gain a more originary path of entry into the hearth itself. In Heidegger's words, by Antigone "taking such being unhomely into her own (*eigenes*) essence, she *becomes* 'properly' unhomely (*eigentlich unheimisch*)."⁵⁰ Here in their rejection of the unhomely one, the words of the chorus bespeak "an uncanny ambiguity that concerns being unhomely itself." At the same time, however, these words also attest to "a knowledge of the hearth." As the one figure in the play who, according to Heidegger, has risked this belonging to the hearth by becoming unhomely, Antigone not only embodies the *ethos* of Sophoclean tragedy but, more importantly for Heidegger, she embodies the *ethos* of Hölderlinian poetizing as the possible pathway for a futural German homecoming.

In this reading of Antigone as "the purest poem itself," as "the telling of the singular *deinon* and its essential ground," we find the core of the Ister lectures as they both intersect with and diverge from the poetizing of Sophocles and Hölderlin. On Heidegger's telling, what is essential here lies in Antigone's putting herself at risk knowingly, in confronting that which remains undecided and indeterminate with a decision about "becoming homely in being unhomely." The chorus enigmatically announces its reluctance to admit anyone to its hearth who forfeits her belonging to the city "for the sake of risk." And yet Antigone responds in a wholly uncanny way. She decides knowingly *for* her belonging to the hearth, but not in a simple, unproblematic sense. Rather, she determines that the conventional definition of the hearth as a congenial space of comfort and domesticity is inauthentic and thus undermines the genuine meaning of the hearth as what is of the home. As she sees it, only by *risking* the home *as* home—by becoming unhomely in relation to the hearth—can one genuinely come into the essence of the hearth as the homely. Hence, in Heidegger's recitation, the last words of the choral ode need to be read as showing us "the risk of distinguishing and deciding between that being unhomely proper [*eigentlich*] to human beings and a being unhomely that is improper and inappropriate [*uneigentlich*]."[51] Simply expressed, Antigone's decision here between an *authentic* and an *inauthentic* sense of dwelling, proper to the home and hearth, will distinguish Heidegger's reading from Hölderlin.

As Hölderlin reads the drama, Antigone's decision to challenge Creon's edict is less a decision for belonging to the homeland than it is a kind of Jacobite rebellion against Creon's monarchic arrogance. Hölderlin characterizes Antigone as ἀντίθεος—that is, acting against the god with a spiritual violence and yet in a godlike manner—in that she seeks union with the earth, even as she seeks such union through death.[52] Heidegger disregards such a reading and focuses on the question of dwelling authentically. What preoccupies him throughout these lectures is the German task of appropriating what is properly theirs, namely, what the Böhlendorff letter terms "the national." But again, as Hölderlin made all too clear to his friend, "the *free* use of *one's own* is most difficult." Because what is one's own lies all too near, properly dwelling in such nearness (*Nähe*) is the most difficult precisely because its proximity unthinkingly inures us to what is genuinely our own within it. For this reason we first need to journey into the foreign in order to come into what is our own, since this very movement away from the proper brings with it a "remembrance" or *Andenken* of the proper. According to Heidegger, the dramatic action within the play *Antigone* by the character Antigone brings about just such a movement since it confronts us with the decision of dwelling authentically within the uncanny, and indeed doubly so, since the uncanny here appears as what is foreign to the Germans—namely, as the *Greek* form of being unhomely precisely as a way of (authentically) becoming homely.

What Heidegger takes up, then, in his attempt to educate the Germans in the proper way of appropriating the national, is Hölderlin's claim that "the Greeks are indispensable for us." This means that they cannot serve as a model to be imitated since what is great in them involves a reversal of their own national endowments. Authentic German homecoming must involve an encounter with the Greeks, but understood in its properly German sense as an "Aus-ein-andersetzung": a confrontational setting-asunder of the one (the proper) from the other (the foreign or the improper) with the aim of returning back to the proper or national by way of, and in contradistinction to, the improper or foreign.[53] For Hölderlin, this sense of finding one's own home amid the experience of expulsion from the home occurs most powerfully in hymnal song. It is there in the poetic articulation of the pain of severance and being set asunder that "song becomes a sanctuary or asylum for the homeless ones, those who have lost their place—the authentic refuge from the vacuity and bleakness of a destitute world."[54] The hymn, as Hölderlin conceives it, seeks to find a home for human beings, to secure shelter from the desolation of the world's night that has descended upon humankind since the departure and flight of the gods. Conceived in this larger sense, all of Hölderlin's hymns point to a pathway out of such nihilistic desolation by pointing ahead to the futural coming of the gods, a coming that at the same time foretokens a genuine "homecoming" for humankind. As Heidegger puts it, "this homecoming is the future of the historical essence of the Germans."[55] In the river hymn "The Ister" this movement of the self from out of the homeland into the foreign occurs by way of a reversal of the river's own course so that "it appears almost to go backwards."[56] In this reversal Heidegger finds a pathway out of the nihilism of the world's night, one that identifies the poetizing of the poet with the very movement of the Ister itself. That is, Heidegger understands Hölderlin's poetizing of the river in this hymn as bound up with the selfsame movement of the Ister as a river in its journeying. Both "say" the Holy; each in its own way "brings the dwelling of historical human beings into its essence."[57]

Conclusion

If in Sophoclean tragedy it is the chorus who offers the most uncanny and ambiguous utterances about human dwelling as the site of an at times insuperable homelessness, then within the German language it is Hölderlin's river hymns that express this irreconcilable conflict. All of Heidegger's efforts here are aimed at opening this relation to our notice, of attempting to make us ever more mindful of our need to address the uncanny essence of our own canny attempts to evade that which cannot be evaded: the abyss at the heart of being, the *Abgrund* that, as the ungrounded ground of all that is, pervades every human venture to ground its own home. As Heidegger brings his lectures to a close, he confronts his listeners with the underlying meaning of these lectures themselves, which he finds above all in the language of the poet's words. He writes:

> This poetry demands of us a transformation in our ways of thinking and experiencing, one that concerns being in its entirety.[58]

As part of this transformation, he enjoins us to "let go of . . . our presumptive measure of truth, so as to enter that free realm in which the poetic is." He then raises a question which Hölderlin famously posed in one of his late poems, "In lovely blueness":

> Is there a measure on earth?

and he reminds us that Hölderlin answered this question by avowing "There is none." As we confront this lack of earthly measure as the "token of hopelessness and despair," Heidegger asks us to think a different measure, perhaps even a poetic measure, that might shelter the truth of the poetic word. In turning to such a word, Heidegger's thinking holds forth the hope that in intimative nearness to this word "we might suddenly be struck by it[s]" unrelenting power. To live in nearness to this word would then open the possibility of what it might mean were we to live commensurately with the promise of poetic dwelling.

Notes

1. Heidegger, GA 66: 426.
2. Hölderlin, "Brot und Wein," v. 147.
3. Hölderlin, "Germania," v. 6.
4. Hölderlin, "Brot und Wein," v. 122.
5. Heidegger, GA: 8: 229; GA 14: 75; GA 16: 748.
6. Hölderlin, DKV III: 459–62.
7. Hölderlin, EL: 150.
8. Dennis J. Schmidt, *On Germans and Other Greeks: Tragedy and Ethical Life* (Bloomington: Indiana University Press, 2001), 135–42, 165–67, as well as "The Ordeal of the Foreign and the Enigma of One's Own," *Philosophy Today* 40, no. 1 (1996): 188–96. Cf. also Friedrich Hölderlin, E&L: 207–209; DKV III: 459–62.
9. Heidegger, GA 4: 115.
10. Heidegger, HHI: 137/170–71.
11. Heidegger, GA 39: 87.
12. Heidegger, GA 34: 88.
13. As I will argue here, the Ister lectures offer an *ethical* interpretation that gets at the heart of Heidegger's understanding of the Other. Yet, at the same time, we also find an understanding of the native and foreign that threatens to undermine the very relation between *das Eigene* and *das Fremde* that stands at the center of the Ister lectures. The difficulty for us, reading them through the history of the last century and its relentless violence, lies in attempting to draw upon Heidegger's own powerful insights into the tragic nature of human dwelling on the one hand *and* in then reading them through the tragic blindness of Heidegger's own provincial assertion of German exceptionalism and its attendant metaphysics of racial exclusion and exclision. While I will not pursue the eminently *political* implications of this reading here, I do attempt it in depth in my forthcoming book, *Of an Alien Homecoming: Heidegger's Encounter with Hölderlin*.

Heidegger's insistence on the singularity of an inner, "essential" Greek-German bond that remains inaccessible to other nations and languages blinds him to the complexity of Hölderlin's own polychromatic understanding of the Greek "event." If for Hölderlin the very name and topos of "Greece" represents a contested space of appropriative engagement (and arrogation) of Near Eastern, Jewish, Christian, Asiatic, and "Oriental" influences, for Heidegger this will appear otherwise. "Greece" and its Ionian legacy will be cleaved off from Asia Minor and will stand as the self-generated, autochthonous flowering of pure Hellenic genius, the inception of a Western history in which "Jerusalem" will stand as the Other to "Athens." It is this kind of monocular focus on the Hellas-Hesperia axis that will lead Heidegger to claim: "There is only *Greek* tragedy and no other beside it" (P: 90/GA 54: 134). Likewise, Hölderlin's allusions to the "Indus" river in "The Ister," to "brown women" and the sailors' voyage to "the Indies" in "Remembrance," as well as to the wisdom tradition of Judaism in essays and poems will be suppressed in favor of the pure and singular Graeco-Germanic Hölderlin of Heidegger's own *Inszenierung*. As this self-identical topos of Graeco-German difference, Heidegger's masterful presentation in the Ister lectures needs to be grasped both as a narrative about Germany's path toward poetic dwelling *and* as an assault upon those who threaten such dwelling in the form of Americans, Russians, Jews, Asians, and other non-Germans.

In this gesture of exclusion, suppression, denial, and disinheritance, Heidegger both instantiates and thematizes/achieves his own uncanny form of the monstrous. And even though the Ister lectures themselves do not boldly and forthrightly proclaim a vision of racial exclusion and removal, their way of configuring the question of the native and foreign reveals a dangerously nativistic privileging of what is one's own that philosophically supports the ontological racism evident in the *Black Notebooks*.

14. Heidegger, HHI: VI/GA 53: V.
15. Heidegger, HGR: 264/GA 39: 291.
16. Heidegger, HGR: 259/GA 39: 285.
17. Heidegger, HGR: 130/GA 39: 148.
18. Heidegger, HGR: 106/GA 39: 117.
19. Ibid.
20. Heidegger, EHP: 54/ GA 4: 36.
21. Heidegger, HGR: 119/GA 39: 135.
22. Heidegger, HGR: 106/GA 39: 117.
23. Heidegger, HGR: 227/GA 39: 250–51.
24. Heidegger, HHI: 142/GA 53: 178.
25. Heidegger, HGR: 204/GA 39: 223.
26. Heidegger, PM: 271/GA 9: 356.
27. Heidegger, GA 12: 70, 166, 169f.
28. Heidegger, PLT; 160/ GA 7: 163.
29. Heidegger, HHI: 43/GA 39: 257.
30. Heidegger, HGR: 34/GA 39: 36.
31. Heidegger, P: 79/GA 54: 117.
32. Heidegger, HHI: 67/GA 53: 82.
33. Heidegger, HHI: 77/GA 53: 94.
34. Heidegger, HHI: 76/GA 53: 94.
35. Heidegger, HHI: 77/GA 53: 94.
36. Heidegger, HHI: 90/GA 53: 111.
37. Heidegger, HHI: 115,102/GA 53: 144, 126.
38. Heidegger, HHI: 99/GA 53:123. Here in *Antigone*, vv. 95–96, Heidegger's translation is quite different from Hölderlin's DKV II: 864 as "das Gewaltige" (the violent); Reinhardt's *Antigone* translates it as "das Schreckliche" (the terrible) and Zimmerman's *Antigone* "das Ungeheuere" (the monstrous)—all of which miss the ontological play of *deinos*.
39. Heidegger, HHI: 103/GA 53: 127–28.

40. Heidegger, HHI: 109–10/GA 53: 136–37.
41. Heidegger, HHI: 104/ GA 53: 129.
42. Heidegger, HHI: 121/151.
43. Heidegger, HHI: 103,109/ GA 53: 128, 136.
44. Heidegger, HHI: 85/ GA 53: 105.
45. Sophocles, *Antigone*, 1.457. Heidegger, HHI: 117–18/ GA 53: 147.
46. For Heidegger what matters is that Antigone knowingly embraces the uncanny, whereas Oedipus comes into it through his own blindness. Oedipus's later self-blinding then appears as a kind of retrospective imposing of a penalty upon himself, as if unable to confront the reality of what he had done. For other readings of *Antigone* in terms of "religion" versus "state"—family versus polis; psychological, gender, cf. Otto Pöggeler, *Schicksal und Geschichte* or Bonnie Honig, *Antigone Interrupted*, which focuses upon Judith Butler and Jacques Lacan. Cf. also Heinrich Weinstock, *Sophokles* (Leipzig: Teubner, 1931), as well as Dennis Schmidt, "The Monstrous, Catastrophe, and Ethical Life: Hegel, Heidegger and Antigone," *Philosophy Today* 59, no. 1 (2015): 61–72.
47. Heidegger, HHI: 119–20/ GA 53: 148–50. See Friedrich Nietzsche, *Birth of Tragedy* (Cambridge: Cambridge University Press, 1999), secs. 4–7.
48. Heidegger, HHI: 107, 110, 114/ GA 53: 133, 137, 143.
49. Whether they focus either on Creon *or* Antigone does not matter; Heidegger focuses almost exclusively on Antigone because she is the figure of risk and daring for being's sake.
50. Heidegger, HHI: 117/ GA 53: 146.
51. Ibid.
52. Friedrich Hölderlin, *Essays and Letters*, 329/DKV II: 917.
53. Heidegger reinforces this logic of privileging the *return* to one's own by way of the foreign in GA 52: 123, 190, where he writes: "The stay [*Aufenthalt*] in the foreign and the learning of the foreign, not for the sake of the foreign, but for the sake of one's own, demands that enduring waiting that no longer thinks of one's own."
54. Hans-Georg Gadamer, "Hölderlin und George," in *Gesammelte Werke* IX (Tübingen: Mohr-Siebeck, 1993), 234.
55. Heidegger, EHP: 48/ GA 4: 30.
56. Heidegger, GA53: 178/HHI: 142–143/178.
57. Heidegger, GA53: 173/HHI: 139/173.
58. Heidegger, GA53: 205/HHI: 166–67.

References

Christen, Felix. *Das Jetzt der Lektüre: Hölderlins 'Ister.'* Frankfurt: Stroemfeld, 2013.
Gadamer, Hans-Georg. *Gesammelte Werke*. Tübingen: Mohr Siebeck, 1993.

Heidegger, Martin. *Elucidations of Hölderlin's Poetry*. Translated by Keith Hoeller. Buffalo: Humanity Books, 2000.

———. "Europa und die deutsche Philosophie." In *Europa und die Philosophie*, edited by Hans-Helmuth Gander. Frankfurt: Klostermann, 1993.

———. GA 4; *Erläuterungen zur Hölderlins Dichtung*. Frankfurt: Klostermann, 2012.

———. GA 7; *Vorträge und Aufsätze*. Frankfurt: Klostermann, 2000.

———. GA 8; *Was heisst Denken?* Frankfurt: Klostermann, 2002.

———. GA 9; *Wegmarken*. Frankfurt: Klostermann, 1976.

———. GA 12; *Unterwegs zur Sprache*. Frankfurt: Klostermann, 1985.

———. GA 14; *Zur Sache des Denkens*. Frankfurt: Klostermann, 2007.

———. GA 16; *Reden*. Frankfurt: Klostermann, 2000.

———. GA 34; *Vom Wesen der Wahrheit* Frankfurt: Klostermann, 1988.

———. GA 39; *Hölderlins Hymne Germania und 'Der Rhein.'* Frankfurt: Klostermann, 1980.

———. GA 53; *Hölderlins Hymne 'Der Ister.'* Frankfurt: Klostermann, 1984.

———. GA 54; *Parmenides*. Frankfurt: Klostermann, 1992.

———. GA 65; *Beiträge zur Philosophie (Vom Ereignis)*. Frankfurt: Klostermann, 1989.

———. GA 66; *Besinnung*. Frankfurt: Klostermann, 1997.

———. GA 77; *Feldweg-Gespräche*. Frankfurt: Klostermann, 1995.

———. GA 94 *Überlegungen*. Frankfurt: Klostermann, 2013.

———. *Hölderlin's Hymns 'Germania' and 'The Rhine.'* Translated by William McNeill and Julia Davis. Bloomington: Indiana University Press, 2001.

———. *Hölderlin's Hymn "The Ister."* Translated by William McNeill and Julia Ireland. Bloomington: Indiana University Press, 2014.

———. *Parmenides*. Translated by Andre Schuwer and Richard Rojcewicz. Bloomington: Indiana University Press, 1998.

———. *Pathmarks*. Translated by William McNeill. Cambridge: Cambridge University Press, 1998.

———. *Poetry, Language, Thought*. Translated by Albert Hofstadter. New York: Harper and Row, 1971.

Hölderlin, Friedrich. *Sämtliche Werke und Gedichte*. 3 vols. Edited by Jochen Schmidt. Frankfurt: Deutscher Klassiker Verlag, 1992.

———. *Essays and Letters*. Translated by Jeremy Adler and Charlie Louth. London: Penguin, 2009.

Honig, Bonnie. *Antigone Interrupted*. Cambridge: Cambridge University Press, 2013.

Nietzsche, Friedrich. *Die Geburt der Tragödie*. Leipzig: Kröner, 1930.

Pöggeler, Otto. *Schicksal und Geschichte: Antigone im Spiegel der Deutungen und Gestaltungen seit Hegel und Hölderlin*. Munich: Fink, 2004.

Reinhardt, Karl. *Sophokles*. Frankfurt: Klostermann, 1933.

Roeske, Kurt. *Antigones tödlicher Ungehorsam: Text, Deutung, Rezeption der 'Antigone' des Sophokles*. Würzburg: Königshausen & Neumann, 2009.

Schmidt, Dennis. *On Germans and Other Greeks*. Bloomington: Indiana University Press, 2001.

Sophocles. *Antigone: Griechisch-Deutsch*. Edited by Bernhard Zimmermann. Düsseldorf: Artemis u. Winkler, 1999.

———. *Antigone*. Translated by Karl Reinhardt. Göttingen: Vandenhoeck u. Ruprecht, 1961.

Weinstock, Heinrich. *Sophokles*. Leipzig: Teubner, 1931.

7

Remains

Heidegger and Hölderlin amid the Ruins of Time

WILLIAM MCNEILL

Introduction

The centrality of Hölderlin's poetry for Heidegger's thinking from the mid-1930s onward is widely acknowledged, yet the reasons for Heidegger's turn toward Hölderlin are still not well understood. Undoubtedly, the Hölderlinian themes of national identity and "a people," of the homeland, the flight of the gods, *Innigkeit*, the holy, ancient Greece, and of the relation between the Germans and the Greeks, between one's own and the foreign, were all critical issues and constitute recurrent themes in Heidegger's dialogue with Hölderlin throughout his lecture courses and published essays. They have also tended to draw the most attention, understandably enough, given the problematic political dimensions surrounding Heidegger's appropriation of these issues. In the present essay, however, I deliberately set aside such themes, essential though they are, in order to focus on questions of time and language in Heidegger's embrace of Hölderlin. In particular, I am interested in how Heidegger's encounter with Hölderlin both continues and inflects his understanding of Being as originary time or "temporality," as analyzed in his earlier, phenomenological work, and in the role that language and poetizing play in that inflection. In this exploratory and tentative account,

I first provide a thematic reading of these issues centered on the 1936 essay "Hölderlin and the Essence of Poetizing," and then consider how that thematic is further unfolded in Heidegger's 1941–42 reading of Hölderlin's hymn "Remembrance." I conclude with a few brief remarks concerning what has changed in Heidegger's understanding of time when compared to the earlier phenomenological project.

For Hölderlin, the essence of time is that it "tears": it is *die reißende Zeit*. Yet this has a twofold implication. On the one hand, such tearing is something that we humans undergo, something to which we are subject. Torn into past and future, we are continually torn away from the present—or the present is torn from us—such that we are unable to remain in the same moment of presence. More than that, because we are torn into past and future, we are never wholly or entirely within the moment. The tearing of time as something we undergo is poetized, for instance, in Hölderlin's elegy "The Archipelago," which ends with the lines:

> . . . und wenn die reißende Zeit mir
> Zu gewaltig das Haupt ergreifft und die Noth und das Irrsaal
> Unter Sterblichen mir mein sterblich Leben erschüttert,
> Laß der Stille mich dann in deiner Tiefe gedenken.

> . . . and if the time that tears
> Should seize too violently my head, if need and errancy
> Among mortals disrupt for me my mortal life,
> Leave me then to remember the stillness in your depths.[1]

According to these lines, "the time that tears" threatens to seize the human being, to transport the poet into a realm beyond that of mortals, into what, in his "Remarks on Oedipus," Hölderlin calls "the excentric sphere of the dead."[2] Time itself, according to the "Remarks . . . ," is divine: the god is "nothing other than time";[3] what time accomplishes in its divine intervention is a displacement or transport into an excentric sphere: the dimension of the excentric that exceeds the human. Henceforth, the human being can never be in the center and can never be the center, never coincide with the present moment: he or she is always outside, always somewhere beyond, always displaced, transported in a kind of rapture, *entrükt*, as

Hölderlin puts it.⁴ The tearing of time as an intervention is an interruption, a rupture with properly tragic dimensions, for it opens up both a relation to the gods and a relation to the dead. Yet we know of the dead only by way of remembrance and commemoration, only by remembering those who once were and once have been. It is by this relation to the dead that mortals first properly become mortals, those who know of death and of its necessity. Only the disruption or shattering of the trajectory of mortal life and its destiny lets such a life become truly mortal, understand itself as mortal, undergo its own mortality. This rupture that is wrought by the tearing of time is, according to Hölderlin, what is marked and commemorated poetically in Greek tragedy. Structurally, in terms of the rhythm of representations through which the plot unfolds, the interruption is what Hölderlin calls a "caesura," and in both Sophocles's *Oedipus Tyrannos* and *Antigone*, the caesura, Hölderlin claims, is marked by the speeches of the seer Tiresias. Tiresias, he remarks,

> intervenes in the course of destiny, as one who watches over the power of nature, which, for the human being in his sphere of life, tragically transports [*entrükt*] him from the midpoint of his inner life into another world and tears him into the excentric sphere of the dead.⁵

The "power of nature" is the power of time itself, "the spirit of time and nature, the heavenly," as Hölderlin calls it, which "seizes the human being"; as "the spirit of time that tears" it is, he states, something to which we are helplessly exposed, it offers no protection: "it is unsparing, as the spirit of the eternally living, unwritten wilderness and of the world of the dead."⁶ The time that tears is both: the spirit of eternally living, unwritten nature, and the spirit of the world of the dead, for it is the rupture instituted by nature herself that first opens our access to the world of the dead—which is to say, of memory.

Yet "the time that tears" is not only something that humans undergo, a relentless and unsparing force to which we are exposed. Torn by time, we are torn apart. Yet it is not only we who are torn. That our very Being, the fabric of our existence, is torn into past and future entails that time itself is torn apart—that it is what Heidegger, in the treatise *Being and Time* (1927), called "ekstatic," "the ἐκστατικόν pure and simple."⁷ Already in *Being and Time* Heidegger had used Hölderlin's word for tragic transport, displacement, or rapture, in characterizing the ekstases of time (the relational displacements of having-been, future, and presencing) as *Entrückungen*: raptures.⁸ In his first lecture course on Hölderlin, on the hymns "Germania" and "The Rhine," delivered in 1934–35, Heidegger explicitly relates the raptures of ekstatic temporality to the Hölderlinian "time that tears." As such, ekstatic transport is an oscillation (*Schwingung*) between having-been and future:⁹

> This originary time transports [*entrückt*] our Dasein into future and having-been. . . . I have provided an account of the essential constitution of this originary temporality and its essential possibilities in *Being and Time*.
>
> The poet on a number of occasions names this time the "time that tears," because it is within itself the oscillation that tears us away [*der in sich schwingende Fortriß*] into the future and casts us back into having-been.¹⁰

And in his Rome lecture of the following year, "Hölderlin and the Essence of Poetizing," Heidegger uses another word from the 1927 treatise to describe ekstatic displacement: "stretching," *Erstreckung*, which he had previously used to designate the "movedness" and "happening" within the oscillation of temporality, a movedness and happening that constitute historicality.¹¹ Here, in "Hölderlin and the Essence of Poetizing," he emphasizes time's being torn open into its three dimensions of past, present, and future; and this occurs in the context of his interpretation of the temporal implications of Hölderlin's claim that human beings are "a dialogue" (*ein Gespräch*), a claim found in the following lines from the unfinished poem "Conciliator, you who never believed . . .":

> Viel hat erfahren der Mensch.
> Der Himmlischen viele genannt,
> Seit ein Gespräch wir sind
> Und hören können voneinander.
>
> Much has the human experienced.
> Named many of the heavenly,
> Since we are a dialogue
> And can hear from one another.

Heidegger reads the "since" here not in a causative sense, but in accordance with the temporal sense of "ever since" that the German *Seit* indeed conveys, and in his remarks further emphasizes that "a dialogue" also means "one dialogue." Given this temporal sense of "since," the German use of the verb *sein*, "to be," really implies "to be and have been," something I shall mark in brackets in the translation below. Heidegger comments:

> Since when are we [have we been] a dialogue? Where there is to be *one* dialogue, the essential word must remain related to One and the Same. Without this relation, even and precisely a dispute is impossible. One and the Same, however, can only be manifest in the light of something that remains and is steadfast. Steadfastness and remaining, however, come to appear whenever persistence and presence light up. Yet this happens at that moment when time opens itself in its stretchings [*Erstreckungen*]. Ever since the human being has placed himself into the presence of something that remains, only since then has he been able to expose himself to what is changeable, to that which comes and goes; for only that which persists is changeable. Only since the "time that tears" has been torn open into presence, past, and future does there exist the possibility of agreeing upon something that remains. We are [and have been] *one* dialogue ever since the time that there "is [and has been] time."[12]

Yet what constitutes the steadfastness of something steadfast, the remaining of something that remains? The "lighting up" of "persistence" and "presence," an illumination, emerging from darkness and concealment, occurs in the moment (*Augenblick*) that time is opened up, torn open as such, thus to become manifest and to *be* as time. The opening up of this moment, in which Being is first opened up as such, that is, in which presence first emerges, differentiating itself from what was and what will be, past and future, occurs as the "event" (*Ereignis*) of language, whose essence is dialogue. Dialogue, Heidegger emphasizes, is in this sense (Hölderlin's sense) not one possibility among others of the use of language (distinguished, say, from naming, designating, questioning, and so on), but constitutes "the essential event of language."[13]

In being opened up, in being torn into presence in the tearing open *of* time, our Being is simultaneously torn *into* time, itself torn apart in being exposed to the tearing of time, to the ravages of having been and being yet to come. If our Being is to withstand this—if Being itself as such, the Being of anything, is to withstand this—it must gather itself from out of and amid this dispersion, it must come to a stand and attain a certain steadfastness, not by eradicating such dispersion (since it itself, as presence, first is by virtue of this dispersion, the tearing of time), but in such a way as to also let this dispersion itself be. Being must be gathered, instituted and founded, as "One and the Same," as that which remains, first enabling the one dialogue that we are and that transpires in our openness to presence, in our ability to "hear from one another." Yet how is this to happen? Who could accomplish such a thing? "Who," asks Heidegger dramatically, "will grasp, amid the time that tears, something that remains and bring it to stand in the word?"[14]

The answer is already given in the closing words of Hölderlin's hymn "Remembrance" (*Andenken*):

> Was bleibet aber, stiften die Dichter.
>
> Yet what remains, the poets found.

That which remains is not found in the sense of finding something already present, coming upon it as something—a being—that is already there. It is found in the sense of being founded, instituted, a founding that Heidegger will proceed to understand as a "free creating" or "free bestowal." This free creating does not proceed from already existent beings (for it first gives rise to Being as such, first lets things "be"), nor, therefore, from the existence of a "Subject" or individual. It occurs in and through "the word," this conceived as the "essence" of language, an essence that is intrinsically "poetic," that is, that happens as the very event of *Dichtung*, "poetizing." Amid the time that tears, such founding first gathers into presence that which remains—Being—and lets it be. Heidegger states:

> Poetizing is founding through the word and in the word. What is founded in this way? That which remains. Yet can that which remains be founded? Is it not that which always already lies present at hand? No! Precisely that which remains must be brought to a stand against the tearing away; what is simple must be wrested from confusion, the measure must be set before what is measureless. That which carries and permeates beings as a whole must come into the open. Being must be opened up, so that beings may appear.[15]

"The word" here does not refer to what we ordinarily understand as the written and spoken words of a language, which, as beings, are a mere surface phenomenon, even though they remain essentially dependent upon the more originary event of language, that is, upon the poetic founding of that which remains as "One and the Same": Being itself, as the "ground" or "essence" of the dialogue that first enables human Being. This, the Being of humans, remarks Heidegger,

> is grounded in language; yet language first authentically happens in the dialogue. The latter, however, is not just one way in which language occurs; rather, only as dialogue is language essential. What we otherwise refer to as "language," namely, a stock of words and rules of grammar, is only a foreground of language.[16]

Nevertheless, this foreground points back to and is indicative of the more originary, poetic event that comprises the ground and essence of language as the dialogue. This ground is not other than the foreground in the sense of lying independently somewhere over and beyond beings, for it "carries and permeates beings as a whole";[17] nor is it an abyss in the sense of an absence of ground: "We never find the ground in the abyss."[18] Ground here means grounding, as the founding event of Being that first opens and enables human dwelling. This founding of Being is the more originary language (*Ursprache*), conceived as the happening of the dialogue: "The ground of human existence [*Dasein*] is the dialogue as the authentic happening of language. Originary language, however, is poetizing as the founding of Being."[19] The ground is this happening, an event, the event of poetizing that first enables language in the commonly understood sense:

> Poetizing, therefore, never takes up language as a working material that lies present at hand, rather, poetizing itself first makes possible language. Poetizing is the originary language of a historical people. Therefore, the essence of language must, conversely, be understood from out of the essence of poetizing.[20]

What, then, is "the essence of poetizing" that lends Heidegger's essay its title, and how are "essence" and "poetizing" to be understood here? "Essence" (*Wesen*), for Heidegger, is another word for Being (*Sein*), understood as the foundational (and in this sense essential) coming to presence of something and its prevailing, or remaining, in and through this very event of coming to presence. It is thus never to be understood as essence in the sense of *essentia* or "whatness," as something timeless, or as an abstract or universal concept or idea. For such essence, as Heidegger explains in his introductory remarks to the essay, is only the "inessential essence." The task of the essay is not "to read off the general essence of poetizing from the work of an individual poet."[21] "Essence" in Heidegger's sense refers, rather, to the force of a certain remaining, of that which remains amid dispersion, amid change and becoming: a force of presencing that asserts itself amid "the time that tears." As essence thus understood, such remaining, however, is not timeless, not outside of or beyond time. It remains as the temporalizing of time that gives rise to presence, and as historicality—as time's remaining and being time.[22]

How are we to understand the essence of poetizing that Hölderlin's poetizing presents, or better, enacts, according to Heidegger's reading? What is poetizing, as the originary—that is, originating—event of language that first founds Being? In what way "is" poetizing, if and when it is? If poetizing, *Dichtung*, first makes possible language, it follows that poetizing does not mean the writing or composing of poetry or poems in the narrow sense of verse (what Heidegger calls *Poesie*). And for this reason, it is misleading to translate the title of the 1936 essay as "Hölderlin and the Essence of Poetry." Heidegger's essay is not about poetry and its essence, but about poetizing, *Dichtung*.[23] Not just all poetry, but all language, is grounded in poetizing. Yet when does poetizing, as the originary event of language, happen? Heidegger states: "Where the human capacity for language is present and is exercised, there is not yet without further ado the essential event of language—the dialogue."[24] It is "not yet"—and yet, it must already have happened for there to be language in the foreground sense. That it is "not yet" means that this event (*Ereignis*) must itself be retrieved, remembered as that which has happened and which once already was—remembered in the sense of poetically founded in the word of Hölderlin's poetizing. However, Heidegger does not simply say that the essential event of language is "not yet." He says that it is not yet "without further ado" (*ohne weiteres*). In a sense, therefore, it already "is"—"is" in the sense of remaining, of something that remains, unremarked and unnoticed by our conventional use of language, yet remaining as a trace that can be re-marked and thus itself poetized (presented in poetry, as in Hölderlin's poetry—yet also potentially in other ways, such as Heidegger's essay itself) as poetizing's essence. And this, according to Heidegger's reading, is what Hölderlin's poetizing does, its distinctive and exceptional accomplishment in "poetizing the essence of poetizing." Hölderlin's work understands itself not just as poetry or the composing of poems, but as poetry poetizing—as poetry poetizing the "essence" of poetizing itself as the inaugural event of Being and time.

What is important here, however, is that the essential event of language is not earlier than the foreground use of language: it is not a historically or transcendentally prior ground anterior to the naming power of language. The time that is marked by the "since" is not an earlier time, a time before time, as it were. This is why, when explicating Hölderlin's lines, Heidegger states:

> Since we are and have been a dialogue—the human being has experienced much and named many of the gods. Ever since language has happened authentically as dialogue, the gods have come to word and a world has been appearing. Yet again the point is to see that the presence of the gods and the appearing of the world are not first a consequence of the happening of language, rather they are simultaneous with it. And this is so much the case that it is in the naming of the gods and in the becoming-word of the world that the authentic dialogue consists that we ourselves are.[25]

The presence of the gods is not a consequence of their being named, for their naming is not prior to their coming to presence. Likewise, the appearing of a world is not the result of some earlier happening of language, but happens at the same time as the event of language: it is "simultaneous" (*gleichzeitig*) with it. What is poetized and founded in Hölderlin's poetizing is, in a sense, Being as "what remains"; yet what remains and is remembered in Hölderlinian remembrance is neither something past, not something that can be drawn from the past, from that which can pass or is subject to passing. For the past can *be* the past only through the instituting or founding of Being as that which remains amid the time that tears. The poet, Heidegger remarks,

> names the gods and names all things in what they are. This naming does not consist in simply providing something that was previously already familiar with a name. Rather, in the poet's speaking the essential word, beings first come to be named as what they are through this naming. Thus they first come to be known as beings. Poetizing is the founding of Being by way of the word. That which remains is therefore never drawn from that which can pass [*dem Vergänglichen*].[26]

We can now better appreciate, perhaps, what transpires in Heidegger's rethinking of temporality in terms of poetic founding when compared to the account given earlier, in *Being and Time*. Heidegger's marginal note in his copy of the second edition of the *Erläuterungen zu Hölderlins Dichtung*, which refers the discussion of "that moment when time opens itself in its stretchings"—thus of the inaugural moment of the opening of time—back to the earlier account, is not just a reference back to some of those pages of *Being and Time* where the "stretching" of time is mentioned. It is not simply referring back to an earlier, phenomenological account that would help us better understand what is at stake in the stretching of time. Indeed, there are other sections of *Being and Time* that better and more incisively describe this phenomenon. The note, I would suggest, contains rather a hidden directive for thinking through what is at stake in the inaugural moment of time's opening, for understanding what was problematic about the earlier account and what has changed in the meantime. The sections that the note refers to all address the way in which the ekstatic temporality of Dasein manifests itself, but indirectly and in a refracted manner, so to speak, within the time of Dasein's everyday and worldly concern. The time of everyday concern, Heidegger explains, understands itself in terms of a "now," which is not free-floating, but always a "now when . . . this or that is happening." This structure, which Heidegger calls datability, is, moreover, implicit in the most trivial everyday speaking and addressing of things in their Being: When I say, "It is cold," I implicitly also mean, "Now it is cold."[27] Furthermore, Heidegger argues, in saying "now" (which for the most part occurs tacitly, without any vocal utterance), Dasein is also speaking itself—its own Being-in-the-world as ekstatic temporality: it is interpreting itself, or literally "laying itself out" (*sich auslegen*), in its addressing of worldly things and events.[28] In section 79 of *Being and Time*, this is elucidated as follows:

> Das gewärtigend-behaltende Gegenwärtigen legt *sich* aus. Und das wiederum ist nur möglich, weil es—an ihm selbst ekstatisch offen—für es selbst je schon erschlossen und in der verstehend-redenden Auslegung artikulierbar ist.

> Making-present in awaiting and retaining interprets *itself*. And this in turn is possible only because—ekstatically open in itself—it is in each case already disclosed for itself and can be articulated in interpretation that discursively understands.[29]

If we compare this with the account of the opening of time given in "Hölderlin and the Essence of Poetizing," we can immediately see what has changed. Our Being, as temporality, is not *already* ekstatically open, that is, it is not already ekstatically disclosed to itself in advance, such that discursive articulation and self-interpretation would be possible only on its basis. Rather, in the 1936 essay, language itself—originary language as poetizing—happens as the inaugural, founding event that first opens time in its ekstatic stretchings. Language and its articulation as discourse are not consequent upon an already disclosed and unitary ekstatic horizon that constitutes world; rather, the poetic "essence" or happening of language is itself the inaugural event that first opens time and a historical world. "Only where there is language, is there world."[30]

That which remains and is founded poetically in and as the event of language is thus Being: the event of presencing as "One and the Same"—that is, as the ground that enables the dialogue that we are. However, poetic naming, in Heidegger's reading of Hölderlin in the essay "Hölderlin and the Essence of Poetizing," is not in the first instance a naming of beings. It is a naming of Being, as that which remains and, in remaining, first lets beings be. Yet it is a naming "of" Being in a twofold sense. First and foremost, in the sense that this naming belongs in advance to Being and is freely bestowed in and by the event of Being, Being as event. But secondly, in the sense that this poetizing—while itself something that "is" and that comes to be in *also* naming beings—names Being as that to which it belongs in advance, as that which remains. It thus poetizes the "essence" and Being of poetizing, as event, and this for Heidegger is the distinctive and exceptional accomplishment of Hölderlin's poetizing, distinguishing him as the one who poetizes the essence of poetizing:

> Hölderlin's poetizing is sustained by the poetic vocation of specifically poetizing the essence of poetizing. Hölderlin is for us in an exceptional sense *the poet of the poet*.[31]

This vocation, as we can now appreciate, is not that of a vain self-absorption on the part of the poet. It is not a poetic subjectivity concerned or preoccupied with itself or turned back upon itself. It is not indicative of "a misguided self-mirroring," of a desire for self-presence that betrays a "lack of worldly content," a withdrawal from worldly engagement. Above all, being "the poet of the poet" does not mean "poetizing about the poet."[32] For there is no Subject and no poet, no presence, prior to the event of poetizing that first founds that which remains, Being as One and the Same, as presence that can be shared by those who partake of the dialogue that we are, and who, by virtue of this opening up, this founding of Being and of presence, "can hear from one another."

Hölderlin's poetizing is thus, in Heidegger's reading, a commemorative remembrance of that which remains, of Being. It lets Being be as the concealed stillness in the depths of all coming and going, all presencing and absencing, the stillness that remains amid the time that tears. Yet what remains, remains and "is" only by virtue of the temporalizing of naming as poetic founding, that is, only by virtue of the temporality implicit in the event of the essence of language. Its remaining does not survive time, does not live beyond "the time that tears," but comes to be only in its midst. What is founded poetically is not something that endures beyond the time of poetizing, therefore. "Being is never a being."[33] It is, rather, an excess that comes to be in and through the poietic work of this distinctive temporality. What remains, remains not as a supra- or extra-temporal endurance, but as remains—in the sense of the ruins of time. These ruins are those of the house in which the human being "poetically dwells," in Hölderlin's words, which Heidegger's essay proceeds to recall. These ruins are left as something that remains to be retrieved, to be remembered, in and through an appropriate remembrance, one poetically attuned to the remains of Being.

That these ruins of time remain as something to be retrieved in thoughtful remembrance entails, however, that not only are they not past; rather, they are fundamentally futural in their temporality. They remain as always yet to be remembered, in a remembrance that must be undertaken ever anew. In the second part of this essay, I shall briefly explore how this futural temporality of Being is thought in Heidegger's 1941–42 reading of Hölderlin's hymn "Remembrance" (*Andenken*), the hymn that closes with the line that supplied the central insight of the 1936 essay.[34] In translation, the hymn reads as follows:

> The Northeasterly blows,
> Most beloved of the winds to me,
> For it promises fiery spirit
> And good voyage to mariners.
> But go now and greet
> The beautiful Garonne,
> And the gardens of Bordeaux

There, by the steep bank
Where the footbridge crosses and into the river
Deep falls the brook, yet over it
Keep watch a noble pair
Of oaks and silver poplars;

Still indeed it thinks of me and like
The wide-ranging peaks inclines
The elm forest, over the mill,
But in the courtyard grows a fig tree.
On holidays go
The brown women thereat
On silken ground,
In March time,
When night and day are equal,
And over slow footbridges,
Heavy with golden dreams,
Lulling breezes draw.

Yet may someone reach me,
Full of dark light,
The fragrant cup,
That I may rest; for sweet
Would be the slumber among shadows.
It is not good
To be soulless of mortal
Thoughts. But good
Is a dialogue and to say
The heart's opinion, to hear much
Of days of love,
And deeds that occur.

Yet where are the friends? Bellarmine
And companion? Many a one
Is shy of going to the source;
For wealth indeed begins
In the ocean. They,
Like painters, bring together
The beautiful of the Earth and do not spurn

> The winged war, and
> To dwell in solitude, year long, beneath
> The defoliate mast, where there gleam not through the night
> The holidays of the town,
> Nor the music of strings nor native dance.
>
> But now to Indians
> The men have gone,
> There on the breezy headland
> On vineyard slopes, where down
> Comes the Dordogne
> And together with the magnificent
> Garonne the river
> Spreads into the ocean. Yet what takes
> And gives memory is the sea,
> And love, too, fixes with intensity our eyes.
> Yet what remains, the poets found.

In a condensed commentary of just a few pages, Heidegger in his 1941–42 course on "Remembrance" claims that the fifth line of the poem, the single line "But go now and greet," conceals the entire mystery of what is called remembrance.[35] Remembrance, *Andenken,* is poetized as a greeting. As a greeting, it is a thoughtful turning toward that which is greeted. Yet this thinking in the direction of what is greeted does not simply lose itself in something past, in the poet's past experience of Bordeaux. Something more than a personal "lived experience" (*Erlebnis*) is at stake, Heidegger insists, something that demands of us an "other thinking";[36] and the mystery of this "other thinking," as remembrance, is perhaps that of thinking itself, the very essence of thinking, which is something entirely other than what Western philosophy conceives as "logic."[37]

Yet Heidegger unfolds the structure of greeting, thus of remembrance, from a meditation on the opening line of the poem, "The Northeasterly blows . . ." For earlier in the lecture course he had indeed insisted that with this opening line, in its naming of the Northeasterly wind, there begins the mystery. The first three words contain "the mystery of the entire poem"; this opening line "resonates in every line that follows."[38] Yet what can be so mysterious about what seems to be so straightforward and self-evident as the blowing of the wind? For one thing, the time and space of this blowing. Heidegger articulates it thus:

It might now appear as though we were looking for mysteries even in those places where "rational human beings" find none. And yet, we must assert the following: "The Northeasterly blows"—taken by itself, this word indeed leaves indeterminate the point in time and the location of that of which it speaks. Nevertheless, it names the time-space from out of which comes the attuning favor of the poetizing that is now needed and is yet to come, in order that this poetizing may fulfill its essence and that poets may be. "The Northeasterly blows"—that is to say: the time-space of the poetizing that is poetized in this poem stands open. We avoid saying that the first line is an "image" for this "thought." We are indicating only that, if the first line says what we have named, then between the beginning of the poem and its conclusion there lies an essential relation that at once embraces this poem in its totality: "The Northeasterly blows"—"Yet what remains, the poets found."[39]

Notably, whereas Heidegger in his earlier, 1936 essay "Hölderlin and the Essence of Poetizing" had understood poetizing as the originary event (*Ereignis*) that first opens and founds a historical time, here he now writes of an opening of "time-space," a notion already found in the *Contributions to Philosophy: Of the Event* from 1936–38.[40] In the present remarks, in the interests of tracing a certain continuity with the earlier essay, I shall focus on the temporal aspect of this founding. The opening line of the hymn is a naming, a poetic naming that institutes or founds "the poetizing that is now needed and is yet to come." The opening line, therefore, is not just the first line, the beginning of the poem, but the line that opens and founds the time-space of the poetizing: indeed, it poetizes and names this very opening, the event that inaugurates the time-space of the poetizing itself. And this, as we have seen, is of course one of Heidegger's central claims about Hölderlin's hymns: that they poetize the essence of poetizing, and do so in inaugurating a new time.[41] Yet this inaugural event, this opening that originates the poem, is not straightforward. It names something that has happened and that is thus, presumably, to be remembered and commemorated through the poetizing itself. Yet this event is not identifiable as a particular moment, a particular point in time or location. The poetizing, Heidegger is careful to insist, "is *now* needed *and yet to come*": the "now" of the poetizing is already the trace of the inaugural event, the event whose essence, however, lies in its being yet to come. Heidegger here reads the opening line in terms of that same temporality which is more explicitly poetized in the opening line of the "Ister" hymn, on which he would lecture the following semester: "Now come, fire!" The "now" names something that has already happened, an inaugural event or *Ereignis*, and yet the time of its being poetized, its "now," is already that of a coming.[42]

"The Northeasterly blows . . ." Yet the blowing of the wind, Heidegger elucidates, the wind's movement, its going, is possible only as a coming: "The wind goes in that it comes. 'The Northeasterly blows' means: it is arrival [*Ankunft*]."[43] The line "But go now . . ." does not dismiss the wind or send it away, does not seek to stop its blowing. It means "go," certainly, but in the first instance means "Blow, wind, and be." The being of the wind is its remaining (*Bleiben*) as the wind that it is, its prevailing in its blowing, in a going that is at the same time its coming, a going that is inseparable from its arrival. The poetic addressing of the wind holds the wind toward this very naming, beckons it, yet in so doing does not stop or arrest it, but lets it be the wind that it is. It is a letting-be of the wind that calls upon the Northeasterly to be, to be the "most beloved." Letting-be, as love, is here a going with the wind on the part of the poet, an accompanying.

Yet the "going" of the wind enunciated in the fifth line is ambiguous. It means, certainly, for the wind to blow and thus to be, to fulfill its essence as the most beloved of the poet. Yet it also marks a departure (*Abschied*), marks it by the word "But" (*aber*): "But go now, and greet. . . ." The departure, however, is not a dismissal (*Verabschiedung*); it neither sends the wind away nor abandons it. Rather, Heidegger insists, the poet remains within the blowing of the wind by going with or accompanying (*Mitgehen*) the going of the wind.[44] His going with the wind is not a traveling or journeying in the wind itself that takes its actual path toward the Southwest, but a remaining with the wind in the manner of its greeting. "Just as the blowing of the wind is a coming and a going that reciprocally exceed one another, so a greeting is a remaining back and yet an accompanying that reciprocally demand one another."[45]

In what way is the phenomenon of greeting to be understood as both accompanying and remaining back? In the act of greeting someone we send a greeting to them. But the sending of a greeting is not the conveyance of any kind of report about ourselves. It does say something about us, but what it says is merely that we seek and wish nothing for ourselves, but rather are entirely turned toward the one who is greeted, so that he or she may present themselves in, as Heidegger puts it, "everything that behooves the one greeted as the one that they are." Genuine greeting, as an address

(*Zuspruch*) turned toward the one greeted, is recognition: the recognition that recognizes the one greeted in "the nobility of their essence" and through such recognition lets them be what they are. Greeting is thus "a letting be of things and of human beings."[46]

While greeting manifests itself in various forms, from what Heidegger identifies as the fleeting, conventional form, to the seldomness of a genuine greeting, it is "the uniqueness of this poetic greeting" of Hölderlin's that is his focus here, as a letting-be that is at once belonging and departure, unfolding as the supreme intimacy (*Innigkeit*) of the poetic embrace. I would like to quote at some length Heidegger's further elucidation of greeting that meticulously unfolds the phenomenality of such embrace, only to interrupt itself at a certain, decisive point, in order to let Hölderlin's words speak for themselves, as though for the very first time:[47]

> Greeting is a reaching out to what is greeted, a touching that yet does not touch [*ein Rühren an . . . das doch nicht berührt*], an embracing [*Fassen*] that yet never has need to "take hold," because it is at the same time a releasing. . . . Greeting in this way always remains a will to belong to the one greeted, and yet never in the manner of imposing oneself or of a calculative reckoning with one another. In the genuine greeting there even lies concealed that mysterious stringency whereby, each time, those greeting one another are directed into the remoteness of their own essence and its preservation; for everything essential is, by virtue of what is its own, in each case unconditionally remote from the other. Yet this remoteness alone also assures the moments of transition from one to the other. Genuine greeting is one instance of such transition. The most simple, yet at the same time most intimate greeting is that whereby that which is greeted itself first returns to its essence anew, appears as something inceptive, and finds itself as though for the first time. Only if we think the greeting in such an essential manner may we have some intimation of how Hölderlin, by way of the Northeasterly and its "going" lets be greeted:
>
>> The beautiful Garonne,
>> And the gardens of Bordeaux
>> There, by the steep bank
>> Where the footbridge crosses and into the river

> Deep falls the brook, yet over it
> Keep watch a noble pair
> Of oaks and silver poplars;

The essential greeting of the poetic embrace not only lets beings first come into Being, letting them appear and come to stand in "the radiance of the poetic word."[48] It also at the same time directs them into the remoteness of their own essence, preserving them and letting them prevail from out of this very remoteness. It first raises those beings that have been greeted and appear in the naming of the poetic word into their actuality and their truth, as the "pure illumination" of what has been poetized. The actual landscape of Bordeaux once experienced by Hölderlin has now been poetized by way of this greeting. What was once actually experienced by the poet, notes Heidegger,

> has presumably long since changed—and yet—how much everything remains, how preserved [*gerettet*], despite the indefiniteness of the whole, everything comes to shine. The beautiful river, the gardens of the town, the footbridge that crosses the steep bank, the deep falling brook—are brought together in the rapture of one *single* embrace [*in* ein *Entzücken*]:
>
> > . . . yet over it
> > Keep watch a noble pair
> > Of oaks and silver poplars;[49]

For what appears here as something inceptive, finding itself as though for the very first time, is preserved in its staying power by virtue of the poet's love—a love that has taken the course of a departure, and that yet itself precisely remains, prevailing out of such departure: "an enduring love, over which the magnificent silence of these words lies."[50] That which remains is thus not only that which is manifestly poetized in this greeting—the beings themselves—but also the poet's love, which stays behind, remaining back, and from out of this remoteness remains mindful of that which once was and which still now prevails in its essence (*des Gewesenen und jetzt noch Wesenden*).[51]

"Still indeed it thinks of me . . ." (*Noch denket das mir wohl . . .*), reads the opening line of the second strophe. This "Still" (*Noch*), Heidegger comments, names the same time as the "now" (*nun*) of the line "But go now and greet . . ." from the first strophe: it names the moment of the poetic greeting itself. And yet, it introduces something else into the greeting, the greeting that the poet, remaining behind, sends on its way with the words "But go now and greet . . ." It is almost as though the moment of poetic greeting, the "now," were suddenly and unexpectedly arrested, detained in the very moment by the countermovement marked by the word "Still." As though this "Still" (*Noch*) first let the greeting unfold into the full richness of its essence, "radiating an intimacy that must come from a source of its own."[52] For the poet does not say what one might expect here: he does not say, "Still indeed I think of it," or, "Still well I remember this,"[53] but quite the reverse: "Still indeed it thinks of me," the "of" here translating the German dative *mir*, literally: "to me." Remarks Heidegger: "That which is greeted itself inclines toward the one greeting, thinking toward the one greeting. So mysterious is this greeting assigned to the Northeasterly."[54]

The line "Still indeed it thinks of me," Heidegger comments, appears to interrupt the greeting and our tarrying in the presence of what is greeted. Yet "in truth, it is like a catching breath in the midst of the fullness of that which is simple, which the greeting Northeasterly blows toward the poet, even though this wind goes away from the poet."[55] In remembrance, it seems as though our thinking departs in the direction of what once has been, in so doing taking leave of the present. Yet at the same time, that which once has been comes in the opposite direction, approaching the one who is thinking. That which returns in this way, Heidegger insists, does not merely become present: it does not take up residence in the present so as to become a kind of substitute for what is past. Rather, when we let that which is remembered unfold entirely in its own essence, when we in no way disturb its prevailing, then we experience the following: "That which is recollected oscillates over beyond our present and stands suddenly in the future. It comes toward us, and is in some way still unfulfilled . . ." It is, Heidegger says, a buried treasure, *ein ungehobener Schatz*, whereas if we consider it something past, we take it to be somehow finished and unalterable.[56]

The poet's thoughtful greeting that gives itself over to the wind and lets itself be carried off by the wind now suddenly comes to stand in the counter-wind of this very wind—in the wind that comes in its very going, comes toward the poet from out of the future. It is, Heidegger comments, "as though a river that runs out and goes into the sea suddenly flowed backward in the opposite direction, toward the source."[57] It is not only *as though* this were the case, for this is of course what is poetized by Hölderlin, not only in the closing lines of the hymn "Remembrance": ". . . Yet what takes / And gives memory is the sea," but also in the "Ister" hymn, which poetizes the apparent backward flow of the river Danube or "Ister" toward the source.[58]

    We might note, finally, the central importance of the "*Andenken*" course for the last lecture course that Heidegger would deliver, some ten years later in 1951–52. *What Is Called Thinking?* is in essence a further unfolding of, and meditation upon, the essence of thinking itself as *Andenken*. Its central claim, "*What is most thought-provoking is that we are not yet thinking*,"[59] is an invitation to think precisely this "not yet," the futural "essence" of thinking. Thinking occurs as our being drawn in and by the wind or draft (*Zug*) of a withdrawal (*Entzug*), a withdrawal that, in its approach, draws us toward and into it, such that we point into this very withdrawal, and are thus, in Hölderlin's words, "a sign that is not read."[60] Socrates himself, "the purest thinker of the West," is characterized as having done nothing else, his life long, than hold himself into the wind of such withdrawal.[61] Yet, in identifying the essence of thinking from its very first page as remembrance, *What Is Called Thinking?* also alludes unmistakably to the earlier readings of both "Remembrance" and "The Ister." Memory, mother of the Muses, the gathering of remembrance, conceals within it that which is to be thought, before all else, in everything that claims us in its essential presencing (*Wesen*), as prevailing, presencing in its having once been (*als Wesendes, Gewesendes*). Memory, Heidegger writes, is *Andenken*, remembrance directed toward what is (yet) to be thought, and as such is the wellspring and source of poetizing. "Poetizing is thus the waters that, from time to time, flow backward toward the source, to thinking as remembrance."[62]

Concluding Remarks

In drawing these reflections to a close, this brief consideration of the thinking of time in Heidegger's dialogue with Hölderlin may suggest the following assessment, however tentative and incomplete: In the phenomenological account of *Being and Time*, the issue of founding had yet to be adequately articulated, and this because both the status of the ontological difference qua difference and the phenomenon of discourse (as the existential foundation of language) had yet to be adequately thought through.[63] With respect both to originary time as ekstatic-horizonal temporality and to historicality (as the movedness and stretching within such temporality), the account of founding given there was ambiguous at best. On the one hand, ekstatic-horizonal temporality was conceived in a quasi-transcendental manner, as the a priori ontological constitution of Dasein's Being that would first found such phenomena as the now-time of our everyday concern. On the other hand, *Being and Time* was insistent throughout that the ultimate foundations of the ontological were ontic, the ontic referring to the factical existence of Dasein and to its historicality. Through Heidegger's encounters with Hölderlin, philosophical thinking at the limits of phenomenology (as *Being and Time* was), understanding time as the "horizon" of Being—a horizon involving both opening and closure—turns into the poetic opening of time accomplished by the inaugural event of language, which in its saying may open a new time and new possibilities of Being, founding them in the word. From "Hölderlin and the Essence of Poetizing" onward, founding will be understood as the poetizing "event" (*Ereignis*) of language, an event neither purely ontic nor ontological, but opening the time-space of the difference itself, as that of the possible nearness and necessary remoteness of all things, the time-space of what remains, for love and for memory, amid the ruins of time.

Notes

1. Friedrich Hölderlin, "Der Archipelagus." *Sämtliche Werke und Briefe* I, 304. Henceforth: SW. For other references to *die reißende Zeit*, see Hölderlin's "Remarks" on *Oedipus* and *Antigone*, discussed briefly below; also the unfinished poem "Wenn aber die Himmlischen . . ." (SW I, 401).
2. Ibid., II, 311.
3. Ibid., II, 316.
4. Ibid., II, 311.
5. Ibid., II, 310–11.
6. Ibid., II, 370.
7. SZ 329.
8. Andrzej Warminski, while not specifying particular terminology, suggests provocatively that "one can with justice argue that "all" Heidegger does is to bring (back) to Hölderlin's poetry only what he had taken from it in the first place: already in *Being and Time* Heidegger's language is saturated by Hölderlin's so that Heidegger cannot easily be accused of forcing a "foreign" ("philosophical") language upon the ("literary") language of Hölderlin's poetry." *Readings in Interpretation: Hölderlin, Hegel, Heidegger* (Minneapolis: University of Minnesota Press, 1987), 46–47. On *Entrückung* in Heidegger and Hölderlin, see David Farrell Krell, *Ecstasy, Catastrophe: Heidegger from* Being and Time *to the* Black Notebooks (Albany: State University of New York Press, 2015), ch. 1 and 2.

9. The term *Schwingung* and other cognates of *schwingen*, "to oscillate," are used by Heidegger especially in the 1928 lecture course *Metaphysische Anfangsgründe der Logik im Ausgang von Leibniz.* Gesamtausgabe Band 26. (Frankfurt: Klostermann, 1978), §12. Translated as *The Metaphysical Foundations of Logic* by Michael Heim (Bloomington: Indiana University Press, 1984).

10. Heidegger, GA 39, 109.

11. A marginal note of Heidegger's in the second edition of the volume in which this essay appears reads: "see *Being and Time*, Sections 79–81," directing the reader to precisely those sections in which the discussion of the ekstatic stretching of time is integrated into the "world time" of everyday concern—thus of Dasein's worldly Being as dwelling. The significance of this will become apparent below. On the ekstatic stretching of temporality, see also SZ, 371, 374–75, 390–91.

12. Heidegger, ED, 37.

13. Ibid. Heidegger states: "The Being of the human being is grounded in language; language, however, first authentically happens in the *dialogue*. The latter, however, is not just one way in which language takes place, rather, only as dialogue is language essential" (ED, 36).

14. Heidegger, ED, 38.

15. Ibid.

16. Ibid., 36.

17. Ibid., 38.

18. Ibid.

19. Ibid., 40.

20. Ibid.

21. Ibid., 31.

22. Cf. Heidegger's commentary on Hölderlin's elegy "The Archipelago" in his lecture course on "The Ister," where he remarks that the Greek πέλαγος, "the sea," names that which "remains and abides within itself in its surging," "abides amid change and becoming." The associated verb πέλειν means "that remaining that is what it is precisely in journeying and flowing" (GA 53, 88).

23. In the first Hölderlin lecture course of 1934–35, Heidegger discusses the meaning and etymology of the verb *dichten*, "to poetize," tracing it back to the Old High German *tithôn*, related to the Latin *dictare*, itself an intensified form of *dicere*, "to say." The original sense of these terms, Heidegger there suggests, can be found in a Greek word of the same root: δείκνυμι, meaning to show or point, to make something manifest by way of a specific pointing (GA 39, 29). Cf. the somewhat different and briefer discussion in the 1942 course that is content to relate *dichten* to *dictare* and to the possibility of writing: "*Dichten*—in Latin, *dictare*—means to write down, to fore-tell something to be written down" (GA 53, 8).

24. Heidegger, ED, 36–37.

25. Ibid., 37.

26. Ibid., 38.

27. Heidegger, SZ, 407.

28. Heidegger writes: "Why does Dasein, in addressing what it is concerned with, though mostly without vocalization, also express a 'now that . . . ,' 'then, when . . . ,' 'on the former occasion, when . . .'? Because its interpretive addressing of . . . [things] also expresses *itself*, that is, its circumspective, understanding *Being alongside* the ready-to-hand which lets the latter be uncovered and encountered; and because this addressing and discussing that also interprets *itself* is grounded in a *making-present* and is possible only as such" (SZ, 407–408).

29. Heidegger, SZ, 408.

30. Heidegger, ED, 35.

31. Ibid., 32.

32. Ibid.

33. Ibid., 38. Nevertheless, the relation between Being and beings should not here be understood in terms of the "ontological difference." Although, as an excess, Being is never reducible to beings, and in this sense "never a being," it also never happens apart from beings as something different from their presencing.

34. The following is a somewhat revised version of a presentation given at the forty-fourth annual meeting of the Heidegger Circle, held at Stony Brook University, New York, in 2010.

35. Heidegger, GA 52, 45; 55.

36. Ibid., 50.

37. Ibid., 55. The theme of remembrance as the essence of thinking would be further developed by Heidegger in his 1951–52 lectures on *What Is Called Thinking?*, discussed briefly below.

38. Ibid., 32.

39. Ibid.

40. *Beiträge zur Philosophie (Vom Ereignis)*. Gesamtausgabe Band 65. (Frankfurt: Klostermann, 1989), §§238ff. Translated as *Contributions to Philosophy (Of the Event)*, by Richard Rojcewicz and Daniela Vallega-Neu (Bloomington: Indiana University Press, 2012).

41. Heidegger, ED, 44.

42. See *Hölderlin's Hymn "The Ister"* (GA 53), §1. It is important to note that Heidegger explicitly says there that the time of this "now"—unlike the "now" of everyday time in *Being and Time*, §79—cannot be dated. For the "fire" called upon in the opening line of "The Ister" does not simply refer to the rising sun, but to "the holy" that "ignites the poet" (GA 53, 193). Precisely because it first inaugurates a time, it cannot be dated in relation to an already existent entity or event within the world. As Heidegger noted in "Hölderlin and the Essence of Poetizing," the essence of poetizing that is poetized by Hölderlin indeed belongs to a determinate time. But it does not simply accommodate itself to an already existing time. "Rather, in Hölderlin's founding anew the essence of poetizing, he first determines a new time" (ED, 44). Heidegger had made the same point already in the first Hölderlin course,

concerning the "event of the true" poetized in the hymn "Mnemosyne" (. . . *Lang ist / Die Zeit, es ereignet sich aber / Das Wahre*). The time of this event (*Ereignis*), he there remarked, "cannot be 'dated'" (GA 39, 55–56).

43. Heidegger, GA 52, 48.

44. This account of the poet's accompanying the going of the wind should be compared to Heidegger's rich account in the following semester of the poet's "going with" the rivers, an account that explicitly relates this to the "tearing" of time and to Hölderlin's "Remarks" on *Oedipus* and *Antigone*. See GA 53, §6.

45. Heidegger, GA 52, 49.

46. Ibid., 50.

47. Ibid., 50–51.

48. Ibid., 53.

49. Ibid., 52.

50. Ibid., 53.

51. Ibid. Cf. 81, 87.

52. Ibid., 53.

53. Such, for example, is the translation offered by Michael Hamburger in his otherwise generally inspired renditions of Hölderlin's poetry into English. See *Friedrich Hölderlin: Selected Poems and Fragments*, 251. (London: Penguin Books, 1998).

54. Heidegger, GA 52, 54.

55. Ibid.

56. Ibid. Cf. Heidegger's assertion that what is greeted is first "raised [*gehoben*] into its actuality" through the greeting (GA 52, 52).

57. Ibid., 54.

58. See Heidegger's lecture course from the following semester on *Hölderlin's Hymn "The Ister"* (GA 53).

59. Heidegger, *Was heißt Denken?* (WHD) (Tübingen: Niemeyer, 1984), 2.

60. Ibid., 5–6.

61. Ibid., 52.

62. Ibid., 7.

63. Notably, the section on "The Temporality of Discourse" (§68d) is conspicuously short and curtailed.

References

I. Works by Heidegger

ED *Erläuterungen zu Hölderlins Dichtung*. Frankfurt: Klostermann. Fünfte Auflage, 1981. Pagination cited refers to the second edition, indicated in the margins. Translated as *Elucidations of Hölderlin's Poetry*, by Keith Hoeller. New York: Humanity Books, 2000. All translations are my own.

GA 39 *Hölderlins Hymnen "Germanien" und "Der Rhein."* Gesamtausgabe Band 39. Frankfurt: Klostermann, 1980. Translated as *Hölderlin's Hymns "Germania" and "The Rhine,"* by William McNeill and Julia Ireland. Bloomington: Indiana University Press, 2014.

GA 52 *Hölderlins Hymne "Andenken."* Gesamtausgabe Band 52. Frankfurt: Klostermann, 1982. Translated as *Hölderlin's Hymn "Remembrance,"* by William McNeill and Julia Ireland. Bloomington: Indiana University Press, 2018. (Note: Translations offered in this essay differ somewhat from the published translation.)

GA 53 *Hölderlins Hymne "Der Ister."* Gesamtausgabe Band 53. Frankfurt: Klostermann, 1984. Translated as *Hölderlin's Hymn "The Ister,"* by William McNeill and Julia Davis. Bloomington: Indiana University Press, 1996.

SZ *Sein und Zeit.* Halle: Niemeyer, 1927. Translated as *Being and Time,* by John Macquarrie and Edward Robinson. New York: Harper and Row, 1962. Translations modified.

WHD *Was heißt Denken?* Tübingen: Niemeyer, 1984. Translated as *What Is Called Thinking?* by J. Glenn Gray. New York: Harper and Row, 2004.

II. WORKS BY HÖLDERLIN

SW *Friedrich Hölderlin: Sämtliche Werke und Briefe.* 3 Bände. Hrsg. M. Knaupp. München: Carl Hanser Verlag, 1992.

8

The Poietic Momentum of Thought

Heidegger and Poetry

KRZYSZTOF ZIAREK

Heidegger's engagement with poetry reaches significantly beyond his encounters with the work of poets, whether in his lecture courses on Hölderlin or his essays on poetry and language. Heidegger's interest in *Dichtung* concerns in fact the very shape of thought, especially the difficult task of preparing a style of thinking that, in view of the history of Western philosophy, might be called nonmetaphysical. His readings of poetic texts, from Sophocles's *Antigone*, through repeated elucidations of Hölderlin, to essays devoted to Trakl, Rilke, and George, examine primarily language, specifically what Heidegger sometimes calls its "naming," that is, the way in which language brings to word. At issue are not poetic devices or literary means of description and expression but a more basic, though often unnoticed or forgotten, movement that each time brings what manifests into words. This momentum—the way of language into language's appearance as words or signs—is always and already underway *as* language, namely as the manner in which language gathers its saying so that it constellates into signification. Such elucidations directed toward poetic texts are not readings or interpretations of poetry but instances of undergoing an experience with language, since for Heidegger it is poetry that expressly concerns itself with the occurrence, the "way," of language. This experience with language is occasioned not simply out of interest in poetry, let alone literary criticism or interpretation, but for the sake of thinking. What matters in the experience with language undergone through encounters with poetry is the opening onto the possibility of a different, nonmetaphysical language *of* and *in* thinking. Such a language is intimated specifically by the poietic "tropes" of language, which here mean not literary figures in their etymological sense but the turns of language occurring in and shaping its poetic traversal. The significance of poetry in the context of Heidegger's work, especially for its preparation of the thinking that we might now be ready to evolve further, lies in the distinct way in which poetic texts allow for the experience of traversing the very movement of poetic language, proceeding alongside its turns, images, figures, and expressions.

To parse this out, it is necessary to maintain a distinction between literary or poetic tropes, that is, figurative uses of language, on the one hand, and the poietic tropism of language, on the other. By "poietic troping" I understand the momentum inherent in language, which is already moving language through the turn of its saying into words. The way of language is tropaic in just this sense that it turns the yet unvoiced, "wordless" saying of manifestation into words, into language signs. This momentum is poietic because it opens up the world into its linguistic expression, letting its dimensions unfold and reach signification. Poietic here is meant in the sense of an originative opening up, that is, as an actuation of emergence, irreducible to the meaning of presence and the paradigm of representation. While poetry can be, and in fact most of the time remains, representational, the poetic *tropos* of language actuates the emergence into presence and naming, thus clearing the room for representation in the first place. It is this actuative force that marks the distinctiveness of the poietic from any understanding of poetry or poetics conceived in aesthetic or literary terms. The poietic here pertains to the manner, the way, or the fashion (*tropos*) in which language occurs by issuing (into) words. The poietic is therefore not a feature or a property, aesthetic, literary, or linguistic, but instead describes the entire traversal—its momentum, tonality, and rhythm—through which language brings itself (its saying) to words: to signs and signification. With this distinction in mind, one can say that while poetic language or composition can indeed be poieitic on occasion, it is not so either always or necessarily. In other words, poetry can be poietic only when and to the extent that its text can indeed actuate the tropaic momentum characteristic of the saying of language and in this gesture set into motion an experience with its poietic force.

This distinction between the poietic and the poetic can be marked more explicitly and directly in German, which has a double terminology for poetic matters: *Poesie* and *Dichtung*. While *Poesie* refers to the literary genre of poetic composition, *Dichtung* is both broader in its scope and more versatile in its connotations. It refers to poetry but also to literature more broadly, as well as indicating the type of composition, configuration, or "art," whose manner of formation can be described as "poetic." Like English "poetry," *Poesie* derives from the Greek notion of *poiesis* (making, producing) and its Latin cognate *poesis*. Aesthetic and literary conceptualizations of certain writings as poetic arise within the broader aesthetic context in which the notion of *poiesis* evolved so that art and poetic composition are understood primarily with regard to literary skill and artistic achievement they exhibit. *Dichtung* in turn describes a range of compositional configurations and practices, which are not limited to literary arts but extend to all types of artistic production and beyond. For instance, what in English is referred to as "symphonic poem," a piece that evokes nonmusical sources, most often literary or artistic, is called in German "*symphonische Dichtung*," which can be taken to mean that *Dichtung* indicates not so much a specific kind or genre of work as a particular modality of composing. What is important in the context of Heidegger's use of *Dichtung* and related terms is the fact that, unlike the English "poetry," the German word draws a relation to but, in the same stroke, also a distinction from *Poesie*, that is, from poetry in the narrower aesthetic sense of a literary composition or genre. This is one of the reasons why translating *Dichtung* in Heidegger's texts as "poetry" is problematic, since the term evokes too strongly the identification of *Dichtung* with the literary field of poetry and obscures the continuous play between *Dichtung* and *Poesie* pivotal to Heidegger's writings. This double terminology in German allows for invoking poetry and yet in the same gesture opening the scope beyond literature and other arts.

One more reason why Heidegger plays up the more expansive sense of *Dichtung* is its possible etymological connection to the Latin verb *dictare*: to compose, to draw up, or to dictate. Although this etymology is not certain, it is assumed that the German verb *dichten* derives from Middle High German *tihten*, which comes from Old High German *tihtōn, dihtōn*, probably an early borrowing from Latin *dictare*. The word *Dichtung* thus has the advantage of indicating both a poetic composition and a composition, not necessarily literary, whose essence is poetic. Its possible connection to the Latin *dictare* suggests a double sense of *Dichten*, which becomes crucial to Heidegger's thinking. As a mark of the composition, of an artwork, or even of thinking, *Dichten* principally indicates that such a composition occurs already in response to the saying ("dictation") of language. If the term *poetry* emphasizes literary creation and invention, *Dichtung* and *Dichten* draw attention to how the human language and its creations, poetic or otherwise, arise as a reply (*Antwort*) to the saying, to "the word of being": "The foreword [*Vorwort*] in the answer [*Antwort*] of the word [*Wort*] of the thinking of the history of beyng."[1]

This more expansive reach of *Dichtung* serves to delineate precisely such a distinction between the poietic, on the one hand, and poetry and poetic language, with its images, figures, and expressiveness, on the other. The poietic force is disclosive and compositional at the same time, composing the momentum of the clearing, which draws up and opens the time-space for the disclosure of the play of un/concealment. In a famous juxtaposition in "The Origin of the Work of Art," Heidegger makes clear that at issue for his thought is not poetry as a literary art (*Poesie*) but *Dichtung* as the poietic momentum initiating and molding the way in which truth occurs in different types of artworks, from literature and music to visual arts and architecture. "Truth, as the clearing and concealing of beings, happens in being composed [*indem sie gedichtet wird*]. *All art*, as the letting happen of the advent of truth, is as such, *in essence, poetry* [*Dichtung*]."[2] "In essence," translates here "*im Wesen*," which, given Heidegger's emphasis on the verbal sense of *Wesen* and *Wesung*, highlights the fact that *Dichtung* does not consist in a specific form or type of artwork, say a poem or a literary text, but pertains to how the work of art unfolds singularly and keeps open its play of truth. In fact, *Dichtung*, as the above quotation indicates, concerns the very manner in which truth composes itself, and expressly does so poietically. The phrase "*gedichtet wird*" does not mean that truth is formed into a poem but that the constellation of un/concealment, its characteristic clearing and sheltering, works poietically, that is, it keeps actuating the opening up of the clearing and prompts the coming to presence of beings within its openness.

It is, then, correct and yet also misleading to suggest that Heidegger simply privileges language arts, specifically poetry, over other genres of artworks. When Heidegger approaches various types of artworks through the prism of language, he can be understood to do so not so much to suggest reducing their specificity or subordinating them to the priority of linguistic expression, but instead to try elucidating the whole spectrum of artistic practices in terms of the saying, which each time distinctly comes to the fore in them. This saying is not simply linguistic or verbal, since it can compose itself into the *Gestalt* (figure) not only in literature but also in architecture, painting, or music. For Heidegger, all artworks, if they are genuinely art, bring forth and keep working in them a saying, that is, an unfolding of truth as the play of concealment and unconcealment.

> If all art is in essence poetry [*Dichtung*], then the arts of architecture, painting, sculpture, and music must be traced back to poesy [*Poesie*]. That is pure arbitrariness. It certainly is, as long as we mean that those arts are varieties of the art of language, if it is permissible to characterize poesy by that easily misinterpretable title. But poesy is only one mode of the clearing projection of truth, i.e. of poetic composition [*Dichten*] in this wider sense. Nevertheless, the linguistic work, poetry [*Dichtung*] in the narrower sense, has a privileged position in the domain of the arts.³

This quotation introduces an important distinction between poetry as a literary genre, that is, poesy (*Poesie*) or the language work that is a kind of poetry (*Dichtung*) irrespective of whether it occurs in poetry, prose, or another literary genre, on one side, and the more broadly conceived poietic composition of truth (*Dichten*), whether in literature, other arts, or elsewhere, on the other. In this view, it is the setting to work of truth, or in other words, its saying, that holds various types of works under the umbrella terms *art* or *arts*. The working of truth as saying is thus inherently and intrinsically plural in arts, and yet it is so in a manner that still allows gathering those distinct kinds of saying with regard to their actuative, poietic momentum, that is, their *Dichten*. At the risk of perhaps oversimplifying the picture, one could say that *Dichtung* in the role that Heidegger assigns to it emerges as the plural ways of *Dichten*, which could be rendered into English, though with a good deal of difficulty and somewhat awkwardly, as diverse ways of "poietizing."

It should not be forgotten, though, that even this awkward translation, by necessarily basing itself on the Greek/Latin roots of the English word *poetry*, disregards and obscures the actual terminological and semantic differences between *Dichtung/Dichten* and *Poesie* in German. What in English becomes a forced and inelegant verb, whether we render *Dichten* as "to poetize" or in the context of Heidegger's remarks even more idiosyncratically as "to poietize," does exist as a word in German with its ordinary idiomatic force. The existence of *Dichten* as a verb and a substantive should not be underestimated in its significance for Heidegger's thought and for our understanding of it. For it is indeed the verbal resonance of *Dichten* that becomes critical to the poietic tropism of language. This resonance focuses attention on the poietic not as a feature or a characteristic of a language or a text but as the momentum and the actuation, in short, as the event, of language's idiomatic turn to words. When one thinks of the different modes of *Dichten*, those are not to be conceived as various traits or qualities of specific art forms but rather as the distinct ways in which the poietic momentum stirs the saying (of the play of un/concealment) distinctly in various genres of artworks.

This is why as early as "The Origin of the Work of Art," much in advance of his writings and essays on language, Heidegger insists that "the right concept of language is needed."4 What is meant is clearly not language understood as a system of signs, composed of written and audible expressions of meaning (signifiers and signifieds), formed in order to be communicated. Instead, language is to be conceived as bringing "beings as beings into the open for the first time."5 As Heidegger puts it, "Language, by naming beings for the first time, first brings beings to word and to appearance. Only this naming nominates [*Dieses Nennen ernennt*] beings *to* their Being *from out of* their Being. Such saying [*Sagen*] is a projecting of clearing in which it is said [*angesagt*] what it is that beings come into the open *as*."6 What undergirds any system of language signs and the rules for signifying is the poietic movement of the saying, through which languages name beings, that is, bring them into appearance and into words. Named, that is, appearing as present through their relation to signs, beings come into the open as what they are, manifesting through the play of un/concealment. What Heidegger calls the saying is not the production of meaning but the preverbal projecting open of a clearing, in which what appears, what is called or named *to* and *in* its being, does so as "said," that is, as held in relation to being thanks to words.

Dichtung, poetry, or more precisely *Dichten*, poetizing, is precisely this projective saying as the actuation of the clearing: "Projective saying is poetry [*Dichtung*]: the saying of world and earth, the saying of the arena [*Spielraum*] of their strife and thus the place of all nearness and remoteness of gods. Poetry is the saying of the unconcealment of beings."7 Language comprehended as a system of signs in a signifying play is in each instance always already the occurrence of the above named saying. This projective saying prepares the sayable, that is, the expression which language achieves through signification. The saying is nothing other than the poietic momentum of language itself, and as such it makes way for and sets in motion the play of signification. At the same time, this saying continues to stream through and thus "say" itself in signs and the domain of meaning or sense. This is why Heidegger can write: "Language itself is poetry in the essential sense,"[8] that is, not as poetic composition or literary language but as the unfolding of the poietic momentum, which conveys what appears into words, that is, brings it in relation to signs and signification. In this sense, "Language is not poetry [*Dichtung*] because it is the primal poesy [*Urpoesie*]; rather poesy takes place [*ereignet sich*] in language because language preserves [*verwahrt*] the original essence of poetry [*Dichtung*]."[9] While poems (poesy; *Poesie*), that is, poetry (*Dichtung*) in the narrower sense, are indeed poetizing (*Dichten*) in its original momentum, it is so not because poetry can simply claim a superior or special status among arts but rather because the movement of language is itself poietic in the sense that it begins as the projective saying of the clearing for beings.

These comments from "The Origin of the Work of Art" make amply clear the role of *Dichten* and its force as the poietic momentum of the saying that occasions signs and meaning. Though only in passing, Heidegger notes in "The Origin of the Work of Art," that this expansive sense of *Dichtung* extends beyond art: "Poetry is thought of here in so broad a sense and at the same time in such intimate essential unity with language and word, that we must leave open whether art in all its modes, from architecture to poesy, exhausts the essence of poetry."[10] While *Dichtung* may be the essence of all arts, that is, the mode in which art each time comes into and maintains its work, its scope extends beyond art. Yet such extension is only possible if *Dichtung* names the poietic momentum of language, that is, the originative projective saying, which makes room for language as a system of signs.

Heidegger's reflections on poetry, as well as his remarks on other arts, can be approached, then, as ways of understanding, elucidating, and becoming conversant with the poietic momentum of language. Even though language is not always the explicit focus of those discussions, an overall concern with the working of language as a saying, especially with how the preverbal resonance of such a saying finds its way into language signs and maintains itself there as the "unsaid" of language, continues to motivate these texts. At issue is the specificity of the language of poetry, and more precisely, of what constitutes the *Dichten*, the poietic momentum, of poetic language. In this context, it is particularly instructive to note an important shift in Heidegger's take on poetic language with regard to the role of the image. In *The Event*, written 1941–42, Heidegger draws a contrast between poetry (*Dichtung*) and thinking (*Denken*) that hinges specifically on the image. "Poetry, although it exists only in the 'element' of language, constantly possesses in its words an 'image,' i.e., something to be intuited, through which and in which it poetizes its compositions."[11] The context here appears to be primarily Heidegger's engagement with Hölderlin and, to a lesser degree, Rilke, as the positioning of the poetic with regard to the holy (*das Heilige*) makes clear.

The role of words in poetry is presented in terms of their necessary link to the image, which, though it appears through words, seems to take priority over them. This attachment to the image becomes the benchmark of poetic language, the condition of poetic expression, which makes the relation to word in poetry something other than in thinking:

> The assignment to words in the thinking of beyng is essentially other and is more inceptual, i.e. altogether inceptual [*überhaupt anfänglich*], in comparison with poetry.

Because of the image, poetry gives emphasis to what is said rather than the act of saying.

> In poems of every kind, the composition incorporates the word; in thinking, on the other hand, that which is to be thought, i.e. the enduring of the difference, is ordained back into the word. The obedience [*Folgsamkeit*] in word is, in thinking, of an inceptual essence; what is shown exclusively therein is that this word is image-less [*bild-los*], i.e. is *only* [*nur*] word, which refers singularly to the twisting free [*Verwindung*] of beyng.[12]

In poetry, word is already an image, while in thinking it is only or simply word in its inceptual, poietic force. That is why "[w]ord in the thinking of the history of beyng is not means of expression and presentation but the essential answer [*Antwort*], the countering word of the human being of the history of beyng."[13] As formative to poetic language, the image displays and propagates the propensity to shape, form, and picture. What is, and what can be apprehended and understood as existing, can be so only as susceptible to being "pictured," that is, as needing to submit to the grasping power of imaging. In its reliance on the image, poetry obscures the poietic force of the word, which, by contrast, can come more expressly into the open in thinking. Thinking, at least in the shape and role allegedly prepared by Heidegger's own work, can be instantiated as an image-free word, that is, as the word-traversal of the image-less poietic momentum. It is this freedom from having words fettered to images that becomes pivotal to the attempt to envisage a nonmetaphysical momentum of thinking.

The Poietic Momentum of Thought 193

If these remarks about poetry and the image from the early 1940s seems to be motivated by Heidegger's proximity to Hölderlin, his later essays, which extend the scope of his interest in poetry to Trakl and George, offer an interestingly altered take on poetic language. Paradigmatic in this context is the discussion of Stefan George's poem "The Word" ("*Das Wort*") in two essays from *On the Way to Language*, "The Essence of Language" and "The Word."[14] In these essays, the focus is no longer the image but instead the word. The most trenchant part of Heidegger's reading of the poem concerns its last line: "Where word breaks off no thing may be." / "*Kein ding sei wo das wort gebricht.*" According to the Grimm dictionary of the German language, *gebrechen*, now largely outdated, is a verb that intensified the sense of breaking indicated by the verb *brechen*, to break.[15] The concluding line of George's poem thus underscores not only the force of the word's breaking but also the reliance of the thing's being on the word. Heidegger uses the line to propose his most poignant redefinition of the word, at least before the recent publication of the manuscripts of *GA* 71 and *GA* 74.

The word, the one indicated by the title of George's poem and invoked in its last line, is not a language sign, that is, not a linguistic or a dictionary term. Signs or language terms (*Wörter*) are a response (*Ant-wort*) to the word as the saying (the poietic momentum) of language. On several occasions Heidegger hyphenates the German *Antwort* precisely to underscore the fact that words-as-signs are *Ant-worte*, already in relation to and a response to the word, here named so by George's poem. Only with this distinction between word and sign, *Wort* and *Ant-wort*, can Heidegger's idiomatic explanation of "the word" in George's poem register its import. The distinction is provocatively suggested in the following remark from "The Essence of Language":

> When thinking tries to pursue the poetic word, it turns out that the word, that saying has no being. Yet our current notions resist such an imputation. Everybody, after all, sees and hears words in writing and in sound. They are; they can be like things, palpable to the senses. To offer a crude example, we only need to open a dictionary [*Wörterbuch*]. It is full of printed things. Indeed, all kinds of things. Plenty of terms [*Wörter*], and not a single word [*kein einziges Wort*]. Because a dictionary can neither grasp nor shelter the word by which terms become words and speak as words ["*Denn das Wort, wodurch die Wörter zum Wort kommen, vermag ein Wörterbuch weder zu fassen noch zu bergen*"].[16]

Terms (language signs) become words thanks to the word, the word that does not coincide with any language terms or signs found in a dictionary or within language systems. This is the case because the word in the idiomatic sense given to it by Heidegger names no being but simply the poietic momentum of language.

Another quotation from "The Essence of Language" makes this evident specifically by invoking the concluding line of George's poem: "The word—no thing, nothing that is, no being, but we have an understanding of things when the word for them is available. Then the thing 'is.'"[17] The word is not a thing, say a sign or a term, but only gives being. "If our thinking does justice to the matter, then we may never say of the word that it is, but rather that it gives—not in the sense that words are given by an 'it,' but that the word itself gives. The word: the giver [*Das Wort: das Gebende*]."[18] At the crucial moment in the text, Heidegger elides the sign "is" and replaces it with a colon to emphasize the manner in which what he understands as "word" is not to be mistaken for language signs, which exist as beings/things, which means that an "is" can be predicated about their existence. By contrast, the giving of being to signs/terms cannot be signified in this way, for the momentum of giving is nothing that gives itself or can ever be given, named, or signified. What the final line of George's poem indicates is not the breaking up or cessation/silencing of a language sign, that is, the decomposition of words taken as linguistic terms (*Wörter*), but rather the breaking off of the poietic momentum of giving, on which language, its signs, and its operations of signifying all hinge. Giving to be, the "word" occurs or "eventuates." The word takes place as event, for, as Heidegger puts it, "The event words" ("*Das Ereignis wortet*").[19]

This poietic momentum, *Dichten*, can signal itself in language at any point. It does not require a poetic composition, poetry or poems, yet poetic texts—due to their inherent preoccupation with the poetic exercise of language—can indeed provide a uniquely focused experience of such a momentum. The force of this poietic giving should not, therefore, be equated with poetry itself, even if this force (*Dichten*) can be particularly intense in poetic composition (*Poesie* as *Dichtung*). The import of the poietic giving for Heidegger cannot be easily ascribed to any poets Heidegger himself engages, not even Hölderlin, whom he names the poet of poets. In fact, this poietic momentum or force can be more pronounced in poets with whom Heidegger never engaged or, as in the case of Paul Celan, with whom Heidegger's engagement, though extended and apparently important, remains largely a matter of reporting. But this is also why in this context the names and the figures of the poets are not the most important. What matters—as *die Sache*—is the way in which their poetic compositions bring to the fore the force of the poietic momentum of language.

This brief explanation of the word in Heidegger's idiomatic approach between Hölderlin and George opens upon the understanding of *Dichten* (the poietic) as the momentum proper to words, actuated when they give being by conveying what appears to words/signs. Rephrasing Heidegger, one can write therefore: the word: the poietic momentum. This copula-less, nonpredicative formulation uses the colon to indicate precisely the tropaic way of language, through which language as word turns into signs. Where Heidegger's work provides a unique impetus to thought is in this undertaking to open in philosophy, or in fact in thinking that occurs "beyond" or "otherwise" than philosophy, expressly the force of the poietic momentum of language. This means specifically that Heidegger's texts, especially those most adventurous with regard to language, pursue thinking distinctively through the poietic momentum of words. In those texts, thought does not operate on the presentational or representational model. Its primary force does not derive from statements and propositions, or from proofs and arguments. This means that such thinking no longer proceeds on the model of grasping thought, which would not only remain in control but also purposefully try to assert such control through aspiration to clarity and exactness. As Heidegger explains, such thinking does not seek correctness or logical precision but a more stringent and demanding poietic rigor, which challenges the apparent comfort, transparency, and control afforded by assertions and by propositional language more broadly.

Yet, as Heidegger's remarks on poetry and images make clear, this different rigor, which defines the port or bearing of thinking, is not to be identified with poetic language, its figures or images, or with literary playfulness more broadly. At issue in this juxtaposition between poietic rigor and logical exactness is the distinction between the force of *Dichten* in thinking and the power—machinational and calculative—of grasping thought. What surprises and prompts thinking, sometimes sending it down an unexpected or even an issueless path, is the intrinsic poietic bearing of language. Much of Heidegger's effort in his many unpublished manuscripts is directed toward allowing words precisely to open thinking in such unprethinkable and non-machinational ways. Whether through the use of hyphens or by creating directional/dimensional constellations of prefixes, Heidegger releases the poietic energy of words.[20] What his writing does is, recalling his discussion of the word in George, to let signs become words. Signs, for instance, *Dasein, Ereignis,* or *Sein,* become dislocated from their ordinary meaning, their poietic potential liberated, initiating the experience with language. Instead of presenting or representing, these signs, now become words, open toward the unprethinkable, active in their capacity—in his discussion of George, Heidegger uses the word *Vermögen*—to hold word/being open to the future. In this manner, thinking becomes redirected from the (re)presentation of what already appeared or has become present, toward proceeding alongside the temporal momentum of being and language. It is this poietic charge of language that comes to move thinking, which no longer focuses on grasping, assertion, or calculation but instead explores the parameters of its attunement to the unfolding of being, in the process participating in deciding what tonality this revealing takes.

This poietic momentum is deployed and underlined by Heidegger specifically at moments when this thinking attempts to unhinge metaphysical modes of thought in order to prepare the way for nonmetaphysical thinking. Because of this juncture, what matters most in Heidegger's project is the *Dichten* within his own thinking, the manner in which this thinking opens itself and lets itself be guided by what I have termed here the poietic force or momentum. That is why it is Heidegger's own *Dichten*, his thinking as poetizing thought (*dichtendes Denken*) that needs to be foregrounded more in relation to Heidegger's encounters with poetry. For this reason Heidegger's forays into poetry or other arts—predominantly painting, architecture, or occasionally music—are not to be considered as exercises in aesthetics or philosophy of art, for example, as an attempt to propose a fresh approach to art or a new aesthetics oriented by the thought of being. As "The Origin of the Work of Art" makes evident, Heidegger breaks with aesthetics precisely in order to try and recognize how art matters with regard to the unfolding of truth, specifically its poietic momentum. Poetry and art more broadly come to matter to Heidegger not for historical, literary, or aesthetic reasons but because an encounter with artworks can allow for undergoing an experience with the poietic momentum of language, and thus let one become attuned to the giving of being from the event. This viewpoint on poetry and other arts should not be mistaken for an instrumental use of poets and their poems. Heidegger does not employ poetry as a springboard for philosophical reflection but rather brings thinking into proximity to poetic writing in order to open thought to the ways in which the poietic momentum (*Dichten*) courses in distinct manner in art and in thought. Furthermore, this gesture, often forceful with regard to both poetry and thought, is prompted by the fact that the long-standing metaphysical tradition has had a deadening effect on thought, and by extension also on art, so that as a result thought has become oblivious to its own distinctly poietic bearing. Repeated invocations by Heidegger of thinkers who preceded Socrates and Plato, whether Parmenides, Heraclitus, or Anaximander, have in view an engagement with texts that do not easily support the metaphysical categorization into distinct domains of philosophy and literature, or of thought and poetry. They also constitute a nod toward the type of writing, and also toward a kind of poietic thinking, that hold in proximity what later became distinct philosophical and literary languages and do so expressly with regard to their shared, and mutually reinforcing, momentum of the unprethinkable.

This is why the change in thinking Heidegger wants to prepare is not about thought becoming poetic, that is, somehow more "literary," metaphoric, or imaginative. It also does not involve focusing more on the playful disposition of words for the sake of aesthetic or literary inventiveness. This shift is clearly more about the way Heidegger's own writing moves and advances, and in the process alters the language *of* and *in* thinking. The change Heidegger introduces concerns manifestly the actuation in thought of the poietic momentum of language, where the poietic becomes the matter of textuality, and thus also of the new patterns of reading. The traversal of such thinking and response to it cannot continue to pay attention only, or even primarily, to points or turns of argument, to propositions or to key statements, but need to experience thought in its "textuality," that is, in its poetic configuration, rhythm, and word texture. This amendment is meant to precipitate evolving a style of thinking that is no longer motivated by traditional or conventional philosophical modes of comprehension but unfolds idiomatically through the tropaic movement of language and its unprethinkable poietic measure. If we ask why such a change matters, Heidegger's texts on poetry and language provide the following answer: it does because the unfolding of world and of Dasein has precisely such a tropaic momentum, and this is why their experience and understanding call for a poietic, and not a calculative, measure.

The matter of thinking concerns the guiding force of the poietic momentum, which translates into a difficult, poetically rigorous mode of thinking, no longer calibrated to effective grasp or calculation but instead "attuned" to the giving momentum of being. As attuned to this unprethinkable manner of giving, that is, to the disposition into which being allows thought to adapt itself, thinking finds itself challenged to stay abreast with the unforeseen and shifting bearings of the event. It is in those zones of thinking that Heidegger is his own best "poet." This is the case not because he writes what he calls *Gedachte,* that is, thought gathered or composed in parallel to *Gedichte* (poems) and poetic forms. Rather, we need to look for poietic composing directly in Heidegger's own language: in the openings and new trajectories for words brought forth by his use of hyphens; in the collapsing grammatical structures that, with phrases such as "*Die Welt weltet*" or "*Das Ereignis ereignet,*" undermine the conceptual power axis of subject-object; in the translational vectors initiated within apparently used up and conventionalized terms. This language initiates a new language of thinking, whose momentum is not propositional or argumentative but instead poietic, in tune with what Heidegger recognizes as the unprethinkable disposition(s) of being.

Notes

1. Martin Heidegger, *The Event,* trans. Richard Rojcewicz (Bloomington and Indianapolis: Indiana University Press, 2013), 227.
2. Martin Heidegger, "The Origin of the Work of Art," in *Basic Writings,* trans. and intro. David Farrell Krell (New York: HarperCollins, 1993), 197.
3. Heidegger, *Basic Writings,* 198.
4. Ibid.
5. Ibid.
6. Ibid.; trans. modified.
7. Ibid.
8. Ibid., 199.
9. Ibid.
10. Ibid.
11. Heidegger, *The Event,* 226.
12. Ibid.; trans. modified.
13. Ibid., 227.
14. The English translation of the essay renders the title as "Words," losing the singular in the German title. Martin Heidegger, *On the Way to Language,* trans. Peter D. Hertz (New York: HarperCollins, 1971), 139–56.
15. Deutsches Wörterbuch von Jakob Grimm und Wilhelm Grimm Online: http://woerterbuchnetz.de/DWB/?sigle=DWB&mode=Vernetzung&lemid=GG0296; accessed November 17, 2015.
16. Heidegger, *On the Way to Language,* 87. The German original can be found in *Untwerwegs zur Sprache, Gesamtausgabe,* vol. 12 (Frankfurt am Main: Vittorio Klosterman, 1985), 181.
17. Ibid.
18. Ibid., 88; trans. modified.

19. Martin Heidegger, *Zum Wesen der Sprache und Zur Frage nach der Kunst*, *Gesamtausgabe* 74 (Frankfurt am Main: Vittorio Klostermann, 2010), 99.

20. A more substantiated discussion of this issue, in the context of the overall understanding of language in Heidegger, can be found in Krzysztof Ziarek, *Language after Heidegger* (Bloomington and Indianapolis: Indiana University Press, 2013).

References

Heidegger, Martin. *Basic Writings*. Translated and introduction by David Farrell Krell. New York: HarperCollins, 1993.

———. *Das Ereignis (1941/42)*. *Gesamtausgabe* 71. Frankfurt am Main: Vittorio Klostermann, 2009.

———. *The Event*. Translated by Richard Rojcewicz. Bloomington and Indianapolis: Indiana University Press, 2013.

———. *On The Way to Language*. Translated by Peter D. Hertz. New York: Harper Collins, 1971.

———. *Unterwegs zur Sprache*. *Gesamtausgabe*, vol. 12. Frankfurt am Main: Vittorio Klostermann, 1985.

———. *Zum Wesen der Sprache und Zur Frage nach der Kunst*. *Gesamtausgabe* 74. Frankfurt am Main: Vittorio Klostermann, 2010.

Ziarek, Krzysztof. *Language after Heidegger*. Bloomington and Indianapolis: Indiana University Press, 2013.

9

Learning from Poetry

On Philosophy, Poetry, and T. S. Eliot's *Burnt Norton*

GÜNTER FIGAL

*For A.M.E.S.—remembering Great Russell Street
and Sir Percival David*

Though art in general has always been a prominent topic of philosophical reflection, poetry has been of particular importance for philosophy, not at least at its very beginning. The reason for that is not difficult to discern. Philosophy is, like poetry, an eminent manifestation of language and as such not always clearly distinguished from it. Philosophy thus can appear as if it were poetry, most obviously with its linguistic form. Parmenides, for instance, has adopted Homer's and Hesiod's epic meter so that one may call his work "Parmenides's poem," and nevertheless Parmenides very likely did not regard himself as a poet. Taking distance to poetry, however, cannot in every case avoid confusion or irritation. Plato, an explicit and radical critic of poetry, articulated his doubts and objections concerning the reliability of poetry and especially of drama in his own theatre plays, which, though not meant for performance on stage but only for reading, are poetical texts. If poetical genres such as epical verse and drama appeared to philosophers as adequate articulations of philosophical thought, it seemed even more urgent to draw otherwise a strict line between poetry and philosophy. Philosophy should appear as something new and superior compared with poetry, and this could only be marked by a substantial distinction.

This distinction, as a philosophical one, becomes explicit with the philosophical claim of truth. At the beginning of his poem, Parmenides imagines a voyage beyond the realm of normal human experience that leads the voyager, very likely an ideal projection of the philosopher, to a gate, governed by a goddess, Dike, who is persuaded to open it for him. Inside, another goddess, who remains anonymous, welcomes the voyager with a promise. As she says, the voyager will "learn all things, both the unshaken heart of the well-rounded truth, and the opinions of mortals, in which there is no true reliance."[1] Plato takes up the Parmenidean distinction but he develops it in a remarkably different version. According to the *Republic*, more precisely to the famous simile of the cave, it is still a way that leads to truth, but it is a way human beings really can take, and they can take it afoot. There is also no longer need of a flying horse-drawn cart and of divine guidance. A human being, obviously a philosopher, would free another human being from his bonds and lead him—there seem to be no women in the cave—outside, that is to say, outside the normal dwelling place of human beings. Philosophers as such know the way out. As "lovers of the sight of truth" (τῆς ἀληθείας . . . φιλοθεάμονες),[2] they must know what they love and also how and where to find it. Without the experience of truth one could not love it.

It is this experience that, according to Plato, distinguishes philosophers from poets. Whereas philosophers seek to find out what something or someone, including the gods, truly is, poets content themselves with stories and images articulated in words.[3] Thus, they conceal truth and impede philosophical research. As to this, even thinkers such as Parmenides and Heraclitus appear as poets or at least like poets. As Plato's Socrates states in the *Sophist*, every of these thinkers has told us a story, a myth, as if we were children, without taking care whether the things told are false or true.[4]

Philosophical resistance to poetry as sketched has more or less explicitly and more or less rigidly been effective throughout the history of philosophy as long as the philosophical claim of truth remained beyond question. This claim had been solidly confirmed by the Aristotelian understanding of philosophy as "science" and even as the most superior one. Though impressively restored in Hegel's system of philosophy the Aristotelian structure did not remain stable. Nietzsche questioned the traditional understanding of philosophy, most strongly and effectively, and in doing this he doubted philosophy's capacity to realize truth in whatever respect, and he assumed that philosophers would not truly conceive and describe the world, but rather invent images of it. Philosophers, as Nietzsche sees them, create perspectival worldviews, and they evaluate what they present due to their respective perspectives. Instead of being contemplators, "lovers of the sight of truth," in Plato's sense, philosophers for Nietzsche are poets. They write dramas to be performed not on stage, but in everyday life.[5]

Nietzsche's rehabilitation of poetry has not generally been taken in Nietzsche's sense. The philosophical claim of truth may also be questioned without giving up an orientation to truth in every respect. As a consequence, poetry may be understood as the truth guarantor, so that philosophy can only follow particular poetical prescriptions and stress their philosophical relevance. In this sense Heidegger and Gadamer have argued, and they have done so in two remarkably different ways. Whereas Heidegger in his own particular way radicalizes Nietzsche's view of poetry as invention of human life in its structures, Gadamer ascribes the achievement of truth to poetry in adherence to the Platonic tradition. According to Heidegger, poets "venture language" and thus overcome a normal everyday understanding of life in order to found anew the openness of being as the world of a historical people.[6] Gadamer, in contrast, regards poetry as a transformation of something turning its everyday appearance into the appearance of its essence. Poetry shows anything whatsoever in such a way that listeners to or readers of poems can only say, "So it is," or, "That is the true."[7] In any case, however, the philosophical claim of truth has been delegated to poetry. Philosophy can only achieve a formal characterization of truth and so clarify as to what and where truth can be sought.

This quite short and sketchy reminder of "the old quarrel between philosophy and poetry"[8] gives no philosophical solution, but rather provokes a fundamental question. Since the mentioned positions are at least partly contrary, it is up to oneself to decide how to understand philosophy's relation to poetry. From a philosophical point of view the question concerning this relation cannot be left open, since with it philosophy as such is at stake. Following Plato or Nietzsche or Heidegger or Gadamer, one will be led to a more or less different conception of philosophy, and accordingly as a philosophizing person one has to clarify and to decide what one's own kind of thinking as philosophizing is or should be. In any case, however, this clarification and decision will be concerned with the problem of truth. Is truth something philosophically, but not poetically available, or can it only be manifest poetically? Or should the claim of truth as such be abandoned?

What is truth? Such are the questions one will soon find oneself entangled in, taking the "old quarrel between philosophy and poetry" seriously. Pursuing these questions, however, one might lose the most simple and perhaps most evident question, namely, what reading poetry can mean to philosophical thinking—not just poetry in general, but the work of particular authors, or, what is even more concrete, of particular poetical works.

Taking up these questions and making attempts to find an answer or answers to them one has to presuppose or, even better, to be certain that philosophizing is possible, and this, again, means that truth is available to human thinking. Without this presupposition or certainty it would be consequent to abandon the claim of philosophy. One may seriously doubt, however, whether such abandonment is possible. Is it possible not just to forget philosophy but to overcome it and to leave it behind? Most prominently, Richard Rorty has argued for a positive answer to this question. For him the attempt to go beyond philosophy in order to become "entirely free of it" can be realized because it goes along with an alternative conception of intellectual life. According to Rorty it is poetry or, he says more generally, "literature," that enables what philosophy only had promised: a life in freedom without dependence on whatever authority.[9] Rorty, however, cannot exclude the question whether "freedom" should be understood in such a way. There is no reason to take just for granted that freedom is adequately and sufficiently characterized as "freedom from authorities." Such a consideration, again, only makes sense if there is something that truly can be called "freedom," in contrast to something else that is not freedom even if it is called so. It makes sense only if linguistic determinations apply to something in the world at all. If this cannot seriously be doubted, philosophy as established by Parmenides and even more by Plato still is valid. The claim of truth cannot be deconstructed as a clever suggestion in order to gain authority. It is inevitable since seeking truth can and should be experienced, and it can be reflected. The elaborate reflection of the experience of truth is philosophy.

Is poetry "true"? In order to answer this question maybe no extensive conceptual discussion of truth is needed, but rather, as already indicated, just attention to a particular poem led by the question how such a poem can be read and understood. Does a poem closely read reveal something about something in the world, a long and complex poem, for instance, like the first of T. S. Eliot's *Four Quartets*?[10] At least the title of this poem, "Burnt

Norton," seems to refer to something, and as one can find out, it refers to a manor house in Southwest England. The poem, however, says little about this place. A garden is mentioned, possibly or even likely the garden of Burnt Norton, but what is said could hardly be verified by a visit to the place. The poem does not even pretend to describe the place. Instead, it associates the place with something that "might have been," but is no longer possible and can only be present in words independent from factual present or past situations:

> What might have been is an abstraction
> Remaining a perpetual possibility
> Only in a world of speculation.

"What might have been" is only present in a self-contradicting memory, as something remembered that did not take place. It is only an echo and thus an acoustical reflection in the words of the poem. Words are echoes, reverberations of what can immediately no longer be heard:

> Footfalls echo in the memory
> Down the passage we did not take
> Towards the door we never opened
> Into the rose-garden. . . .

The poem takes this passage to places undiscovered, places invisible, with sounds not to be heard. They belong to "our first world," the world that cannot be fixed because it is beyond localization and that also cannot be fixed in time:

> I can only say, *there* we have been: but I cannot say where.
> And I cannot say, how long, for that is to place it in time.

The poem is in search of this "first world," a world beyond—or before—the distinction between the factual and the possible, a world of places, things, living beings, sounds, colors, and names inaccessible in practical life and thus only present with

> The inner release from the practical desire,
> The release from action and suffering, release from the inner
> And outer compulsion, . . .

In this freedom, however, the "first world" presents as "a grace of sense" that cannot be grasped and attached to a particular situation. The poem seeks this sense it evokes "at the still point of the turning world," beyond the distinction of "movement" and "arrest," beyond different directions of movement and thus beyond succession. The poem is an attempt to articulate the world at this "still point" just as a web of allusions and relations. The poem's words may sound when the poem is read, but they are what they are only as this web, which coincides with the "still point" of the "first world." In this coincidence the poem is no utterance, no description of whatsoever but, as "form" or "pattern," has the simple present of an object, a vessel, for instance, without meaning or representational function, just appearing and, in its appearance, being an intertwinement of movement and stillness—movement quieted in stillness and stillness not as an end or a pause of movement, but as the liveliness of appearing:

> Words move, music moves
> Only in time; but that which is only living
> Can only die. Words, after speech, reach
> Into the silence. Only by the form, the pattern,
> Can words or music reach
> The stillness, as a Chinese jar still
> Moves perpetually in its stillness.
> Not the stillness of the violin, while the note lasts,
> Not that only, but the co-existence,
> Or say that the end precedes the beginning,
> And the end and the beginning were always there
> Before the beginning and after the end,
> And all is always now. . . .

The "Chinese jar," possibly a strong and clear vessel with celadon glaze as they were produced during the Song-period, is the measure of the poem. The poem is such a vessel in words.

The poem's attempt to find the stillness of sense beyond factuality and possibility is realized in a rather complex way. The poem is a weaving of its web or "pattern" of sense, bringing places, things, sounds, colors, and names together, and it is also a reflection on the status of this web as a "first world." It begins with such a reflection questioning the order of time, evidently so, if time, more precisely the distinction between past and future as modes of time, enables the distinction between the factual and the possible—all things factual are past, and what is possible can "now," presently, be realized in future. But:

> Time present and time past
> Are both perhaps present in time future,
> And time future contained in time past.
> If all time is eternally present,
> All time is unredeemable.

This reflection is not an assertion. Rather, it is an assumption indicated by the word *perhaps*. The poem does not argue for this assumption. There is no intention to make it plausible. The poem confirms the assumption concerning the unredeemable character of time only in exploring the "first world" as a web or "pattern" of sense in which everything whatever is simply appearing—not as a factual reality and not as a possibility that can be realized. The poetical exploration of the "first world" begins in time, with memory, but always already is beyond time since fitting in a web or a "pattern" is no timely event, and accordingly the experience of such a pattern cannot be temporal:

> To be conscious is not to be in time
> But only in time can the moment in the rose-garden,
> The moment in the arbour where the rain beat,
> The moment in the draughty church at smokefall
> Be remembered; involved with past and future.
> Only through time time is conquered.

The poem is a passage beyond time that starts in time and, with its first word, has already reached the "still point" of appearing sense, which thus is no aim of poetical movement and nothing that could ever get lost. Placing something remembered or a possibility that "might have been" into the web or pattern of poetry immediately transcends the mode of time poetical thinking has started with. This can be articulated in temporal terms fitting the modes of time together, placing present and past in future and future in past and thus forming a temporal sphere that as such has no temporal character.

This sphere, the "first world" of the poem is indicated also otherwise, and this indication is especially interesting because it points to philosophy. The poem *Burnt Norton* is preceded by two quotations taken from the fragments of Heraclitus as they have been collected by Hermann Diels in his *Die Fragmente der Vorsokratiker*. As if it were a philological quotation, the motto includes this German title and the name of the editor. The motto is no part of the poem. In the original edition of the *Four Quartets* it is not placed over the poem's first part, but on a page vis-à-vis the front page with the poem's title, *Burnt Norton*. The two quotations present fragments 2 and 60,[11] both in Ancient Greek without translation:

τοῦ λόγου δ ἐόντος ξυνοῦ ζώουσιν οἱ πολλοί ὡς ἰδίαν ἔχοντες φρόνησιν.
ὁδὸς ἄνω κάτω μία κα'ὠυτή.

It is not difficult to find an allusion to the second quotation in the poem. The characterization of "still point" by the exclusion of movement—"neither [movement] from nor towards, / Neither access nor decline"—can be understood as a more radical version of Heraclitus's sentence according to which "the path up and down is one and the same."[12] Whereas Heraclitus speaks of the sameness of one way that can be taken in two different directions, the poem stresses the intermediate state of the "still point" being neither movement up nor movement down but just the stillness of appearance.

Clarifying the status of the first quotation—"although the Logos is common the many live as though they had a private understanding"[13]—can appear as more difficult. But if the suggested reading of the poem so far is sound, it can be related to the poem's attempt to explore the "first world" of sense, which, like Heraclitus's λόγος, is not experienced by "the many" in everyday life. Pursuing one's particular intentions led by "practical desire" and being limited by "the inner and the outer compulsion," one is not free to feel oneself "surrounded by a grace of sense." One is bound to the modes of time, oriented to the future in which one's aim is to be realized, and constrained by the factual of the past, struggling "now," presently, as an individual person with particular intentions, in the tension of time. Heraclitus's λόγος, however, is different from the "first world" of the poem. It is rather a conceptual structure than a web or a pattern, the rational determinateness of the cosmos that as such can be investigated and described. The poem, in contrast, does not describe anything. It is no set of concepts in accordance with the world order. Rather, its particular elements fit together in such a way that their relatedness is not determinate in every respect. There are moments of vagueness and ambivalence, so that the correspondences between the poem's evocations are not once and for all fixed. Every new reading of the poem may discover new correspondences. Accordingly, no interpretation will ever be able to determine its sense and exhaust the richness of the poem. Though the poem's text is definite and thus the same for every reading, its complexity will allow new and different discoveries again and again. All these discoveries, however, will remain partial. They cannot just be summarized to a consistent and complete whole.

Is poetry or, more concretely, is Eliot's *Burnt Norton* "true"? Is the poem an articulation of truth or of a particular truth that is not accessible except by the poem? Though the poem refers to a particular place, namely the manor of "Burnt Norton"—just as the other three "quartets" also refer to particular places—the poem does not articulate anything about this place. Rather, this place, a real place in Southwest England, is transformed into a web of sense that only exists with the poem. There might be a "rose-garden" at Burnt Norton, but surely only in the poem is this garden connected with the "echoes" evoked by the poem; only in the poem is a walk through this garden placed in the context of reflections on time and on a sphere containing all time and thus on a particular stillness that is beyond time without being separated from time, like a sphere of its own, as if it were another world, neatly separated from the world we live in.

Whereas the poem does not refer to something real, this sphere is no poetical invention. It is there and can be experienced with the poem. The experience of the poem is as such an experience of the world, of the poem's "first world." This is the world we live in as it appears if time, the tension between past and future, is suspended. It is the world of sense as it can be experienced without practical intentions, which can only be pursued if particular activities can be regarded as the truly "right" ones in order to reach a particular aim. Practice cannot do without the claim of truth; as Aristotle has shown, practical reason (πφόνησις) is a specific way of "finding the truth" (ἀληθεύειν)—truth about the situation of practice and the particular means that allow oneself to realize what one has decided to pursue.[14] And, as one should add, the world of sense as the poem reveals it can only be experienced if not only practical orientation is suspended but also conceptual thinking that seeks to grasp the world order in whatever particular way. The poem's "first world," this may again be stressed, is different from Heraclitus's λόγος and also from every other philosophical attempt to characterize the world in its intelligibility.

So, is there any truth in the poem? As one can conclude, the poem is not untrue or deceiving, as Plato's Socrates would have said in consequence of his considerations in the second and third book of the *Republic*. It is beyond truth—if truth can only be found in practical and theoretical thinking. The poem, then, cannot offer any truth that is inaccessible for conceptual thinking, philosophical or scientific, but rather confronts conceptual thinking with "a grace of sense" different from sense as it can be experienced conceptually. Or, to say it with the words of the poem, what it confronts with is

> . . . concentration
> Without elimination, both a new world
> And the old made explicit, understood
> In the completion of its partial ecstasy,
> The resolution of its partial horror.

Though the correspondences of the poem's elements are not without determination they do not "eliminate" indeterminacy. They do not demand concentration on the determinate as do articulations of conceptual thinking. Rather, they open the world differently, suspending the limitations of practical and theoretical rationality.

This does not mean that rational thinking confronted with a poem such as *Burnt Norton*, cannot do anything but surrender. The "first world" or "new world" of the poem is no chaos, and it also does not enable experiences beyond the limits of rationality. Reading *Burnt Norton* is no irrational ecstasy. In its complexity the poem needs attention to its elements and correspondences and words in order to find interpretations, careful and precise as possible, that articulate the poem as experienced in reading. Nevertheless, every reading of the poem is a movement at the verge of precision and determinateness. More or less explicitly, every reading would realize how the determinate as it can be grasped conceptually is embedded in the indeterminate—as the forms and lines of a painting are embedded in the ground of color. Whereas in practical or theoretical contexts words "make sense" only in accordance with predetermined criteria as aims, strategies, methods, or reasons, a poem like *Burnt Norton* allows the experience of non-predetermined sense—sense on the verge between determinacy and indeterminateness. Only this sense allows predetermination and, going along with that, concentration on what is possible and required in predetermined contexts of practical and theoretical rationality. The poem allows experiencing what, in a term of Husserl's,[15] could be called *primordial sense*—sense always already experienced in every limitation and not limited by any.

Primordial sense as such is not inaccessibly beyond conceptual thinking. Speaking of "primordial sense" and distinguishing it from other kinds of sense *is* conceptual. But though conceptual thinking is able to formally grasp primordial sense it cannot explore it. Every attempt to do this would necessarily lead to a more or less consistent set of concepts and thus would miss what was supposed to be grasped. Primordial sense is unlimited, so that its infinite possibilities would always exceed the attempt to conceptually describe it. For conceptual thinking primordial sense is there, but only like the ground of a painting for a view that would solely perceive distinctive lines and forms. Though these lines and forms could not be viewed without the color ground of the painting, their visibility could not be understood unless one would realize that the primordial correlate of visual perception is color and that lines and forms without color could not appear.

This analogy of vision and the visible can be revealing also in another respect. Mostly, and especially under conditions of everyday life, one does not pay attention to colors unless they are signals like traffic lights. One concentrates on particular and, at best, distinctive forms—forms that are determinate, so that they can be identified and also recognized, even if they vary and appear in different matter with differently textured and colored surfaces. Viewing and contemplating paintings, however, especially paintings that do not represent something and are not dominated by distinctive forms, one may experience and understand color as the primordial correlate of visual perception. Contemplating, for instance, one of Monet's late water lily paintings one may find out that it is color from which more or less distinctive forms emerge. This, however, is only possible because the painting has limits. The dense texture of blue and green and some brown and yellow shades slightly merging can be studied because the painting as such is a limited and distinctive object one can face and concentrate on.

If a poem such as *Burnt Norton* is like a painting as described, it could be called an objectification of primordial sense. With such a poem, the infinite is brought into objective limits, not only insofar as the poem is a composed—or woven—and limited text that can be identified and read and reread and interpreted, but also insofar as the poem does not objectify primordial sense as such, but in particular. The poem, though inexhaustible in its sense, is this particular poem—as particular as the place it calls with its title, *Burnt Norton*. With particular places—and never without them—space is experienced, space in a particular concreteness and nevertheless it is not reducible to the concreteness of a particular place. Vessels like the poem's "Chinese jar" are of a comparable kind. They need space and comprise space. Like a vessel, a poem such as *Burnt Norton* comprises the infinite space of primordial sense it belongs to.

Notes

1. Parmenides, VS, B 1, 28–30. Translation quoted from G. S. Kirk, J. E. Raven, M. Schofield, *The Presocratic Philosophers. A Critical History with a Selection of Texts*, 2nd ed. (Cambridge: Cambridge University Press, 1983), 243.

2. Plato, *The Republic* 475e. Translation quoted from *The Republic of Plato*, trans. with notes, an interpretative essay, and a new introduction by Allan Bloom (New York: Basic Books, 1968).

3. Cf. Günter Figal, Die Wahrheit und die schöne Täuschung. Zum Verhältnis von Dichtung und Philosophie im platonischen Denken, in *Kunst. Philosophische Abhandlungen*, 203–20 (Tübingen: Mohr Siebeck, 2012).

4. Plato, *The Sophist* 242c–243b. Cf. Günter Figal, "Beteiligter Blick von außen. Die literaturgeschichtliche Bedeutung der Philosophie als Literatur," in *Freiräume. Phänomenologie und Hermeneutik*, 82–92 (Tübingen: Mohr Siebeck, 2017).

5. Cf. especially section 301 of Nietzsche's *The Gay Science*.

6. The expression translated by "venturing language," "*die Sprache wagen*," is to be found in Heidegger's essay "Wozu Dichter," in *Holzwege, Gesamtausgabe*, Band 5 (Frankfurt am Main: Vittorio Klostermann, 1977), 269–320, 310; English translation, "What Are Poets for?" in *Off the Beaten Track*, trans. J. Young and K. Haynes (Cambridge: Cambridge University Press, 2002).The understanding of poetry as foundation of a historic people is mainly developed in the essay "The Origin of the Work of Art," in Martin Heidegger, *Holzwege*, GA 5, 1–74; English translation in Heidegger, *Basic Writings*, ed. David Farrell Krell, 139–212 (London and New York: Harper Perennial, 1993).

7. Cf. Hans-Georg Gadamer, *Wahrheit und Methode*, in *Gesammelte Werke* 1, 118, and also: Die *Aktualität des Schönen*, in *Kunst als Aussage. Ästhetik und Poetik I, Gesammelte Werke* 8, 94–142, 106.

8. Plato, *The Republic* 607b, trans. Allan Bloom (New York: Basic Books, 1968).

9. Richard Rorty, *Contingency, Irony, and Solidarity* (Cambridge and New York: Cambridge University Press, 1989), 97, 102–103.

10. All quotations are from: T. S. Eliot, *Four Quartets* (London: Faber and Faber, 1944).

11. Hermann Diels and Walter Kranz, eds., *Die Fragmente der Vorsokratiker*, 7th ed., vol. 1–3, vol. 1: Heraclitus B 2 and B 60 (Berlin: Weidmannsche Buchhandlung, 1954).

10

An "Almost Imperceptible Breathturn"

Gadamer on Celan

GERT-JAN VAN DER HEIDEN

Hans-Georg Gadamer opens his most extensive essay on Paul Celan's poetry, "Who Am I and Who Are You?" as follows:[1]

> In his later volumes of poetry, Paul Celan increasingly moved toward the breathless stillness of muted silence in words which have become cryptic. In what follows, I will examine a sequence of poems from the book *Breath-turn*, which was first published . . . under the title "Breathcrystal."[2]

In only two sentences Gadamer discloses two important motives in Celan's poetry. The first concerns the word *breath*: we encounter here three terms including this word: a breathless stillness, a breathturn, and a breathcrystal. As we know from his famous speech *Der Meridian*, this word goes to the heart of Celan's understanding of poetry: "Literature/poetry [*Dichtung*]: that can signify a turn-of-breath [*Atemwende*]."[3] The second motive concerns the stillness, the muteness and the silence of Celan's poetry, which Gadamer combines with the secrecy or mysteriousness to which they give rise: what Celan's poetry is trying to say remains almost imperceptible. As no other,

Gadamer understands that these two motives of breath and stillness are intrinsically connected since nothing is as "quiet and almost imperceptible as the breath-turn."[4]

In this essay, inspired by Gadamer's interpretations of Celan's poetry, I will address the question of why Celan's poetry is so important for philosophical hermeneutics. Clearly, the insights of philosophical hermeneutics also apply to Celan's poems, and it is therefore not surprising that one can trace many aspects of this theory of interpretation in Gadamer's reading of Celan.[5] Yet, this is not what interests me here. The assumption from which my questioning departs is that Gadamer reads Celan's poetry not simply as a reader who interprets this poetry, but rather because this poetry speaks to philosophical hermeneutics, that is, has a particular significance for philosophical hermeneutics, its categories, and its limits. In this way, Gadamer's account of Celan's poetry may be understood as a dialogue between philosophy and poetry in which philosophy aims to *experience* Celan's poetic language. As Gadamer makes clear in his reflections on experience (*Erfahrung*) in *Wahrheit und Methode*, this means in the first place that philosophy experiences that "something is not what we supposed it to be."[6] Therefore, when poetry truly speaks to philosophy, its philosophical framework—concepts, categories, presuppositions, and so on—will be affected and its understanding changed.

To get a sense which dimensions of philosophical hermeneutics are affected by the confrontation with Celan's poetry, consider the following quote in which Gadamer uses three keywords—instant or moment (*Augenblick*), restraint or reserve (*Ansichhalten*), and hope (*Hoffnung*)—to articulate the significance of Celan's poetry:

> I do not want to deny that Celan does not only associate this moment of turning breath, this instant [*Augenblick*] when breath returns, with calm self-restraint [*Ansichhalten*], but that he also allows the subdued hope [*leise Hoffnung*] bound up with every return to resonate.[7]

In what follows, I shall take these three keywords as my guideline and shall explain which philosophical notions are at stake in these three keywords and how they are affected by the confrontation with these two basic motives of Celan's poetry: the breathturn of the poem and the stillness and secrecy of the poem.

The Poem and the Moment

One of the basic insights of philosophical hermeneutics is that a reader always reads texts in context, that is, in the concrete situation in which the reader finds him or herself. Therefore, as Gadamer insists, reading has always been understood as *application* in hermeneutics: How does the text—its opinions about a certain subject matter, its demands, its religious conviction, and so on—apply to the concrete situation of the reader? This, one might say, is the miracle (or the "ideality")[8] of the text: despite coming from another context, the text has the capacity to speak to a reader in another situation. This capacity indicates that the text includes possibilities that could not be brought to light in other contexts; these possibilities are disclosed at the very moment the text is applied to the reader's situation. Gadamer calls this time of understanding the "moment of interpretation" (*Augenblick der Auslegung*).[9]

In this moment, the reader discovers in the text possibilities that concern his or her own situation and which therefore belong to the text as well as to the situation. This double belonging marks what Gadamer calls the *hermeneutic experience* of the interpreter and which means two things at once.[10] First, it means that the text becomes, in this moment of interpretation, significant to the reader since it applies to his or her own situation. Yet, second, the text becomes significant because it has something to say that the reader did not yet (fore)see. The text thus becomes a "vis-à-vis" of the reader—*ein Gegenüber*, as Celan suggests; or, as Gadamer writes, the text becomes a you who brings into play another point of view, another demand, another promise, another judgment, and so on.[11] To apply the text to one's own situation implies that the reader takes these claims or demands of the text seriously and reconsiders his or her own perspectives accordingly. Borrowing Heidegger's concept of resoluteness (*Entschlossenheit*) by which Heidegger describes the moment (*Augenblick*) of disclosure, one might perhaps say, without doing injustice to Gadamer, that an application of a text can only take place, in the moment, if the reader resolutely adopts the task to be open, that is, to reconsider his or her situation in light of the new possibilities the text discloses.[12] The disclosure of the possibilities of the text goes hand in hand with this particular ethos of the reader. Such a moment of interpretation as application might also be called "the event of meaning."[13]

Thus, the moment of understanding is a moment in which an encounter takes place with a text that, as a you that speaks to the reader, says something that is foreign or strange (*fremd*) to the reader but that nevertheless becomes significant and important because it allows the reader to discover his or her own situation in light of other possibilities that are to be taken seriously—whether this situation concerns a philosophical problem, a moral demand, a religious conviction, or something else.[14] All this happens at the moment when the text speaks to the reader, that is, when the reader applies the text to his or her own situation.[15]

This reference to the moment, the you, and the speaking of a text prepares us for a transition to the work of Paul Celan who uses the same vocabulary as Gadamer uses here but who slightly displaces it, thus constituting for philosophical hermeneutics the poetic vis-à-vis that may speak to it. In fact, to make the transition and to grasp the slight displacement with which Celan's poetry confronts hermeneutics, it might be enough to replace the "when" of the final sentence of the previous paragraph by an "if": Celan is not concerned with the moment, the you and the speaking of a poem as terms that describe what can be presupposed as the structure of interpretation—that is, as what always happens when interpreting—but rather as the terms that are at stake in interpretation: they describe what, perhaps, may happen, but may just as well not happen.

One of the main sources in this respect is Celan's famous speech "Der Meridian," which was held on the occasion of his receiving the Georg Büchner Price in October 1960. In order to explain Celan's point of view, I will offer an interpretation of the following passage from the Meridian-speech:[16]

> Literature [or poetry: *Dichtung*]: that can signify a turn-of-breath. . . . Perhaps it succeeds since strangeness [*das Fremde*], that is, the abyss *and* the Medusa's head, the abyss [*Abgrund*] *and* the robots [*Automaten*], seem to lie in the same direction—perhaps it succeeds here in distinguishing between strangeness and strangeness [*Fremd und Fremd*], perhaps at precisely this point the Medusa's head shrivels, perhaps the robots cease to function—for this unique, fleeting moment? Is perhaps at this point, along with the I—with the estranged I, set free *at this point* and *in a similar manner*—is perhaps at this point an Other [*ein Anderes*] set free?[17]

For sake of clarity, let me note that the figures of the Medusa's head and the robot are borrowed from the work of Georg Büchner. According to Celan, Büchner uses these figures to describe how poetry petrifies the natural, and how poetry automates and mechanizes the natural. He interprets this petrification and automation as follows: "Here we have stepped beyond human nature, gone outward, and entered a mysterious realm [*unheimlichen Bereich*], yet one turned toward that which is human."[18] The word *unheimlich* refers to the same direction beyond human nature as the word *fremd* does; yet, at the same time, in a rather Heideggerian style, this realm of the mysterious or the strange is "turned toward that which is human," that is, it concerns and addresses human beings and has something to say about human beings. Celan adds that this characterization of art might also apply to literature and poetry: "perhaps literature [or poetry: *Dichtung*] . . . travels the same path as art, toward that which is mysterious [*das Unheimliche*] and strange [*das Fremde*]."[19] Thus, in its petrification and automation, poetry moves beyond the human realm toward a realm of what is mysterious and strange. The Heideggerian overtones of the terms *mysterious* and *strange* have not gone unnoticed in the literature, yet it is important to see what Celan does with them.[20]

In the above long quote, Celan emphasizes "the abyss *and* the Medusa's head" and "the abyss *and* the robots." By doing so he says on the one hand that the abyss is found in the same direction—beyond the everyday human being—as the Medusa's head and the robot, but also that the abyss introduces something that distinguishes itself from petrification and automation. In *Der Meridian* also the figure of the abyss stems from Büchner's work, namely the latter's story *Lenz* in which the protagonist is said to experience "a sense of uneasiness because he was not able to walk on his head." To this Celan adds, "whoever walks on his head has heaven beneath him as an abyss."[21]

These remarks on abyss and heaven are quoted by Gadamer in his comment on *Mit erdwärts gesungen Masten* of which I quote here the first part:

> With masts sung earthwards,
> heaven's wrecks are sailing.
> Into this wood-song
> you firmly sink your teeth.
> You are the song-firm
> pennant.[22]

This poem clarifies the usage of heaven and abyss in the Meridian-speech because it brings a number of things together (which as such cannot be found in Gadamer's interpretation). The shipwreck is not simply an accident but it expresses a catastrophe. That we indeed have to think here of a catastrophe is affirmed by the fact that these wrecks are sailing upside down, with their masts directed to the earth: catastrophe originally means to overturn; a catastrophe is that which turns everything upside down. Consequently, these ships sail as Lenz wanted to walk, namely upside down, on their heads, with the heaven as an abyss beneath them. Apparently the earth—as ground or as sea—no longer offers any support but is rather exactly what is in need of support and rescue: the song that is sung by the masts has a reversed direction, from the heaven to the earth.[23]

This poem—and this is why Gadamer's reference to the Meridian-speech is so accurate—discloses the double role of the abyss. On the one hand, the abyss is the abyss opened up by a catastrophe that puts the whole world upside down, that destroys the world. "The world is gone," as Celan writes elsewhere, indicating that neither ground nor soil nor earth offers any support: the space in which we were once rooted, that offered us shelter, and that determined our place and significance in the world is gone.[24] The abyss (*Abgrund*) is the opposite of ground (*Grund*): it offers no support and offers no guarantee. On the other hand, however, because the abyss is the space that offers no guarantee whatsoever, it is also the space of a "perhaps," and I will return to this motive of the perhaps more extensively in the next section. Despite being shipwrecked, the masts sing their "wood-song," and it is the figure of the you who clings on to this wood-song by sinking his or her teeth into it; the you is the "song-firm," that is, the one who hangs onto the song and, thus, is the only hope for the poetic song—which is often portrayed by the figure of the I—to have something to sing to the earth. To be able to speak, after the catastrophe that occurred and that put everything upside down, the poem depends on the abyss and on this figure of the you who somehow belongs to this abyss.[25]

The catastrophe of which Celan speaks here has serious consequences for philosophical hermeneutics and its relation to notions such as tradition and *Bildung*. If we ask which world is gone or which world can no longer supports us as it did before, Gadamer includes the following in his answer: Celan's poetry testifies to "being appalled by the weakness [or impotence: *Unkraft*] of the world of *Bildung* [*Bildungswelt*]."[26] This groundbreaking catastrophe therefore puts the hermeneutic presupposition of *Bildung* and tradition upside down. Perhaps one should go even one step farther. The motto to the third part of *Wahrheit und Methode*, borrowed from Schleiermacher, reads: "Everything presupposed in hermeneutics is but language."[27] In German, language or *Sprache* also means speech and is derived from the verb *sprechen*, to speak. Perhaps one might say that it is the hermeneutic presupposition of language and speech that is put into question by the catastrophe to which Celan's poetry bears witness. To put into question—and that means for Celan neither that the poem simply speaks nor that language is simply lost but rather that we are in a space in between these two poles.[28] Therefore, the stakes of Celan's poetry are not only whether the reader listens carefully enough (as Gadamer sometimes seems to suggest), but also whether the poem succeeds in speaking: the unique fleeting moment of its speech is the moment the poem waits for, but without guarantee.

If we return with this reading of *Mit erdwärts gesungen Masten* in the back of our minds to the long quote from the Meridian-speech, we see more clearly the characteristics of the moment to which Celan points. The moment is not simply the moment in which the reader hears the poem, but it is rather the moment at which the poem is granted its capacity to speak. The death of language and the incapacity to speak that resound in the petrification and mechanization of art, and which constitute what is truly mysterious and uncanny (*das Unheimliche*) as well as strange (*das Fremde*) in the era in which we live, waits for something else to happen. It yearns for the "unique fleeting moment" (*der einmalige, kurze Augenblick*) in which the realm of the strange and the uncanny is *bifurcated*: the poetic moment is the moment in which poetry retrieves its capacity to speak. It is of this moment that Celan writes: "perhaps it succeeds . . . in distinguishing between strangeness and strangeness." The time of the poem is, therefore, the moment in which the strangeness of language splits itself into two and in which an abyssal realm breaks away from the realm of a petrified and mechanized language.

In the same part of the Meridian-speech, Celan supplements this complicated account of the distinction between strangeness and strangeness by the following description of the way in which the poem *speaks*. His first statement is: the poem "speaks only in its own, its own, individual cause [*in seiner eigenen, allereigensten Sache*]."[29] Note that Celan writes here "speaks in," which indicates that the poem does not speak *about* its own cause but rather speaks *in defense of* its own cause, that is, testifies to its own cause.

Here, one can once more point out the Heideggerian overtones: the authentic realm is for Dasein its ownmost (*eigenste*) possibility and at the same time, it is exactly what is strange (*fremd*) to itself in its everydayness; therefore, Heidegger uses the category of *Bezeugung*: in attestation, Dasein speaks in its own cause, that is, attesting to its authentic potentiality of being.³⁰ If we follow this suggestion, it becomes clear why Celan places the own, individual cause of the poem parallel to the realm of the uncanny and the strange. Yet, if this is the case, what, then, is this other strangeness identified as abyss? Celan indeed complicates his picture of poetic speech: it does not simply speak in its own case, as if it is closed in on itself, but by this speech, it hopes for another bifurcation, which one might call a bifurcation of the *voice* or the breath of the poem:

> But I think . . . that it has always belonged to the hopes [*Hoffnungen*] of the poem, in precisely this manner, to speak in the cause of the strange—no, I can no longer use this word—in precisely this manner to speak *in the cause of the Other*—who knows, perhaps in the cause of a *wholly Other*.³¹

The phrase "in precisely this manner" refers to the previous quote: by speaking in its own, individual cause, the poem *hopes* to speak in the cause of the other. That is to say, the poem hopes to speak not only as itself but also as an other, to speak for the other, to let the voice of the other be heard. Here we see more precisely in which sense Celan questions the hermeneutic presupposition of language: for philosophical hermeneutics, the text is a you and the text, when it speaks to the reader, speaks as a you to the reader; for Celan, it is rather the hope (and not the given) of poetry to speak as a you and to speak in the case of the other. It is the capacity of the poem to speak for the other and to let the voice of the other be heard that is both the wager and the hope of poetry.

This means that poetic speech not only hopes to enter the realm of the strange—as the realm of what is most own (*das Eigenste*)—but also, and more importantly, at the very moment it enters this realm, hopes to displace and duplicate this realm. When Celan, in the above quote, writes between hyphens that he can no longer use the word *strange*, he once more bifurcates the strange and unfolds the distinction between the strange and the strange as the distinction between the very ownmost and the other. To capture this distinction, and to position it in the right way in relation to the distinction between the everyday ("stepped beyond human nature") and the what is truly one's own, one might use the figure of the cut of Apelles, which is a cut that divides a line not transversally but longitudinally: poetic speech does not only hope to enter the realm of the strange or the uncanny, but hopes to cut the line that separates the strange and uncanny from the everyday and the familiar, into two by dividing it longitudinally, that is, *by dividing it with a meridian*, a line of longitude. Such a longitudinal cut does not lead to another clear-cut division, but rather complicates and displaces the first division.[32]

According to this line of thought, poetry finds its true poetic moment in a breath that cuts, interrupts, and dissects the category of the strange. This dissecting word is not concerned with disclosing the essence of the strange or the mysterious, but rather with disclosing its *remainder* or *reserve,* that is, with what somehow stems from the strange but can no longer be called strange—"no, I can no longer use this word," as Celan writes. Since we are dealing here with the effect of a breathturn, one might call this the pneumatic transformation of the strange that is at stake in Celan's poetry, and the poetic word hopes for and depends on the moment in which the poet's breath turns.

It is both intriguing and telling to considers the poem to which Gadamer refers when addressing this issue of the poem hoping to speak in the case of the other, namely the poem *Harnischstriemen, Faltenachsen*:

> Armored-ridges, fold-axes,
> Breakthrust-points:
> your terrain.
> At both poles
> of the cleft-rose, legible:
> your banished word.
> North-true. South-bright.[33]

In his interpretation of this poem, Gadamer argues (as he quite often does) that Celan's poetry articulates the poetic concern for finding "the true word" (*das wahre Wort*). In the context of this poem, this true word is developed in a particular way. Let me recall that the title of Gadamer's most extensive interpretation of Celan's poetry is *Who Am I and Who Are You?* It refers to the I (*ich*) and the you (*du*) that occur so often in Celan's poems. By referring to I and you, Gadamer directly addresses the heart of the matter, as we have seen: for Celan, poetry succeeds when it speaks in its very own cause, the *ich,* as well as in the cause of the other, the *du*.[34] In *Harnischstriemen, Faltenachsen,* as Gadamer argues, we see how the quest for the true word concerns a word that is not only the poet's or the I's, but is explicitly referred to as the word of the you—the other, or perhaps even the wholly other, as Gadamer suggests.[35] Only if the poem is capable of speaking the word of the you—and thus speaks in the cause of the you, bears witness for the you—the poem truly speaks.

This latter speaking for the you is intensified by Celan's description of the word as "your banished word" (*dein geächtetes Wort*). As Gadamer comments: "The word is 'banished.' This is not simply a strong expression for disdain or scorn. It also means: hated and persecuted. To be banished means to have no legal home [*Heimatrecht*], to be banned and thus outlawed."[36] Because the word of the you is banished, it needs someone to speak for it, to testify for it. Moreover, the cleft-rose refers to orientation—in geology, cleft-rose is an instrument of orientation—based on clefts found in the layers of the earth, that is, in that which cleaves or separates: the word is legible as offering orientation since the word is itself a cleft, a distinction or separation that allows the you and his or her word to be spoken by the poem.

As Gadamer notes elsewhere, this cleft is first and foremost concerned with moving away from the realm of the everyday language. In his interpretation of *Von Ungeträumten geätzt*, a poem which speaks of a deep hunger, Gadamer describes this as follows: "the I renounces all the richly filling words to which one resigns oneself in life—in order to be prepared for the true, luminous word [*das wahre, erleuchtete Wort*]."[37] Hence, the poet turns away from the everyday usage of language in its hunger for the true word, the word that brings brightness and light. He reaffirms this insight as follows: the poem "means language, which is deposited over the entire experience of life like a covering burden. It is language which is probed, that is, tested for its permeability, for the possibility of maybe somewhere permitting the breakthrough into brightness."[38] In poetry, language is probed, examined, to see whether it allows for a "breakthrough into brightness."

In both of these poems, Gadamer remains close to what we discovered in Celan's Meridian-speech: the poetic concern for the true word is a concern for a word that bring brightness by a *breakthrough*. Thus, the true word is a *dissecting* word, a cleaving word. Yet, one might wonder whether this word can truly be captured in terms of brightness, if it is banished and if it depends on the breathturn of the poem: should the breakthrough not be towards the you rather than into a certain brilliance or radiance of appearing? In the next section, we will explore this more carefully.

For now, let me recall that I started this section with a reflection on the moment of interpretation in Gadamer's hermeneutics as the moment in which the text as a you speaks to the reader and receives its significance. Using similar categories, Celan places these categories under the experience of a catastrophe that places everything upside down and this catastrophe is for the poet a crisis in language. Due to this catastrophe, the poem can no longer trust language because in this crisis it was infected by "death-bringing speech" (*todbringende Rede*) and marked by a "terrifying falling silent" (*furchtbares Verstummen*).³⁹ Therefore, poetry as well as language has to *retrieve* its own capacity to speak; it has to find another breath. In this way, the hermeneutic presupposition is put into question by the poem and the poem is concerned with retrieving for language the capacity to speak and for language to become significant again.

The Poem and the Reserve

In both Celan's speeches and his poetry, the significance of the breathturn is surrounded by uncertainty and indecision. As Gadamer notes, Celan's poetry expresses "the uncertain position between belief and disbelief, between hope and despair."⁴⁰ This is reflected in the Meridian-speech: when speaking about the breathturn and the unique, fleeting moment, Celan repeats the word *perhaps* (*vielleicht*) twenty-five times accompanied by three times "who knows," thus removing all ground and certainty of his statements. In Celan's poetry, this "reserve of the 'perhaps,'" as Derrida writes, its uncertainty and its accompanying indecision are reflected in a high degree of discretion, an "indescribable discretion," as Gadamer writes.⁴¹ In fact, Celan's is so much subdued and discrete, that it comes into close proximity of falling silent; Celan's poetry is "the breathless stillness of muted silence [*Verstummen*]," as Gadamer suggests. This stillness indicates the exact place where the poem is located: as it departs from the experience of the terrifying falling silent of language and its death-bringing speech, the poem is placed at the point where stillness reigns, but not as a sheer empty stillness. This is why the word of the poem needs to be discrete: its subdued speech, verging on mere muted silence, is a discrete speech, that is, it holds itself back and thus holds something in reserve, but in the way as someone holding his or her breath tensely while waiting for something crucial to happen without knowing whether it will or can happen.

This particular place of the poem, located on the threshold of silence, also implies that the poetic word does not simply release its meaning; its significance is to be found elsewhere. Gadamer acknowledges this when he writes: "What appears to be a word, bursts as it were, and evokes in its being burst in disseminated [*bedeutungsdifferente*] splinters of word [*Wortsplinter*] a new significance [*Bedeutungseinheit*]."⁴² Although the poem resists our normal attempts to find meaning, it does offer its own significance. What this means, is elaborated, for example, in Gadamer's interpretation of *In die Rillen*.⁴³ In this poem, Celan writes:

> when with trembling fists
> I dismantled the roof over us,
> slate by slate,
> syllable by syllable,[44]

Gadamer emphasizes that the roof that is torn down here is the roof of language. Language gives us shelter; language constitutes a world of meaning and thus allows us to live in the world. Celan's poetry, the I, tears down this roof; this means that what appears to be a meaningful word is torn apart by the poem, leaving us with only splinters of word, or with syllables as the slates of the roof. Yet, by deconstructing word and language, the poem sets free another horizon, namely the horizon of "the unfamiliar," as Gadamer writes, or in Celan's own term that seems to follow immediately from the poem, the horizon of the heaven.[45] In the first part of this poem, it is made known that there we find the you:

> Into the grooves
> of heaven's coin in the doorcrack
> you press the word,
> from which I unrolled[46]

It is highly instructive to see that Gadamer's attempt to interpret these sentences leads him to questions rather than answers or meanings since it shows his appreciation for the particular indecisiveness characterizing Celan's poetry; I will turn to the significance of this indecisiveness in what follows. For now, whatever these four sentences may exactly mean, it is clear that they state that the way to the you is opened up by tearing down the house of language, and with that also the possibility of a revival of language is brought near; yet, at the same time, this possibility is presented in terms of the sheer difficulty for the I to reach the you.[47] Despite this latter difficulty, this poem suggests that the bursting of language—of words in syllables, slates, and splinters—does evoke a new direction, and this is its very significance. Yet, this new significance can hardly be called the meaning or the sense of the poem: it rather concerns its breath—as Celan writes, "breath, that is direction."[48]

If one would argue that interpretation is a process that ends in finding a meaning or a sense, one would have to conclude that these poems resist such an interpretation. This resistance is amplified and supported by the indecision of interpretation to which Celan's poems give rise. When commenting on Gadamer's reading of Celan and especially on the many questions that Gadamer raises—consider, e.g., his reading of *In die Rillen* or of *Wege im Schatten-Gebräch* to which Jacques Derrida refers—Derrida writes: "I admire the respect Gadamer shows for the indecision."[49] This indecision thus goes hand in hand with the interpreter's *incapacity* to find the particular meaning of a poem or of its parts, leaving the interpreter with no other option but to raise questions. To a certain degree, this incapacity belongs to the account of interpretation that marks philosophical hermeneutics: after all, all important texts are marked by the fact that they always offer other possibilities of reading and, thus, hold something in reserve that will only be disclosed when they are applied to new situations and other contexts. Yet, the indecision of Celan's poetry is not identical to the interpreter's incapacity to exhaust its meaning; rather, the indecision belongs to the poem itself; it is part of its very significance. As Celan writes in *Sprich auch du*:

> Speak—
> But keep yes and no unsplit,
> And give your say this meaning:
> give it the shade.[50]

Poetic speech should not separate the no from the yes. By this indecision between yes and no, poetic speech withholds judgment and thus maintains its reserve. In fact, this restraint or reserve is the ethos the poem has explicitly assumed because it is only in this way that it receives significance: it is only by the shadow, the indistinctness and indecision between the no and the yes, that the poem gains its significance.[51] If the poem would already be able to clearly affirm (or deny) something, and would already have secured the results of its own speaking, its waiting for the unique, fleeting moment would be superfluous and there would be no abyss opened up by it. Hence, its significance is to be found in its indecisive relation to this unique fleeting moment of the breathturn and the abyss opened up for it.

More than anything, it is the repetition of the word *perhaps* that indicates the importance of the indecision for the poem; it approaches the unique, fleeting moment in light of its possibility and chance alone: the breathturn is not a result of the poem, but it is what it may hold in reserve, as its secret. Therefore, it need not surprise us that Celan himself describes this breathturn in terms of a secret, a *Geheimnis*. It is important to note that in German, the word *Geheimnis* comes with the adjective *heimlich*—secret. These two words thus constitute the opposite of *unheimlich* and *das Unheimliche*.

Whereas the latter two words stem from the distinction between what is familiar, where we are at home, and where we are not at home, *unheimlich,* the words *Geheimnis* and *heimlich* differentiate between what belongs to the home and its closed circle, and thus a certain interiority or private sphere, on the one hand, and the public realm and everything that does not belong to the interior of the home, on the other. Celan's account of the breathturn as the moment that distinguishes between strange and strange may now also be understood as the moment that distinguishes between *das Unheimliche* and *das Geheimnis.* The *Geheimnis* is concerned with, on the one hand, poetry finding a place to be (a *Heim*) not on earth but in a place that is poetically named heaven and, on the other hand, keeping this place a genuine secret, which is the place of an intimate encounter with the other, in a nonpublic space, a new interiority, which is the "*Geheimnis der Begegnung.*"[52]

The Poem and the Hope

For Celan, the indecision we discussed above is related to the Heideggerian figure of being on the way. He uses this figure in his Bremen-speech when describing the poem as "being *on the way,*" as an "attempt to find a direction."[53] For Celan, to be on the way means to be on the way "toward something open [*Offenstehendes*], inhabitable [*Besetzbares*], an approachable [*ansprechbar*] you, perhaps, an approachable reality."[54] The poem is on the way to a you that can be spoken to (*ansprechen* means to speak to or to address), and it hopes to find the chance to speak to the you by moving toward "*etwas Besetzbares.*" The verb *besetzen,* which is here translated as to inhabit, actually means to occupy, and it is also used in the sense of keeping a place free for someone: the poem hopes to find a refuge in language where the you may take place.

Also in this Bremer-speech, in his account of the poem's being on the way, Celan insists on the word *perhaps*. The poem is not on its way as toward a preestablished or pregiven goal. To be on the way is indeed nothing but an attempt to find *direction*. In the Heideggerian register of being on the way, one should always hear the German expression *auf dem Holzweg sein,* which means to be on an erring way, to make detours, or not to have a clear and definite goal, and thus to be on the way to something unclear and still hidden. This form of being on the way is often also related to the problem of the aporia, to the non-passage and the non-way: after all, to be on the way to a direction means that one moves where one did not yet find a passage or a way. This combination of being-on-the-way and the non-way is present most insightfully in Gadamer's reading of *Wirk nicht voraus*:

> Do not work ahead,
> Do not send out,
> stand
> inward:[55]

In these first sentences of the poem, the I addresses the you. The phrase *wirk nicht voraus* can be translated as don't work ahead, that is, don't set any clear or fixed goal toward which to work—there is no predestined or predetermined goal, as Gadamer affirms in his reading.[56] Also, it indicates: don't send anything or anyone out to announce where you are or to announce your word.[57] Both of these sentences suggest, in light of the poem's being on the way, that there is no direction given in advance leading to the you and that no announcement of the you can help the I to reach the you. The I can only be helped in one way, and therefore the I asks the you: *steh // herein*. Thus, the I asks the you to stand and to stand still: *steh*. The you is asked to stand firm (*standhalten*).[58] Gadamer uses this standing firm also to interpret the *herein*: it is not so much concerned with standing inside—as if the I welcomes the other and says, "please do come in"—but rather with the German expression *"etwas steht herein,"* something stands in the way. Hence, as Gadamer notes, the I asks the you to stand in the way: "be there in such a way that I cannot pass you by."[59] Yet, this particular *aporia* or nonpassage turns out to be an *euporia*, the good way: the I is going nowhere unless, all of a sudden, in a unique, fleeting moment, the you stands in the way in such a way that the I cannot miss the you. It is this unforeseen obstacle and chance encounter that gives significance and direction to this disoriented movement.

This standing in the way of the you has a counterpart in the standing of the I evoked in "Standing, in the shadow" (*Stehen, im Schatten*):

> Standing-for-nobody-and-nothing.
> Unrecognized,
> for you
> alone.[60]

The I or the poem, stands for nothing and for nobody, that is to say, it cannot be known or recognized. Thus, the poem has nothing—no meaning, no object, no person—to offer but itself. Yet, the two other lines indicate that there is one exception: the I stands for the you, stands in the place of the you, in the sense of keeping its place free. Or, as Gadamer writes, "Standing and standing firm means bearing witness to something," that is, to the you.[61] Combined with the previous poem, it becomes clear that this particular testimony will only succeed if it encounters the you—an encounter the poem can only hope for, in its being on the way, if the you stands and stands firm in such a way that the I cannot pass it by, that is, cannot miss it.

In this encounter, the poem "becomes dialogue," as Celan writes, albeit "often despairing dialogue."[62] Also with regard to this ultimate hope of the poem to become dialogue, we discern a particular displacement of the normal philosophical hermeneutic account of dialogue. For Celan, the poem becoming dialogue concerns the following:

> Only in the realm of this dialogue does that which is addressed take form and gather around the I who is addressing and naming it. But the one who has been addressed and who, by virtue of having been named, has, as it were, become a [you], also brings its otherness along in the present, into this present. In the here and now of the poem . . . only in this immediacy and proximity does it allow the most idiosyncratic quality [*Eigenste*] of the other, its time, to participate [*mitsprechen*].[63]

The poetic way to the other requires of the poem a capacity *to speak for* the other (or to speak in the cause of the other, as we saw before). In the common conception of dialogue, one speaks with someone else about a shared subject matter aiming to reach a better understanding of this subject matter. Celan's poetic dialogue puts into question one of the presuppositions of a "normal" dialogue, namely, that both speakers are *present* and *can* speak. The catastrophe by which the world is gone thus gives a particular place to the you. I already quoted the first part of the final sentence of *Große, glühende Wölbung*: "The world is gone." This second part of this sentence reads: "I have to carry you." The you whom the poem addresses is not simply present; he or she retrieves a voice by being named and by being addressed. In this sense, the poem speaks for the you, and the poem's speech is speaking for the you. It does so—and this is the poem's ultimate hope, which cannot be separated from its despair since it cannot assure itself of this hope—not by making the you a puppet of the I, but by letting the voice of the you be present in such a way that it is truly with its very own (*eigenste*) voice that the you takes part in the dialogue, has a say in this dialogue and matters in this dialogue. The turn of breath, on which everything depends, thus concerns the question of whether, when the poem holds its breath, the you gives its breath to the poem.[64] The poem thus speaks for the you, but in such a way that it actually meets the other in its otherness, in its other time and with the other's own voice. In this way, the poetic dialogue aims at a speaking for . . . so that the you may speak "your word," which indeed is a word banished from the dialogue as long as the I does not carry the you.

Conclusion: The Inspiration of Poetry

Celan's attention to words such as *breath, wind,* and *storm,* which are forms of air in movement, lays bare the original meanings of the Hebrew *ruach,* the Greek *pneuma,* and the Latin *spiritus.* The breathturn might be seen as a form of inspiration, as the inspiration of poetry, in both the objective and subjective genitive: poetry breathes its breath in the you and poetry depends on the you for its other breath. The insistence that poetic speech does not stand for anything or anybody else but itself and, at the same time, that poetic speech stands for the you indicates that this speaking for the you, this testimony of the you, of the word and of the breath of the you, is the very core of Celan's poetry. To a certain extent, the words that are spoken by the poem are themselves already too much, except if they take in the other, as Celan beautifully writes in *Unten*: "And the too much of my speaking: / heaped up round the little / crystal dressed in the style of your silence."[65] It is the silence of the you that carries around a small crystal that is taken in or adopted by the speech of the I. To avoid the superfluousness of its words, the poem speaks as discrete, dense, and subdued as possible. Yet, when adopting the silence of the you, these superfluous words of the I become the testimony of this small crystal. In the final poem of the series of poems called *Atemkristall* (published also as the first part of *Atemwende*), this is said in even more clarity. Deeply hidden away, as the poem's secret, there waits "a breath-crystal, / your irrefutable witness," and as Gadamer writes: "This tiny detail is, nonetheless, witness."[66]

The importance of this speaking for . . . is not absent from philosophical hermeneutics. As Gadamer notes, in a wording that is reminiscent of what he writes in *Wahrheit und Methode,* "Reading always means allowing something to speak. The pale, mute signs need articulation and intonation in order to say what they want to say."[67] Yet, this awareness of the interpreter's speaking for the text is always mitigated by the conviction that the text speaks for itself so that it can speak to the reader in the moment of interpretation. If Celan's poetry makes one thing clear, it is that the catastrophe of language requires a more profound reflection on this speaking for . . . ; it is not clear that the words have something to say; rather, they are dispersed in splinters, in letters, syllables, and fragments. Yet, these remainders are still in hope for a unique fleeting moment in which they become the testimony of the you, thus constituting a turn that releases breath for another speech.

Notes

1. The main texts of Gadamer on Paul Celan are collected in Hans-Georg Gadamer, *Ästhetik und Poetik II, Gesammelte Werke 9* (Tübingen: Mohr Siebeck, 1990); hereafter *GW 9*. Some of these texts are translated in *Gadamer on Celan*, tr. and ed. Richard Heinemann and Bruce Krajewski (Albany: State University of New York Press, 1997). When referring to these translated texts, I will refer to the German original as well as the English translation by #a/#b, where #a denotes the page number in the *GW 9* and #b the page number in *Gadamer on Celan*.

2. Hans-Georg Gadamer, "Wer bin Ich und wer bist Du?," in *GW 9*, 383–451/67–165; at 383/67.

3. "Dichtung, das kann eine Atemwende bedeuten" (Paul Celan, *Gesammelte Werke in sieben Bände. Dritter Band* (Frankfurt: Suhrkamp, 2000), 195; hereafter *GW III*). For references to Paul Celan, "Der Meridian," in *GW III*, 187–202, I'm using the translation by Jerry Glenn: "Appendix: The Meridian," in *Sovereignties in Question: The Poetics of Paul Celan*, ed. Thomas Dutoit and Outi Pasanen (New York: Fordham University Press, 2005), 173–85.

4. Gadamer, "Wer bin Ich und wer bist Du?," 388/73. I adapted the translation slightly: rather than "barely perceptible," I put "almost imperceptible," which is a more literal translation of Gadamer's German: "fast unmerklich."

5. See, for a good overview, Gerald L. Bruns, "The Remembrance of Language: An Introduction to Gadamer's Poetics," in *Gadamer on Celan*, 1–51.

6. Hans-Georg Gadamer, *Wahrheit und Methode, Gesammelte Werke 1* (Tübingen: Mohr Siebeck, 1990), 360. Translated as *Truth and Method*, trans. Joel Weinsheimer and Donald G. Marshall (London/New York: Continuum, 2004), 349.

7. Gadamer, "Wer bin Ich und wer bist Du?," 388/73.

8. Gadamer, *Wahrheit und Methode*, 396/392.

9. Ibid., 314/307.

10. Ibid., 360–68/349–55.

11. Celan, *GW III*, 198/181; Gadamer, *Wahrheit und Methode*, 352–53.

12. Consider the following telling quote: "To the anticipation of resoluteness there belongs a present in keeping with which a resolution discloses the situation. . . . We call the *present* that is held in authentic temporality, and is thus authentic [*eigentliche Gegenwart*], the Moment [*Augenblick*]" (Martin Heidegger, *Sein und Zeit* (Tübingen: Niemeyer, 1967), 338; translated by Joan Stambaugh as *Being and Time* (Albany: State University of New York Press, 1996), 311).

13. Gadamer, *Wahrheit und Methode*, 476/468.

14. One might be inclined to refer also at this point to the Heideggerian inspiration: for the reader, the possibilities belonging to the situation and disclosed by the text are, at first, foreign and strange to him or her; that is, the text speaks to the reader with a voice that is experienced as *fremd*, but discloses something that is most proper (*eigen/eigentlich*) to the reader's situation. This seems to be the philosophical hermeneutic rephrasing of what Heidegger says about the discovery or disclosure of Dasein's authentic potentiality-of-being, which is foreign or strange (*fremd*) to Dasein in its everydayness (Heidegger, *Sein und Zeit*, 275/254). Of course, the discussion of *das Eigene* and *das Fremde* in the relation of Heidegger and Celan should also take into account the relation with Hölderlin, as Charles Bambach has shown, cf. Charles Bambach, *Thinking the Poetic Measure of Justice: Hölderlin—Heidegger—Celan* (Albany: State University of New York Press, 2013).

15. To a certain extent, one might read this concern of Gadamer's philosophical hermeneutics as showing the hermeneutic significance of the concept of the event.

16. See also Jacques Derrida, "Majesties," in *Sovereignties in Question: The Poetics of Paul Celan*, ed. Thomas Dutoit and Outi Pasanen (New York: Fordham University Press, 2005), 108–34, in which the theme of the present in Celan's Meridian-speech is extensively discussed.

17. Celan, *GW III*, 195–96/180.

18. Ibid., 192/177.

19. Ibid., 193/178.

20. Cf. e.g., Derrida, "Majesties."

21. Celan, *GW III*, 193/179. Also here, as Bambach rightly observes, one may find a controversy between Heidegger and Celan concerning the meaning of ground and groundless or abyss, cf. Bambach, *Thinking the Poetic Measure of Justice*, 189ff.

22. "Mit erdwärts gesungenen Masten / fahren die Himmelwracks. / In dieses Holzlied / beißt du dich fest mit den Zähnen. / Du bist der liedfeste / Wimpel." (Celan, *GW II*, 20); see Gadamer, "Wer bin Ich und wer bist Du?," 407/99.

23. At exactly this point, I tend to disagree with Gadamer's interpretation stating that the wrecks are looking help on earth, cf. Gadamer, *GW 9*, 408/99.

24. "Die Welt ist fort, ich muß dich tragen" (Celan, *GW II*, 97).

25. In a similar way, Gadamer notes that in *Fadensonnen* Celan hopes for the songs to be sung beyond the human being: in the human landscape—the realm

of the human—there is nothing to hope for and nothing elevated or sublime to find; yet a thought high as a tree (*baumhoher Gedanke*) reaches into the heaven and finds that there are still poetic songs to find there; Gadamer, *GW 9*, 416–17.

26. Ibid., 381.

27. Gadamer, *Wahrheit und Methode*, 387/383.

28. As Celan writes: "Sie, die Sprache, blieb unverloren, ja, trotzdem allem. Aber sie mußte nun hindurchgehen durch ihre eigene Antwortlosigkeiten, hindurchgehen durch furchtbares Verstummen, hindurchgehen durch die tausend Finsternisse todbringender Rede" (Paul Celan, "Ansprache anlässlich der Entgegennahme des Literaturpreises der freien Hansestadt Bremen," in *GW III*, 185–86).

29. Ibid., 196/180.

30. Heidegger, *Sein und Zeit*, 267/247.

31. Celan, *GW III*, 196/180. I've changed "expectation" to "hope" as a translation of *Hoffnung*: the word *expectation* does not capture the deep uncertainty with which Celan surrounds the word *Hoffnung*.

32. The cut of Apelles is also used in Giorgio Agamben, *The Time that Remains: A Commentary on the Letter to the Romans*, trans. Patricia Dailey (Stanford: Stanford University Press, 2005), 49–50. Agamben uses it here to understand in which sense the Pauline notion of *pneuma* does not add a new division (spirit vs. flesh) but complicates the old one installed by the law (Jew vs. non-Jew). Terms such as *breath* (*Atem, pneuma, ruach*) play a similar role in Celan's poetry, as the above considerations suggest.

33. "Harnischstriemen, Faltenachsen, / Durchstichpunkte: / dein Gelände. / An beiden Polen / der Kluftrose, lesbar: / dein geächtetes Wort. / Nordwahr. Südhell" (Celan, *GW II*, 28). Discussed in Gadamer, *GW 9*, 419–22/115–19.

34. This connection between the other as the du, as the one who is addressed, is made explicitly in the Meridian-speech when Celan writes that the addressee of the poem is turned into the you by being named (Celan, *GW III*, 198).

35. Gadamer, *GW 9*, 421/118.

36. Ibid., 420/117.

37. Gadamer, "Wer bin Ich und wer bist Du?," 390–91/77.

38. Ibid., 391/78.

39. Celan, *GW III*, 186.

40. Hans-Georg Gadamer, "Im Schatten des Nihilismus," in *GW 9*, 367–82, at 368; my translation.

41. "la réserve du 'peut-être' (*vielleicht*)" (Jacques Derrida, *Séminaire La bête et le souverain*, Volume I [2001–02] [Paris: Galilée, 2008], 361). Hans-Georg Gadamer, "Verstummen die Dichter?," in *GW 9*, 362–66, at 363. See also 398–400.

42. Gadamer, "Im Schatten des Nihilismus," 371; my translation.

43. Gadamer, "Wer bin Ich und wer bist Du?," 392–95/78–82.

44. "als ich mit bebenden Fäusten / das Dach über uns / abtrug, Schiefer um Schiefer, / Silbe um Silbe" (Celan, *GW II*, 13).

45. Gadamer, "Wer bin Ich und wer bist Du?," 393/81.

46. "In die Rillen / der Himmelsmünze im Türspalt / preßt du das Wort, / dem ich entrollte" (Celan, *GW II*, 13).

47. It can hardly be called a surprise that Gadamer also hears here a reference to the theme of the *Deus absconditus*, of "the most extreme estrangement from God" (Gadamer, "Wer bin Ich und wer bist Du?," 393/80).

48. Celan, *GW III*, 188/174.

49. Derrida, *Sovereignties in Question*, 145.

50. "Sprich— / Doch scheide das Nein nicht vom Ja. / Gib deinem Spruch auch den Sinn: / gib ihm den Schatten," Paul Celan, *Gesammelte Werke in sieben Bände. Erster Band* (Frankfurt: Suhrkamp, 2000), 135; Hereafter *GW I. Paul Celan: Selected Poems*, tr. Michael Hamburger, Christopher Middleton (Middlesex: Penguin Books, 1972), 43.

51. Once one sees this reference to the skeptic movement, one might be surprised to find that in skepticism the moment of *epoche*, of the suspension of judgment, is compared to a body (*soma*) that is accompanied by its shadow (*skia*), the same figure Celan uses here, and the shadow of the *epoche* is nothing but the passageway or significance that skepticism finds in the very failure of judgment (the *aporia*) the failure of the *aporia* in which it finds itself; this new passage is nothing but the *ataraxia*, see Sextus Empiricus, *Outlines of Pyrrhonism*, I.29. It might be added that the skeptic also describes this newly found significance in terms of a chance (*tuchikos*).

52. Celan, *GW III*, 198. Also the word "hopes of the poem" is Celan's expression, see 196.

53. Paul Celan, "Ansprache anlässlich der Entgegennahme des Literaturpreises der freien Hansestadt Bremen," in *GW III*, 185–86, at 186. Here, Celan also refers to Heidegger's conception of *Ereignis* as well as his account of language as *Be-wëgung*, as developed in Martin Heidegger, *Unterwegs zur Sprache, GA 12* (Frankfurt a.M.: Klostermann, 1985), 200.

54. Celan, "Ansprache," 186. Translation taken from Gerald L. Bruns, "The Remembrance of Language: An Introduction to Gadamer's Poetics," in *Gadamer on Celan*, 1–51, at 16.

55. Gadamer, "Im Schatten des Nihilismus," 371–75. "Wirk nicht voraus, / sende nicht aus, / steh / herein:" (Celan, *GW II*, 328). Translation taken from *Breathturn into Timestead: The Collected Later Poetry*, trans. Pierre Joris (New York: Farrar Straus Giroux, 2014), 316.

56. Gadamer refers to the theological notion of *Vorbestimmung*, predestination ("Im Schatten des Nihilismus," 372).

57. At this point, Gadamer notes the connection to the apostles who are being sent out to proclaim the gospel.

58. Cf. Gadamer, "Im Schatten des Nihilismus," 382.

59. Ibid., 372.

60. "Für-niemand-und-nichts-Stehn. / Unerkannt, / für dich / allein" (Celan, *GW II*, 23). Cf. Gadamer, "Wer bin Ich und wer bist Du?," 411–12/104–105.
61. Gadamer, "Wer bin Ich und wer bist Du?," 411/105.
62. Celan, *GW III*, 198/182.
63. Ibid., 198–99/182.
64. This you comes from the outside, as Gadamer notes so carefully: "Es ist etwas von aussen, was hereinstehen, dasein oder kommen soll" (Gadamer, *GW 9*, 373).
65. "Und das Zuviel meiner Rede: / angelagert dem kleinen / Kristall in der Tracht deines Schweigens." Celan, *GW I*, 157. Translation taken from *Paul Celan: Selected Poems*, 47.
66. "ein Atemkristall, dein unumstößliches Zeugnis." (Celan, *GW II*, 31). Gadamer, *GW 9*, 427/126.
67. Hans-Georg Gadamer, "Phänomenologischer und semantischer Zugang zu Celan," in *GW 9*, 461–69/179–88; at 462/181. A similar remark can be found in *Wahrheit und Methode*, 397/394–95.

References

Agamben, Giorgio. *The Time that Remains: A Commentary on the Letter to the Romans*. Translated by Patricia Dailey. Stanford: Stanford University Press, 2005.
Bambach, Charles. *Thinking the Poetic Measure of Justice: Hölderlin—Heidegger—Celan*. Albany: State University of New York Press, 2013.
Celan, Paul. *Gesammelte Werke in sieben Bände*. Frankfurt a.M.: Suhrkamp, 2000.
———. *Breathturn into Timestead: The Collected Later Poetry*. Translated by Pierre Joris. New York: Farrar Straus Giroux, 2014.
———. *Paul Celan: Selected Poems*. Translated by Michael Hamburger and Christopher Middleton. Middlesex: Penguin Books, 1972.
———. "Appendix: The Meridian." Translated by Jerry Glenn. In Jacques Derrida, *Sovereignties in Question: The Poetics of Paul Celan*, edited by Thomas Dutoit and Outi Pasanen, 173–85. New York: Fordham University Press, 2005.
Derrida, Jacques. *Sovereignties in Question: The Poetics of Paul Celan*. Edited by Thomas Dutoit and Outi Pasanen. New York: Fordham University Press, 2005.
———. *Séminaire La bête et le souverain*, Volume I (2001–02). Paris: Galilée, 2008.
Empiricus, Sextus. *Outlines of Pyrrhonism*. Loeb Classical Library 273. Translated by R. G. Bury. Cambridge: Harvard University Press, 2000.
Gadamer, Hans-Georg. *Wahrheit und Methode. Gesammelte Werke 1*. Tübingen: Mohr Siebeck, 1990.
———. *Ästhetik und Poetik II. Gesammelte Werke 9*. Tübingen: Mohr Siebeck, 1990.
———. *Truth and Method*. Translated by Joel Weinsheimer and Donald G. Marshall. London/New York: Continuum, 2004.

———. *Gadamer on Celan*. Edited and translated by Richard Heinemann and Bruce Krajewski. Albany: State University of New York Press, 1997.

Heidegger, Martin. *Sein und Zeit*. Tübingen: Niemeyer, 1967.

———. *Being and Time*. Translated by Joan Stambaugh. Albany: State University of New York Press, 1996.

———. *Unterwegs zur Sprache*, Gesamtausgabe Band 12. Frankfurt a.M.: Klostermann, 1985.

11

Hölderlin's Empedocles Poems

MAX KOMMERELL
TRANSLATION BY CHRISTOPHER D. MERWIN AND MARGOT WIELGUS

Empedoclean Sorrow

How does a poetry such as Hölderlin's become possible? It becomes possible through an aptitude that is uniquely attuned, understanding all that exists as the harmony of many things. An aptitude attuned to completing the harmonizing unity of every individual thing, divided in itself. An aptitude, and also a self, attuned less to delimiting and asserting itself than to opening and preparing itself for crossing over and completing the universe. This quality of mind, which is only for-itself and only lets things be for it in crossing over, responds to the same quality of the universe that first becomes happy about its wholeness when dividing itself into many. As the universe is happy in this dividedness, so too is the poet of the completion of the self and the world also happy. This is merely a philosophical identification of Hölderlin's grace [*Anmut*].

The special type of poetry attuned to it belongs to this harmony as its joy, inasmuch as the harmony of the world only becomes audible through this aptitude of the mind. Contact with the permanent pains this harmony. Both the poet's for-itself and the for-itself of things is the condition imposed by life. While the poet knows and remembers this, others forget it and exaggerate the for-itself to the point of irreconcilable separation. The world renounces the harmony to which the institution of the poet is attuned and, to the extent to which the world hardens into permanence, its rigid assertions of falsity disturb the poetic mind. Insofar as the dismay of the poetic mind is called an insult, it corresponds to the hierarchy between the world-harmony, constantly held by the poet, and the misjudged strife of life. For Hölderlin, that personality firmly holds its own form means little. Inner life, for him, fluctuates between a sense of separation and a sense of unity. The latter is actually the state of inspiration for the poetic mind; the former, of Hölderlinian sorrow.

As Hölderlin's poetry develops in form, in the harmony of the divided among each other and in the confusion of the distinct sobriety of his mind's own essence with that voiceless and nameless element, Hölderlin's mind develops skill [*Virtuosität*] in unlocking itself, in crossing over, in examining natural forces and the way of becoming. This skill strives beyond contingent life. He who masters this skill becomes awkward in human accomplishments and he whose business is poetry becomes idle and is without object in mortal human life. The series of life stages is not a process of becoming milder; rather, that which is for itself becomes stronger. Childhood did not express itself, but possessed itself. Adulthood expressed itself, but missed something. This sorrow, insofar as Hölderlin bears witness to it from his own experience, assumes different forms for different stages of life. It is the grief of lovers. For, as lovers reconcile their singularity and their personal life as a pair restores the unity of the world, so the lovers' lament is the most impassioned separation. It takes place in three stages whose sequence defines other Hölderlinian themes: in the umbral stage of missing something (that is, a Hades of the soul), in the stage of remembrance (to which the all-advising [*Alleratenden*] ache of love opens the universe), and in the stage of restoration (that mythically displaces the boundary between temporal life and originary life). This is the most powerful formulation of personal sorrow. The sorrow can also express itself as a sorrow of a stage of life (as the sorrow of ebbing youth), as nature's grief (which grieves with the earth over its separation from the sun), or as a reflective historical grief (that, in the time of leave-taking, thinks about the remoteness of the gods and their arrival), or, finally, as the prophetic grief of becoming a stranger to the most trusted. But always, the ground of this sorrow is the separation that conditions real life. The state of pure life, the harmony of nature with itself and with the mind of humans is always missed in this sorrow.

This harmony is not, however, originally given and indestructible. It emerges as a free creation—of the word of God and the response of humans, as delicate and disruptible as the harmony that dwells in the mind of the poet. Its sounding and fading away is a destiny—for Hölderlin, *the* destiny—and, to sound, it requires the very mediation, the very mutual relation, through which, for Hölderlin, the gods step out of their hiddenness and over into actual being. The sorrow that is called separation is, thus, being without gods. This is not a nonbeing of gods but, rather, their absence. Because of Hölderlin's piety, for him, life without the gods is not beautiful. Wherever gods are and act, the dividedness of life is void. Wherever the gods step back into hiddenness, the dividedness dominates.

To derive Empedoclean sorrow from this Hölderlinian sorrow (the two are related, though not the same) requires the mediation of a poem that finds a simple, age-old symbol for the sorrow: blindness. It is reminiscent of another, equally simple Hölderlinian symbol: night. Night is a period of time in folk experience and in the life of nature understood in a historical sense (i.e., nature as an occurrence and a becoming). Blindness is something different: it is the inner night of the poet. "Bread and Wine" answers the question: Why is it the night of the poet? The poem of the "blind bard" says why blindness is night in him. And while the sorrow of separation comes and goes and recurs, night suddenly falls over the humans as it falls around the poet at the moment when sight departs. It became night in the poet when he was blinded. What is it to see? What is it to be blind?

To see is to know nature. Just as one knows a person—their actions, their words, their gestures are construed as coming from within—nature is opened to the poet through its generation, movements, and occurrences. The poet construes these as gestures of nature's innerness because he knows it and because it is present in himself. That while wandering as a youth he saw the wings of the heavens (not the clouds) distinguishes the state of the poet who can still see. This is one of the simplest, yet completely esoteric, descriptions of Hölderlinian nature mythology. The life of nature's movements as gestures of the soul did not become accessible to the poet through study [*Forschung*], but through induction. This enabled him to perform poetic naming, of which, here, one is given as an example for all. This reading, a linking and interpretation based on lore, is a gift to which nature must assent and that is bestowed only upon the open of heart. Since it is a gift, it can be taken away. To live with this blessed understanding means: to see. To be expelled from it means: to go blind. Blindness continually signifies the poet's grief as the indication of a missing state. Seeing, as he saw before, does not return. Conversely, another, more spiritual seeing is freed, exploding from the form of his human *Dasein*.

This is a tragic ode, a poem that borders on the tragic, since it does not proceed to the deciding moment. In the tragic moment of tragedy, in the midst of a rending reversal of opposites, what is actually meant appears meaningful in a way that can only be illuminated in actual death. Hence, what is actually meant does not appear prior to this moment. Empedoclean sorrow attempts to interpret itself, but it is first adequately interpreted in the moment of death. In the moment of death, inasmuch as it can be represented in the play [*Drama*]—the death of Empedocles performs itself in speech before it is truly carried out.

The Empedocles poem, just like every tragic ode, therefore, proceeds from the missing [*Vermissen*] of a pure state to a restoration of the same. If this restoration is death, all of the prior exposition is only significant in view of the meaning of this final moment. What Empedocles expresses about himself in the rapture of his sorrow is conditioned by his death. If his interpretation of his sorrow does not conform to the meaning of the sorrow that comes out of the last tragic moment of restoration, this is no mistake on the part of the poet. Rather, it is the actual process through which Empedocles continually and more truthfully construes himself. The sorrowful Empedocles interprets his sorrow out of indebtedness. It is not as if this were invalid. It is valid so long as it defines the events of the drama from the reversal between human states. Later, the events become apparent in his person and define him. Subsequently, Empedocles no longer mentions his self-destructive guilt, and precisely where he most strongly feels the inevitability of his death he does not find words to grasp it as a death of atonement for his sacrilege. It is not atonement but, rather, the purchase price.

So that the theme of the Hölderlinian gods is not, therewith, exhausted, I must add a word about them here. For, without this, the very sacrilege that Empedocles himself committed would remain unintelligible. What is strange, and what the gods indicate, is the gods' own dependence upon the human soul [*Geist*]. This is opposite to the usual representation. The gods are the spirit of the elements, imparting life to all, the consistently self-establishing unity of life. They dwell within, but it requires a special act for them to come to themselves. In addition, it is necessary that they be recognized. The gods need humans and, indeed, humans that recognize them as the reflective medium, in which the gods recognize themselves. Without humans, the being of the gods is only latent. Now, it lies in the nature of the human soul to misunderstand this act. That humans recognize the gods means that the gods recognize themselves. The misunderstanding is that the human soul supposes that this recognition is the recognition of itself. For, the discrepancy in rank between gods and humans is strangely equalized by the fact that the gods are defenseless and the humans hold the weapon of their soul against them. While together in harmony with the gods, and the gods in harmony with themselves, Empedocles gloried [*genoß*] in himself. And by thinking only of himself, the gods were able to forget themselves in him.

This sacrilege was so convincing in Empedocles's words and expressions and Empedocles was, thereby, so strongly driven into his memory that the gods withdrew from the intimacy in which they lived with him. More loosely considered, the sacrilege is only his life itself, the life that Empedocles, as an individual person, must lead and, thus, not more or less sacrilegious than this whole life in general. As the relationship to the gods is thought here, the soul stands in contradiction with itself. According to its essence, the soul is the self-assertion of the human in the ownness of his individual form. In encountering the gods, the reverse would be credited to him [*wird ihm das Umgekehrte zugetraut*]: that the gods remember themselves while he forgets himself. He must give himself up, whereby he ceases to be Empedocles, or he must assert himself. He can only perform self-assertion in doing violence to the gentle defenselessness of the very gods that still threaten his life with dissolution. He first knows what he has done when he misses them—he does not pluck up real, genuine, hubris in this missing, in the Promethean enjoyment of his own power, although it draws near to him. "Dawn shall rise, from my own flame!"[1]

Now, the fact that the language Hölderlin otherwise connotes with many increments between imperative and prohibition seems to be, here, nothing other than that one such violence comprises the horizon of this poem. This violence offends the gods, above all, through speech. As there is a concrete moment of restored intimacy, paid for by a death that is decided and tasted in advance, so there must also be a concrete moment of affront to the gods. And when one keeps in mind the idea that the soul uses its supremacy against the relatively defenseless gods, the different forms that this violence against the gods takes hang together. These forms are: inwardly setting itself over nature, expressing the intimacy, wantonly expressing what the human soul has achieved in this mediation, directly expressing its own divinity, and, finally, exciting delirium in people by expressing these things. The first form is the subtlest interiority. The last form shows a striving toward reification. It would be a mistake to import the concept (from Hölderlin's hymns into the first and second Empedocles fragments) that the sacrilege is the expression at a particular point in time rather than the expression in itself. Empedocles's spoken sacrilege is a sacrilege in itself, brought about by the pretention of the soul, not by untimeliness. In the last fragment, in which the fermentation of time becomes the central concept, there is not even the slightest hint of that earlier sacrilege. Plainly, as long as the soul persists on the mortal level, the soul is unable to completely replace the gods without preserving itself. Empedocles still truly felt himself and the gods in himself—thus, he named himself a god. In truth, he neither offended the gods, nor did they punish him. He must have missed them, since he gave up the comportment of openness and self-forgetting (the sole comportment in which they were perceptible) and, thus, they were no longer there. The same thing makes itself known in an echo. The gods that had withdrawn from his being [*Wesen*] could no longer be present in communicating this being to others. Thus, Empedocles's divine ecstasy dimmed to a shadow, devoted to a shadow of the gods and recognized the person who remained alone and destitute. Empedocles survived untransformed and had to live on in the way of humans. All of this had to happen so that proceeding humanly was a false continuation of the same intimacy. In that the gods withdrew, they taught him rightly, baited him away from false human self-assertion. He had to exaggerate humanly [*menschlich*] before he humanly extinguished himself.

Prior to every impure moment when the encounter with the gods enmeshed the soul in its own contradiction, there was an earlier, more inspired moment that endowed intimacy. Likewise, every impure communication [*Mitteilung*] of possession that went to the people was preceded by the time of Saturn, when the people, bound by love, presagingly took part in a life on the Empedoclean level together. This, as always, was a crossing over and it had to be broken in the continuation of life. In a true act of communication, Empedocles would only still be if the god passed over into the people through him—he was, however, only given the ability to so mediate in death. "For, if only once,/We blind ones required a miracle."[2]

But why all of this, if gods are gods and if they love the human, as Empedocles loves them? Why this sequence of annihilating him, from intimacy to the soul's entanglement in itself and to the reestablishment of intimacy through free death? Why not the alternative, the religious tradition that protects humans from the gods and the gods from the humans? In Hölderlin's poetry, this tradition is a lie told by the priests, a lie in which the gods themselves have no part; but the sequence of annihilation becomes the enigmatic truth of his alluring lines. He calls it Zeus's arbitrariness. He does not interpret this path from humans, but from the gods themselves. In fact, this path becomes the suffering humans' path of destiny. Divinity is one. It divides itself in order to enjoy its indivisibility and, through the pain of division, wants to return to itself. That is the teaching of the gods' life. This life encloses in itself Empedocles's sorrow and free death as a condition of being-there. This teaching seems to border closely on pre-Socratic doctrines of being: it is not a scientific doctrine and, in it, being announces itself to the mind of the poet, who, out of his human purity, replenishes the fragmented world. Being announces itself in a language that is not, however, perceived but, rather, is and fulfills itself.

The distance between the very highest human organization of the "blessed" from the arbitrariness of Zeus seems far and, yet, the latter returns to the former. The blessed one must be how he is so that divinity plays its game with itself. In this lies the enormous luxury of individuality: that it completes itself in a singular, irreplaceable worth although no one aims for it at all, although it adorns itself only for its own annihilation—not with tragic bitterness, but with vibrant gaiety. Again, it is a human position, the position of the short-lived, to want to squander itself in this way. The human, forgotten by the gods—how gladly he forgets the gods!

Hölderlin—Empedocles

The foreshadowing statement, the concealment in the statements, is Hölderlin's poetic comportment. It determines not only the shape of his language, but also his poetic forms. In his theoretical essays, he admits that the poem progresses by contrasting the basic tone of the poem (its actual mood) with its aesthetic character (its bearing) and that the poem has to protect its true intimacy at the beginning. This law of the conditioned statement ultimately manifests itself in the setting up of a symbol, in the sense of a self-externalization. A content [*Gehalt*] that is not of the poet, and temporal relations of the same sort, and, in the end, a deed that purely expresses the intention, but which does not lie within the poetic profession as such, this is supposed to take the place of the entirety of poetic sensibility. This cannot be done by the immediacy of a poem that dispenses with the symbol. Hyperion, a hermit in Greece and the disappointed hero of a failed renewal (rather than Hölderlin and rather than poets) meets a non-Hölderlinian fate.[3] *Hyperion* thus salvages Hölderlin's life, in its entirety, more than any other poem. Conversely, if Empedocles progresses less lyrically than Hyperion, in contrast to Hyperion with regard to reification, Empedocles distinctively describes a historically particular action (the free death) in a particular environment. Empedocles embodies more of Hölderlin than Hyperion does, to the degree that Hyperion removes himself further from Hölderlin.

In enunciating his name, one does not perceive a means of representation, as in *Hyperion*. But also, compared to the later hymnic declaration, the *Empedocles Poems'* ownmost lies in the fact that it grasps everything abstracted by the directness of the hymns. Empedocles is Hölderlin's unique, unrepeatable mystery, and the only one of his poems that completely contains his personal religiosity.

If this pertains to the veiled nature of the symbol, then tragedy, in Hölderlin's sense, is the genre of unveiling. For, according to his designation, tragedy contains an intellectual assumption, something that cannot be achieved from the concept and that, within the poetic forms, corresponds to the mythical state of life. It is precisely from the perception of particulars in the whole, and the whole in the particulars, in which Hölderlinian concept of intimacy, as a friendly dwelling-in-each-other, can be seen at its most extreme. But this means that the state of life toward which Hölderlin's religiosity aims can only be achieved at the end of life, in a tragic procession of events. For only such an end contains the decision between the abrupt crossover of extremes, the decision in which the pure emerges. This decision completes the course of one's whole life in order to more deeply feel the pain of separation. The death of a man fulfills the return of this whole of life to itself. In this, the endlessness of life is restored to itself. This can be put more precisely. The course is becoming in its decaying and it does not contain the death of the individual as its condition once or arbitrarily, but rather, always and necessarily. Therefore, Empedocles can say, "And what is yet to happen already is accomplished."[4]

Empedocles is not a poet, but precisely for this reason he can communicate something about Hölderlin's poetic vocation that Hölderlin himself cannot immediately communicate. The concealment, the falling silent, is inherent in Hölderlin's speaking. It is also present in the effect of this saying: as the half-heard, as the unheard, of this speaking. In this, one may amend the meaningful, though youthful, remark that Hölderlin is the poet of poets. Hölderlin overturns the essence of the poet itself: his poetry as a riddling expression is knowingly conditioned by the fact that it is unheard.

By its nature, a celebratory saying [*feierliches Sagen*] aims toward celebration [*der Feier*]. At the end of Hölderlinian elegies, instead of celebration, the opposite notion appears. The one who is still enraptured discovers his loneliness and painfully contents himself with grasping the hand of a simple friend.

Beyond the fact that Empedocles is not there to speak, and that a false speaking leads to a false hearing, lies the decision of time. Time is demonized as the spirit of time and finally mythologized as the God of time. Now, in the earlier versions of the poem, where can one grasp this character and power of the moment? Not in Empedocles himself, but in the condition of collective life. We would have to guess at this condition if it were not fixed in a schematic figure, namely, the priest. The priest represents people in their reality, while Empedocles represents people in their ideality. For the grim, soul-crippling magic that originates in Hermocrates and lies over the people is nothing other than the condition of collective life itself, which satisfies itself through an excess of separation. It appears in others besides Hermocrates: in the farmer who sends Empedocles away, in all of the hexes and curses that affect Empedocles, and perhaps also, in his self-destruction. But Hermocrates stamps this condition with the official seal of the false myth, he makes this condition ceremonial [*feierlich*] and sacred.

Hermocrates is an enemy of becoming. He condemns becoming to rigidity. Hermocrates makes the daring that wants to re-entrust something that persists to becoming shrink back by enslaving it. In this enslaving, he strikes humans, in contrast to the gods. To him, religion is anguish, not freedom. He murderously eradicates all of the beginnings that Empedocles wants to bless.

In his striving, Hermocrates is aligned with the striving of time. Hermocrates is the sustainer of all division and the guarantor of all that persists against the strength of the gods. And, like time itself, to release himself, Hermocrates brings forth time's reversal in Empedocles. Hermocrates drives Empedocles into the comportment of a religious reformer, for whom association with the gods is not fixedly established and is not a regulated business. Instead, it must be newly redefined out of his own inner being in correspondence to the truth of becoming. A twofold myth is, thereby, generated: the hearsay of the gods as a false, inflexible, man-made myth, the experienced patron as authentic myth, as dangerous and as endangering. For the priest, it operates as the actual realization of the old titanic powers of turmoil, castigated in old mythology, and his reproach appears right because Empedocles, too, in his sorrow, describes himself as a defiant Tantalus. The distinct versions of the poem differentiate themselves by Empedocles's actions and inactions. As a contingent being, Empedocles's actions and inactions lead out from temporal relationships through opposition, while his innermost predisposition is only conditioned by itself. Nevertheless, in the later versions, this predisposition itself is primordially determined to the equilibrium of hostile extremes by the daemon of time. The daemon of time is no longer merely the fact of occurrences. Rather, it designates itself and not against the gods. It is the contradiction of God with itself.

This is the becoming of the Empedocles-figure in the passage through the different versions. First, he is without destiny, then he has a destiny, then he is destiny. But what is the substance of this destiny? A loving encounter between a human and nature, whereby nature consecrates this human in itself while the human himself enriches nature by the strength of his spirit, better acquaints the spirit with itself so that they trade essences. But this encounter is not poetic in the sense that the poem captures what life transcends but, rather, in that this transcending becomes fatal for the chosen human who knows it and bears himself toward such a death.

More important than demarcating particular versions according to these differences, whereby anticipation and reversion hinder a precise divide, it is important to see the direction. The direction aims, on the one hand, toward the growth of knowledge (Empedocles's self-knowledge, and Hölderlin's knowledge of Empedocles). On the other hand, what the individual is disappears. This is not, however, to be understood in the classical sense. The individual traits, perhaps those of the poet, are smoothed over, becoming more and more generic. Hölderlin is a stranger to this turn from the personal to the commonly human. Rather, it primarily evolves from out of the person, from out of a disposition that is somehow attuned, that something to which a person is attuned: a living out. This carries itself out through a human who is attuned to it. But, in the end, this carrying out no longer emanates from the individual at all. Instead, forces handle their own process with each other through the individual. Thus, out of freedom comes necessity. Empedocles's self-knowledge imitates this process; indeed, it is acted out in him. The process permeates him and annihilates him as individual. In this, the process acquires its primordial conditions, which lie beyond all personality. And, as one who knows, Empedocles loses himself in the elements and beginnings of the world. He is no longer his own ground. This reversal of a predisposition that was attuned to nature due to a calling of destiny and the self-permeating knowledge as the strength of reversal is, however, at the same time, wholly Hölderlin's poetic way. In this respect, his biography is esoterically included in Empedocles. At the beginning of the poem, there was the sorrow as the absence of the good among humans in the real world, toward which the predisposition of the poet was initially attuned. In the middle lies the poetic self-fulfillment that reconciles in another way, like the reconciliation of Empedocles. In this reconciliation, the person is still the medium in which human being-there is voluntarily permeated with the undulations of the universe. At the end of the poem lies the dissolution wherein the human form no longer maintains itself. Rather, the human is torn away from endless becoming or the prophetic statement, that is, the "to-be-said" that was sealed within the poet, which breaks him in order to be revealed. The last stages of the drama and the last stages of Hölderlin's life look strikingly alike. In both, the god of time alone rules.

Yet, Empedocles's self-knowledge has a boundary, to be seen in a poetic symbol that must be explained. But even so, its explanation does not allow for a complete articulation. In fact, Empedocles must articulate the totality of the condition of his life in poetic language that represents the sentiment in the constraint of the moment. The mental acuity of knowing, torn from the moment, must be left to another's mouth. That is, in this poem, it must be left to those who know: first, Panthea and, last, Manes. It must also be left to those who know from a second degree: the young man who, as the spiritual son of the teacher, cannot completely comprehend it and the opponents, the priest and the archon, who both, by virtue of their distant view of and rivalry with Empedocles, however, contribute something indispensable to an interpretation of his essence. Empedocles, in the distance of missing, can completely articulate his previous intimacy with nature. He nurtures himself with multifaceted justifications and interpretations (that hang together through rapture) of the sacrificial death that lies before him, but he does not have the last word. Given that the interpretation of sorrow as the consequence of a sacrilege sounds like the bias of the human "I" is not adequate, so too, then, the notion that a free death would redeem the dishonor of debasement (that not only affected Empedocles, but also the gods in him) seems inadequate. While, at the beginning, Panthea more deeply unravels the sorrow, after the sacrifice was performed, she and the young man together express the meaning of this sacrifice more thoroughly than Empedocles previously could. She clarifies what Diotima actually was, which, here, does not amount to the proper contents of a romantic relationship. Through the consecration of nature, Diotima was the most deeply knowing. Diotima was the interpreter of the world and interpreter of the interpreter—just like Panthea.

Manes was a worthy opponent to Empedocles. He gave full testimony about the Empedocles of this final stage. Manes's fiction makes Empedocles's essence and death a necessary actuality in that, as an unconditioned knower,

Manes derives Empedocles from unending being and from the complete course of time. He offers the interpretation of the moment and, pure in its representation, without referring to Empedocles (whose calling he clearly denies), via the notion of emerging from this moment, Empedocles must appear in the manner of dissipated humans (as described above)—abstract, in a manner of speaking, as he must appear in any sequence of events. If, therefore, in this great dialogue, Empedocles's self-regarding conclusion, whose content is his uniqueness, confronts Manes's intrinsic pronouncement about the particular, necessary, and recurring bearer of an Empedoclean attunement, it is completely coherent that Hölderlin characterizes these contrasting understandings by contrasting Greece and Asia. One rushes through its course in life driven by itself, then in sorrow through itself and, finally, in the voluntariness of self-dissipation. Another thinks of the sequence in precisely the same way, but out of its eternal, for him, constantly recurring evocative premises. This intermittency of occurrences construes the uniqueness of occurrences differently, as this can construe them itself. Fixed being can, in this manner alone, still comprise the most daring transitions of becoming through the notion of repetition, in which becoming ends at the beginning. Empedocles too, for himself, encompasses this manner of observation when, with the words, "Everything recurs,"[5] he sends the student to Egypt where clandestine patrons should be introduced to him. This statement scarcely fails when the old Egyptian man, presumed dead, stands before him.

The Death

As multifaceted as it is, the motivation for Empedocles's free death appears different among the fragments as well as within each fragment. It is not, as might be expected after Empedocles's self-destructive complaints, that he chooses death as atonement for his sacrilege. In fact, Empedocles does not suffer death during the poem. His death is, however, enacted and felt in the rapture of-death anticipated in advance, the condition under which he, in anticipatory exhilaration, established the old relationship to the gods. Any thought of a connection between culpability and atonement is, however, missing in this exhilaration. What has transpired is only thought as the people's offense against Empedocles, not as Empedocles's offense against the gods. His death is, thus, seen as the merely conditional and ephemeral ablution of disgrace. Empedocles's life appears as a whole whose name is "preliminarity" and "stark futility." There are exceptions to this in the opening, solitary moments that Empedocles shares with the young man. These are moments of mythical life, in which earth and light are grasped. What is it toward which these moments internally press? Only now can this question be answered. The moments repeat themselves not only in Empedocles's heightened exhilaration. They also complete themselves in his death, which appears to be the solely authentic, unmistakable, and possible procession of those very moments.

If Empedocles's death is the necessary truth, then his life is the necessary error. What had been deplored as sacrilege is not an independent event, but a constitutive part of the error's necessity. The gods were always around Empedocles. They were never offended. Empedocles only blocked the course of their approach through the false self-assertion of his spirit. When he reopens himself, they pull him back out of vain persistence along the path of becoming, further and more powerfully than ever. This is the course of love.

Empedocles's death discloses another signification, a signification that excludes the signification of atonement: it is a celebration. It is not atonement, it is reconciliation and, yet, it is different from reconciliation. It is the reunification of what was separated. A person strides toward atonement hunched over, but toward celebration gloriously. It is a privilege and, for this reason, it cannot be atonement. Thus, the cause is the effect and the effect, the cause. Empedocles's death is the condition of recovery and the recovery is the condition of death—for he who has been reunited with the gods is only then sufficiently adorned to offer himself up as a sacrifice.

Finally, in contrast to persisting and becoming, this death is Empedocles's affirmation of the same. The anticipation of death, as the headlong rush of becoming, is irreplaceable in Hölderlin's prophetic hymns. Similarly, remaining back behind becoming is also a comportment that stands in contrast to the hastening of time. Empedocles would be guilty of lagging behind becoming if he had remained among the living. The thinkable, though discarded, possibility of Empedocles's continuing to live stands in comparison to the fact that the man is injured in the course of his boyhood years. In the Empedocles poem, the business of the poet (otherwise hurrying ahead to becoming) also appears to be remaining-behind. In Empedocles, Hölderlin portrays only the second half of the path of becoming, in which it hurries back, out of the many and into the one—not, that is, when it hurries out of the one and flows into the many. The return is the jubilant movement of life akin to a bacchanalian parade. This jubilation (which Hölderlin never tires of extolling as the stream that rushes into the ocean) echoes in the mind of the spontaneously devout person. In relation to the divine, such a person knows of nothing serene abiding in the distance. This person is Hölderlin's antithesis to positive religion. By safeguarding human life from the gods, the gods are expelled from positive religion. Empedocles also asserted himself against the destructive nearness of the particularly human ways of relating to the gods, those of a politician, doctor, or poet, and, of course, as a religious leader, who protects himself against the gods by communicating the gods to the people and, thereby, expelling them. The religious leader does not yet understand that his own god-given persistence was only meant as a fleeting crossing over into becoming. Through thorough instruction, the religious leader has unlearned this and holds himself steadfast. Thus, the people call to him, "Abide!"

But why does Hölderlin only portray this second half of the path of becoming? Because it is human history, a history that is only possible after passing through the first half. The destiny of the human condition, which rushes headlong by virtue of becoming, can only come back to humans through dissolution.

Dissolution does not contradict but, rather, corresponds to death as a privilege of higher rank, because only the highest organism freely consents to its own self-dissolution. Hölderlin's unforgettable words give evidence of this: "Through whom the spirit speaks must part betimes."[6] A person of rank necessarily has free will. One can envision it in this way. The divine, in the game of becoming, plays with itself throughout the broad course of nature. The divine needs a person who understands and wants to play the game that is played with him—someone who lends himself to this game though he could also refuse. Since Empedocles's death is inimitable, he also expresses his authoritative rank in opposition to the young man with unexpected brusqueness. For the young man, abiding is beautiful.

Though Empedocles's death is not itself depicted in the poem and is imperceptible in life, his death must exist and be devised in advance. The soul [Geist] only playfully abides in its previous form. It already lives the life of infinitude and still possesses the mortal organs of communication when it reluctantly rushes out. That is the moment of parting, the single real infinitude of finite life. The intoxication of leave-taking, where the one who takes leave is also god, even if previously (in abiding) he was only human, is never so poetically pronounced or philosophically comprehended as it is through Hölderlin.

Death is memory. In death, everything arrives to itself in going out from itself. All of the felicitous moments accumulate in the closing reflection of the last moment, in which time ceases. When a human feels this leave-taking, he performs a gesture in which he does everything that he has always done once again, only more comprehendingly and more beautifully. The meaning of this act is found in its loss of purpose. The parting celebration is to, once again, taste the fruits of the stalk and the juice of the vine—Christ-like, but thanks to the earth. Here, earth reveals what it is: the mother of the gods and the stage of their play, but also the sympathetic friend of the human soul, which has become aged through the human's destiny. The earth signifies that the human is god's affliction, that unending being takes its course through the souls of humans. And if the earth is the green hills of human youth, it is also the chasm of Mount Etna that swallows everything and the goal of the jubilant return. The heavens and the ether are not for themselves; rather, they are earth's playmates.

Even in the first version of the poem, at the presentation of the bequest, an intermediary by the name of the people [*Volk*] (an expression with Hölderinian meaning that one should adopt!) is there, alongside Empedoclean consciousness and the world's unconscious life. Even if in Empedocles's life (now past), which seems idle in retrospect, there was an inaugurating enthusiasm and time well spent with the people [*Volk*]. Even if this time contained literal death, so too the golden "Saturnal days" anticipated the metaphorical death of the people. In this, Empedocles comes across as completely anti-priestly. A priest is someone who sets an absolute boundary between god and human. Priests take human emotion prisoner in churlish fear and they take human awareness of the gods prisoner in the good news that is read to them. Instead of the true myth (which, through its own self-propulsion, agitates communal life), the priest chooses the false security of priestly rule, from which the gods withdraw. These are the same gods that do not want humans to shield themselves against them. By contrast, the priest treats the inner movement of the people as the content of a poem that merely imitates the becoming of the world. Thus, the death of Empedocles is an initial, antecedent gesture. His death is a testament that heartens those who relive his gesture to reach the same spontaneity: "Oh, give yourselves to nature, before she takes you!"[7]

There is a difference between religiously spontaneous people and the religiously oppressed. This difference also prevails between a people that rushes through the period, meted out in advance, between ascent and descent with a hollow sense of hurry and a people that prepare for the end and, upon meeting it, regenerate themselves.

Nature and the religious genius, the two partners in this high game, freely arrange the moment of free death between themselves. History, however, determines the instant for the metaphor of death and for the self-chosen, regenerating death of a people. In other Hölderlin poems, it is also imperative to understand where the poetry begins to admit history as a general form of thought. Already, in the Empedoclean legacy, two historical conditions must be fulfilled. First, a false hardening of mythical life, from which the gods have withdrawn their presence and, second, a yearning that goes through the people, similar to the stirrings of young love that is weary of its burdensome shroud. Then, the legacy itself! It rectifies something that had lapsed in the course of history: leadership by an individual. Empedocles spontaneously led and then the people offered rulership to him in an established capacity. Ever since his youth, Nietzsche remembered Empedocles's answer so well that it came out literally in *Thus Spake Zarathustra*: "The time of the kings is past."[8]

Empedocles's death makes the metaphorical death of a people thinkable. The death comes out of Empedocles himself, as voluntary and necessary as the song that comes from the poet. It is difficult to capture what Hölderlin did to change or rather, to reverse, this relation. Nature disclosed itself to Hölderlin, though not as the language of a timeless soul, perceived in the same timelessness of the poet's mind. Rather, Nature disclosed itself as the language of an occurrence that urges itself forth and narrows itself into a moment only perceptible to him. Henceforth, his poetry is the reception of certainty in the deepest terrified sounding out in the vastness of what has not yet occurred. Through the expression of this reception of certainty in words, his supple voice acquires inevitability. Perhaps the predominant attention and obedience are the actual ground of his poetry, the reason that it serves the style of historical representation.

Up until Hölderlin's attempts at prose (which are, themselves, attempts to clarify the path of the Empedocles-poem) and the latest version of the Empedocles poem (to which the prose attempts roughly correspond), the individual versions' organization stipulated the spiritual law. The hatred of culture came out of their dissonance with human life. But in the latest version, Hölderlin grounds the being of Empedocles, as an unrepeatable person who was his own ground, upon something else: time. Hölderlin does not ground his being upon time in general, but upon its passage, which is as destructive as it is creative. Empedocles is nothing other than the consummation of the passing of time. Again, this does not characterize Hölderlin himself, for Empedocles would fail his purpose if he were a poet and poetized. He is, however, defined in a Hölderlinian way. Moreover, he is defined in that he does not claim to be human. Instead, he is defined in that the becoming of the world plays with him, and, in playing with him, breaks him. The degree to which he is determined does not cease, but becomes much stronger since no one besides him exists—not out of the genius's despotic legitimacy, but because there is nothing other than the balancing of epochal extremes takes place in him. These extremes both exist and balance only once.

This thought admittedly bears an upheaval among Hölderlin's gods as well as among the Empedoclean gods. Empedocles acquires the human name of master of time, the divinely named birth of this disquiet, and he presides over all. Everyone carries the mark and unrest of his rupture. Both of the originary divinities, sky and earth, sympathetically suffer the dispute of time. As two halves of the world that have been torn apart from each other, sky and earth crave reunion. A third, the master of time, reunites them. Empedocles humanly [*menschlich*] completes what he divinely prepares.

> Where patiently before the day begins the heart
> Of earth conceals itself, where all her pains she tells,
> Our darkling mother, tells you, nocturnal one,
> The son of ether! I'd follow you below.[9]

In this new Empedocles, Hölderlin thought a human whose humanity is both an illusion and a contradiction. The human passes by, a flashing spark out of the spans of the eons. It is a human mask through whose eyeholes a telltale primal fire blazes. It is a voice that dissolves all laws with its legislative tone. This ambiguous face is, however, reminiscent of the poet's face, whose beauty is not personal and eludes us in infinitude—beautiful in a way that can only be assumed in the appearance of humanity, in spirit or element. Only Hölderlin could undertake making the captivity of infinitude credible through language. To me, at least, the dialogue of this "Empedocles on Mount Etna" seems to be the greatest thing Hölderlin mastered, not in its individual beauty but, rather, by capturing a course of language.

What is called the people [*das Volk*] here, and what was it called before? Empedocles freed the people from holy angst and, in death, raised the people to his level. This people was nothing other than the material that Empedocles affected. But now it is the substratum of time and its division, nature itself in historical form, that is, in the form of a unique, irresolvable opposition—thus, in the festering discord of the same, which Empedocles is in the reconciliation.

This is reminiscent of Hölderlin's Christology. He calls Christ the reconciler who comes again as reconciled reconciler. Christ is the reconciler, as he always was, but now he is reconciled to his exclusiveness so that, next to him, "yet others are." Thus, his name and vocation, as were also particular to the dogmatic Christ, are obviously reinterpreted! Just as the returning Christ is a god of time marked by the Hesperian moment of equilibrium and remembrance, the former Christ was also a god of time and, therefore, the lightning bolt is his sign. This surely authorized Hölderlin's audacious reinterpretation, an interpretation that was not authorized by the written word of god. To Hölderlin, Christ's speaking signified something concealed. He saw a god forbidden the word by a stronger god: the god of time. Whoever conceals himself, whoever is allowed to conceal himself, must be interpreted by a human—be spoken completely. The mission of this Christ was the same as the mission of Empedocles: to die. But what did Christ, thereby, reconcile? Patmos says it most simply: the anger of the world.

This Christ, whose nature is concealed and whose mission is a reconciling death—a death that does not reconcile God and humans but, rather, the angry forces of the world with each other—is different from the Christ of the Christians. God does not conceal him. Rather, the Christ of the Christians stands manifestly and exclusively between God and humans. He is God become human and he endlessly atones for the humans' endless guilt. This Hölderlinian Christ is, therefore, more than conventional gods and half-gods, a will and hint of time. In his every expression and effect he holds himself back. He does not reveal himself but, rather, reveals a condition. He dies; much—everything—dies with him. But what is this dying called? In that he conceals himself, he conceals his god. In that he conceals his god, all divinity walks with him and in him, out of the state of cause and effects back into the state of concealment. Insofar as Hölderlin's gods have their life in reciprocity, they die—they die a god's death that does not take place at a random time but that is imposed once, at a determinate hour. In this, Christ appears unlike the old gods to whom Hölderlin compares him. His sibling-like relation to Heracles or Bacchus is hidden by the shadow of death. He is god in the attitude of leave-taking. Does this not make his reconciliation dubious? What is reconciled when the gods leave? By describing this (non-Empedoclean) reconciliation as historically unrepeatable, Hölderlin converges with Christian dogma from which he had previously distanced himself. The reconciliation, a consolation for the somnolent, is given to the night, the Hades of time. It is an extinguishing of the eye and a dawning of inner light. It is the gift of the evening meal understood as a gift of the wine-god, who lends strength of memory: remembrance in missing something. This completely esoteric mythos of the night and its gifts as the time since Christ describes an experience, an awareness of the gods, in which they peculiarly stand between being and nonbeing. The eon of god's absence follows the gods' leave-taking, which is Christ. The eon is neither godless nor permeated with gods. The most pious of humans respond to the truth of God's absence during this eon is by closing their eyes, the Christian reckoning of time, not having, but lacking God. Christ (though a divine destiny and not a human destiny) is, thus, also the reconciler of humans. When he tires of them, painkilling consolation trickles onto closed eyelashes.

Built upon his own inner testimony, the poet has the material to portray Christ "as he was"—not construed as a symbol, but real and historical. In this, there was admittedly no room for Gethsemane and Calvary. The death also should not be a death of anguish, done unworthily to the most worthy. It had to have the self-prepared festiveness of Empedoclean dying. With this, the death necessarily reached a boundary. The boundary marks the extent to which its irrefutable occurrence allows for reinterpretation, its own mythos. For, according to Hölderlin's free choice, the death of Empedocles, unbound to a holy tradition, represents reconciliatory death. The death does not, however, open a religiously amorphous epoch absent a comforting afterglow. Rather, advent is in the demise.

In addition to the reconciler and the reconciled forces, to be complete, the poetic coherence of the whole theme of reconciliation requires a meaningful substructure [*Substratum*] of time and its crisis. In the Christology, this is, on the one side, Christ's disciples and, on the other side, the entire Christianity of the Western world. Now, if these both substitute as substrates of time after the appearance of Christ, then they represent both what is missing and the eyeless inner thinking about the absent god. The absence burns twice as much in those who sat so close to Christ. This Christology lacks a substrate for the rupture that occurs before Christ's appearance, the defined space of destiny that belongs to the reconciler, and what Hölderlin calls, "the people" as well as what hangs together with it (i.e., living proof that reconciliation is really complete). That is, it is missing a new mythical condition as the condition of the people subsequent to reconciliation.

The third version, "Empedocles on Mount Etna," meaningfully and completely develops this connection. In it, Empedocles is derived from the strife of time and the people are conceived as the material that substantiates the irreconcilability of the extremes. With the help of theoretical studies, the following train of thought emerges: in their initial approach, the pure nature element and the human's formative strength embrace each other in such a way that the malleability of this element and the humility of the spirit before it (which allows the element to persist as such) created a mediation. Out of this mediation, without either of the two overdoing or renouncing itself, a mythical state emerges. The people is its domain and the soul of the people is the center of this domain. The restless becoming that drives this intimacy then drives both forces over and beyond their pure dispositions, into extremes. Each emphasizes its character, whereby each discovers itself. Subsequently, they discover each other more intimately. But, in this, the spirit unlearns humility and the element loses malleability. This breaks the understanding that had meditated between the two and brings forth the mythical condition. The intimacy turns into pure separation. As the element loses the element and the spirit loses the spirit, they become completely enraged. This rage becomes a lawless structure. This is the time of the soulless regiment of priests. Only a human can reconcile the separation that fetters the extreme within itself and halts becoming by voluntarily reversing the spirit. The mythical life restricts itself to a human mind and the extremes are there in two ways: insofar as the extremes are irreconcilable, they are there as the state of a people. Insofar as they become reconciled, they are there in a conciliatory person. Insofar as the person is human, the person leans toward the elemental. But the person must also have an adequate amount of the element so that the readiness of that element in the person to become malleable again can be actualized. This is a double encounter between nature and human, from the side of nature as much as from the side of the human.

Empedocles's mind is, thus, the possible reconciliation, his death the completed reconciliation. The act of reconciliation can be seen as transcendent or transcendental. It is transcendental as a reconciliation of extremes that takes place in Empedocles and transcendent as a reconciliation between him and nature. That both acts are one and the same emerges from the free death that brings them both, likewise, to a conclusion. The transcendental act is shaped in the first, most succinct moment, especially in the first and second versions of the dialogue, though not so much of the last. It occurs when the earth—like a human—entwines Empedocles's head with its branches and Empedocles makes a death pact with it.

Empedocles is, thus, to be understood as reconciler in that the attribute of self-direction withdraws into his spirit while earth and sky mark his face and are present in his voice. Nature corresponds to this by stepping out of the extreme of imperceptibility and becoming perceptible as a life that resonates in the vibrations of a human soul. This is the transcendental act. It is transcendental in that nature becomes human only in Empedocles's encounters with nature (and nowhere else) as long as he lives. This also means that poetry must not be immediately concluded at its end.

The formative drive [*Bildungstrieb*] now prevails over the nature of the elemental. But, in Empedocles, the element prevails over the formative drive. Thus, like captures like. The elemental captures nature's formative drive [*Bildungstrieb*] and Empedocles's humanity. The elemental captures that same element in Empedocles's nature, insofar as it is a pure primordial life. The individual human is now the field and consummation of a world-process conducted in the human soul and endured for only a moment. If Empedocles were to remain Empedocles, he would, yet again, overturn his act of reconciliation. For, in their freest moments (of self-reversal), the freest forces remain shackled to a passing form. Empedocles must sacrifice himself in order to testify to and glorify the endlessness of this occurrence, in contrast to its human appearance. In sacrificing himself, he avows that what occurs through him is more than just himself.

Manes is the opposite of this new Empedocles. Manes is the timelessness of knowledge and the more predictable path of the stars. Empedocles fulfills more than he knows. What he knows is not so much yesterday or tomorrow, but the one-time-only. He knows this in the midst of the decision. The weak point in Manes's knowledge lies in the actual fulfillment of the actual moment. He is only acquainted with fulfillment insofar as it is general and thinkable. Manes is still a student in binding this merely thinkable thing to the person and events that stand before him. Though he thought he would come as a master, to teach Empedocles what he is not and what he must be, Manes makes himself into Empedocles's student with the skeptical question, "Are you that man? the very one?"[10] Thus, he remains instructed, pointing to the necessity of the free act. He also indicates what most deeply separates this Empedocles from the Hölderlinian Christ: Christ's death took place once in all of time, just like the night in the elegy, "Bread and Wine," is not a recurring night. The Empedoclean sacrifice returns with the rhythm of the predetermined course of the world.

In the outline of a conclusion of the last version, it says, "The human being who felt his country's downgoing so mortally was also able thus to sense its new life."[11] The thought of the deciding god, who yet conceals himself in the earlier community of love that was shared by Empedocles and the people, however, dominates the completed dialogue. This was also the final felicity of death . . . more brusquely than before, the youth is pushed away from taking part in the festival of unification. The humans are not permitted to witness it since Empedocles negates the humanity in himself and proclaims only one interpretation of his act:

> For when a country is about to die, its spirit at the end
> Selects but one among the many, one alone through whom
> Its swan song, the final breaths of life, will sound.[12]

Nevertheless, the people [*Volk*]—the material representation of time, in their strife—suffer the aftermath of the reconciliatory act. The people are implicated in an act at which they are not present. As long as Empedocles lives, the people exist without allotment. If he sacrifices himself, the people are not only allowed an allotment, they must have an allotment. This is because the allotment is first negotiated through the act of sacrifice.

It has been said that the second intimacy was overly intimate. It was overly intimate not insofar as it was a convergence, but a reversal of both fundamental forces and insofar as it fulfilled itself in a human. In this, the intimacy (itself extreme) revealed its own origination from out of extremes. The third state of intimacy, to which the second was a passageway, is to be understood thus: the first intimacy self-consciously repeats itself, possessing its history in such a way that each power is at the same time more itself and readier for unification. This postulates a new mythical state of advent in demise. Hölderlin's posthumous plans provide no answer as to whether this is to be thought as analogous to his earlier attempts to structure [the rise of a new mythical condition] or as altered in accord with modified content.

In attempting to depict Empedocles's encounter with nature in the various versions of the play, I did not, from the start, presume that there is something communal between Hölderlin and us, upon whose basis we can interpret him. My principle was, rather, that one must pursue Hölderlin in his distinctiveness, with understanding or at least the desire to understand. Only then can we see what, for us, follows out of his distinctiveness. Thus, at the end, it behooves me to emphasize once again where this rendering through concepts necessarily fails. It is not only in the well-known difference between conceptuality and poetry. The puzzle lies much more in this: that, in accord with his talent, Hölderlin could experience what, for us, lies at an ungraspable distance and is a hardly thinkable event as the real history of his soul.

Notes

This English translation is of Max Kommerell, "Hölderlin's Empedokles-Dichtungen," avaiable in *Geist und Buchstabe der Dichtung: Goethe, Schiller, Kleist, Hölderlin* (Frankfurt am Main: Vittorio Klostermann, 1956). Special thanks to the Glasscock Center for Humanities Research, Texas A&M University, for providing support of this translation. With special thanks to Tobias Keiling and Andrew Mitchell for their generous assistance with some of the more challenging German locutions: *Translators*.

1. Friedrich Hölderlin, *The Death of Empedocles*, trans. David Ferrell Krell, v.2, Act 1, Scene 3, 333–34 (124). References throughout will be to Krell's translation by page and line number.
2. Ibid., v.2, Act 1, 332–33 (136).
3. See Hölderlin's *Hyperion oder Der Eremit in Griechenland (Hyperion or The Hermit in Greece)*, vol. 1 published in 1797, vol. 2 in 1799.
4. V.3, 182.
5. Ibid.
6. 96–1715.
7. 90–1500.
8. Friedrich Nietzsche, *Thus Spoke Zarathustra*, trans. Walter Kaufmann (New York: Penguin, 1978), 210.
9. 78, ln. 230.
10. 184, ln. 388.
11. 194, ln. 29.
12. 186, ln. 442.

References

Hölderlin, Friedrich. *The Death of Empedocles*. Translated by David Ferrell Krell. Albany: State University of New York Press, 2009.
———. *Hyperion oder Der Eremit in Griechenland*. Stuttgart: Reclam, 1998.
Nietzsche, Friedrich. *Thus Spoke Zarathustra*. New York: Penguin, 1978.

Contributors

María del Rosario Acosta López is professor of Hispanic Studies at The University of California, Riverside. She teaches and conducts research on Romanticism and German Idealism, aesthetics and philosophy of art, contemporary political European philosophy, and Latin American studies. She has edited and co-edited more than ten volumes in these areas in the last ten years, and several special issues for journals such as *New Centennial Review, diacritics, Dialogo, Ideas y Valores,* and *Revista de Estudios Sociales*. She is the author of a book on silence and art in German Romanticism (2006) and a monograph on Friedrich Schiller and the political sublime (2008), and most recently for SUNY Press she has co-edited with Jeffrey Powell a volume on F. Schiller, *Aesthetic Reason and Imaginative Freedom* (2018), and with J. Colin McQuillan a volume titled *Critique in German Philosophy: From Kant to Critical Theory* (forthcoming 2020). She is currently working on two book manuscripts, *Grammars of Listening: Philosophical Approaches to Memory after Trauma* and a new monograph on Friedrich Schiller in English titled *Aesthetics as Critique*.

Babette Babich is professor of philosophy at Fordham University in New York City and teaches, on occasion, at the Humboldt University in Berlin. She is the author of more than 250 articles and book chapters and eight monographs, including two in French, one on Heidegger and politics, another on the political fortunes of university philosophy, and two in German. English monographs include *The Hallelujah Effect: Music, Performance Practice, and Technology* (2016 [2013]) and a study of philosophy and poetry, *Words in Blood, Like Flowers* (2006). A four-time Fulbright scholar, she has edited some fourteen book collections, most recently *Reading David Hume's "Of the Standard of Taste"* (2019) in addition to eighteen issues of the journal she founded (and then co-edited with David Allison), *New Nietzsche Studies*.

Charles Bambach is professor of philosophy at the University of Texas Dallas. He specializes in hermeneutics, contemporary continental philosophy, Ancient Greek philosophy, Heidegger, Nietzsche, Derrida, philosophy and poetry. He is the author of *Thinking the Poetic Measure of Justice: Hölderlin-Heidegger-Celan* (SUNY Press, 2014). He has also published two books with Cornell University Press: *Heidegger's Roots* (2003) and *Heidegger, Dilthey, and the Crisis of Historicism* (1995). He is currently completing a book manuscript with the working title *Of an Alien Homecoming: Heidegger's "Hölderlin."*

Günter Figal is professor of philosophy at the University of Freiburg. He specializes in Heidegger, phenomenology, hermeneutics, and the history of philosophy. He is author of many books and articles in his areas of expertise; his books include *Unscheinbarkeit: Der Raum der Phänomenologie* (Mohr Siebeck, 2015), *Martin Heidegger. Phänomenologie der Freiheit* (Morh Siebeck, 2013), *Kunst. Philosophische Abhandlungen* (Mohr Siebeck, 2012), and *Erscheinungsdinge. Ästhetik als Phänomenologie* (Mohr Siebeck, 2010), *Verstehensfragen. Studien zur phänomenologisch-hermeneutischen Philosophie* (Mohr Siebeck, 2009), and *Gegenständlichkeit. Das Hermeneutische und die Philosophie* (Mohr Siebeck, 2006).

Theodore George is associate professor of philosophy at Texas A&M University. He specializes in continental European philosophy since Kant with emphases in hermeneutical philosophy, Hegel, ethical philosophy, and the philosophy of art and aesthetics. He is the author of *Tragedies of Spirit: Tracing Finitude in Hegel's Phenomenology* (SUNY Press, 2006), and many essays in his areas of expertise. He is also the translator of Günter Figal, *Objectivity: The Hermeneutical and Philosophy* (SUNY Press, 2010).

Gert-Jan van der Heiden is professor of metaphysics and holds the Chair of Fundamental Philosophy at Radboud University, Nijmegen, the Netherlands. His research focuses on problems from metaphysics and ontology in light of recent developments in phenomenology, hermeneutics, and contemporary French thought. His publications include *Ontology after Ontotheology: Plurality, Event, and Contingency in Contemporary Philosophy* (Pittsburgh: Duquesne University Press, 2014), and *The Truth (and Untruth) of Language: Heidegger, Ricoeur, and Derrida on Disclosure and Displacement* (Pittsburgh: Duquesne University Press, 2010).

Contributors

William McNeill is professor of philosophy at DePaul University. He is author of *The Time of Life: Heidegger and Ēthos* (SUNY Press, 2006), and *The Glance of the Eye: Heidegger, Aristotle, and the Ends of Theory* (SUNY Press, 1999). He has translated numerous works by Heidegger, most recently his lectures on *Hölderlin's Hymn "Remembrance"* (co-translated with Julia Ireland: Indiana University Press, 2018).

Christopher D. Merwin is a doctoral candidate in the philosophy department at Emory University in Atlanta. He is currently in Germany on a Fulbright research grant and completing his dissertation entitled *The Metaphysics of Time: Heidegger's Later Concept of Time*. He is the co-editor of *Heidegger on Technology* (Routledge, 2018) and co-translator, with Andrew J. Mitchell, of volume 76 of Heidegger's collected works, *Guiding Thoughts on the Emergence of Metaphysics, Modern Science, and Contemporary Technology*, to be published by Indiana University Press.

Kalliopi Nikolopoulou is associate professor of comparative literature at the University at Buffalo. Her research focuses on the relation of ancients and moderns, particularly on the importance of tragedy for ethics and aesthetics. Her book *Tragically Speaking: On the Use and Abuse of Theory for Life* offers a critical understanding of the reception of tragedy in the continental tradition. She is currently working on vigilance and vigilantism from Aeschylus's *Oresteia* to contemporary revaluations of these terms, as well as on another project exploring the relation between the Apollonian and heroic principles to timelessness in Greek thought.

Christopher Turner is assistant professor of philosophy at California State University, Stanislaus. His areas of expertise include ancient philosophy and Western Marxism. He received his PhD from DePaul University in 2016. His dissertation, "Aristotle and the Cynics on Happiness and Misfortune," which he defended with distinction, was awarded a Mellon/ACLS Dissertation Completion fellowship for 2014–15. His recent works include "Under Adorno's Spell: *Bann* as Central Concept rather than Mere Metaphor" (in *New German Critique*, 2016) and "Misfortune and the Contemplative Life" (in *The Journal of Greco-Roman Studies*, 2017). He has also translated a number of books and articles over the past few years, including *I am Not a Brain: Philosophy of Mind for the 21st Century*, by Markus Gabriel (2017) and *What Happened in the 20th Century?* by Peter Sloterdijk (2018).

Margot D. Wielgus graduated with her PhD in philosophy from the University of Kentucky in 2015 and is now an independent scholar. She wrote her dissertation on the experience of critical self-reflective thinking as described by Plato, Heidegger, Thoreau, and Arendt. Her main areas of specialization are ethics and phenomenology. She has also published other translations, including "Tautóphasis: Heidegger and Parmenides," by Günter Figal and "The Universality of Technology and the Independence of Things: Heidegger's Bremen Lectures Once More," by Günter Figal.

Krzysztof Ziarek is professor of comparative literature at the University of Buffalo. Dr. Ziarek specializes in twentieth-century comparative literature, especially contemporary poetry and poetics, aesthetics, philosophy and literature, literary theory, and Heidegger. His books include *Inflected Language: Toward a Hermeneutics of Nearness* (SUNY, 1994), *The Historicity of Experience: Modernity, the Avant-Garde, and the Event* (Northwestern, 2001), *The Force of Art* (Stanford, 2004), and *Language after Heidegger* (Indiana, 2013), as well as many articles in his areas of expertise.

Index

Abgrund. See abyss
absolute, as term and concept, 67, 80n4
absolute spirit, 65–68, 71–73. *See also* spirit
abyss, 6, 142, 153, 165, 218–22
Achilles, 119, 125, 133n8, 134n9
Adorno, Theodor, 9–10
adventure, 78–80
Aeschylus, 125–26, 129–30, 135n31, 136n41, 136n43
aesthetic freedom, 24–29, 38n15, 49–50, 56–61. *See also* style
aesthetic labor, 68
Aesthetic Letters. See *Letters on the Aesthetic Education of Humanity* (Schiller)
Aesthetics: Lectures on Fine Art (Hegel), 68, 77
Allison, David, 85, 90
Andenken. See remembrance; "Remembrance" (Hölderlin)
Antigone (Sophocles), 13–14, 78–79, 142, 145–53, 156n46, 161
anti-hero, 130–33
Apollo, 119, 128, 132
"Archaic Torso of Apollo" (Rilke), 9
Archilochus, 12, 86, 92–101, 136n41
"The Archipelago" (Hölderlin), 160, 180n22
Aristides, 91

Aristotle: aesthetics of, 13; on courage, 120, 133n4; *Nicomachean Ethics*, 120, 134n9; Schiller on, 59; on tragedy, 92, 101–2, 130, 136n47; on truth, 209
art as language, 66–70, 75–77, 188–91. *See also* Romantic art
atavism, 116–17, 126
Auschwitz, 9–10

Bacchae (Euripides), 125, 129–32, 136n47
Baudelaire, Charles, 130
beauty, 30–34, 42n55
Beethoven, Ludwig van, 99
Behler, Ernst, 74
Being and Time (Heidegger), 14, 161–64, 167–69, 178–79
being on the way, 228–29
Beiser, Frederick, 41n52
Benardete, Seth, 120, 130–31, 136n47
Bezeugung, 221–22
The Birth of Tragedy out of the Spirit of Music (Nietzsche), 12–13, 86–88, 94–95, 121–33, 134n16
Bread and Wine (Hölderlin), 65
breathturn, 10, 16, 215–16, 223–25, 227–28, 231
Büchner, Georg, 218–19
Burnt Norton (Eliot), 15–16, 204–12

267

Cassandra, 129
catastrophe, 146–47, 219–21, 224, 230, 232. See also tragedy
Celan, Paul: "Der Meridian," 6, 215, 218–21, 224–25; *In die Rillen*, 225–26, 227; *Fadensonnen*, 233n25; *Harnischstriemen, Faltenachsen*, 223–24; on language and *ethos*, 6–8, 9, 10; the moment of interpretation in poems by, 217–25; on otherness, 16, 229–31; the reserve of perhaps in poems by, 225–28; *Sprich auch du*, 227; *Von Ungeträumten geätzt*, 224; *Wege im Schatten-Gebräch*, 227; *Wirk nicht voraus*, 229–30
Cervantes, Miguel de, 77–80
Chladni, Ernst, 92, 108n54
Christ, 255–57, 259
classical art, 71–72, 75. See also Romantic art
"Concerning the Spirit and the Letter within Philosophy in a Series of Letters." See "On Spirit and the Letter in Philosophy" (Fichte)
Contributions to Philosophy (Heidegger), 173
courage, 120, 133n4. See also heroic ideal and heroism
Crawford, Claudia, 127–29
Critique of Judgment (Kant), 32–33, 40n28, 43n69

darstellende Schriftsteller, 31, 32–34, 41n42
Dasein: Hegel on, 69; Heidegger on, 14, 143, 162, 165, 168, 179, 180n11, 181n28, 233n14
Davenport, Guy, 94
death, 253–54
Death in Venice (Mann), 130
The Death of Empedocles (Hölderlin). See Empedocles

deiknymi, 3
De Man, Paul, 28–29
"Der Meridian" (Celan), 6, 215, 218–21, 224–25
Derrida, Jacques, 87, 225, 227
"Dialogue on Poetry" (Schlegel), 77
dicere, 3
dichten, as term, 2, 3–4, 180n23, 187–91. See also poetizing and philosophical thinking
dichterisch. See poietic momentum
Dichtung, as term, 164, 185, 187–91. See also poetizing and philosophical thinking, overview
Die Fragmente der Vorsokratiker (Diels), 208
Die Horen (publication), 11, 21, 63n13. See also Schiller, Johann Christoph Friedrich
Diels, Hermann, 208
Dionysus, 89, 96, 121–22, 128, 135n22, 136n49. See also *The Birth of Tragedy out of the Spirit of Music* (Nietzsche)
Diotima, 249
Don Quixote (Cervantes), 77–80

Eckhart, Meister, 6
Eliot, T. S., 15–16, 204–12
Empedocles: death of, 242, 250–61; Hölderlin's embodiment of, 245–47; self-knowledge of, 248–50; sorrow and, 239–45; time and, 247–48
Empedocles Poems (Hölderlin), 246
"end of art" thesis (Hegel), 12, 65, 72–73
epoche, 235n51
Erstreckung, 162, 163
"The Essence of Language" (George), 193–94
essence of poetizing, 165–69. See also poetizing and philosophical thinking, overview

ethos: language as, 6–9, 10; as poetic dwelling, 8–9, 144, 146–47
Euripides, 125, 129–33, 136n47
The Event (Heidegger), 191–92

Fadensonnen (Celan), 233n25
Fichte, Johann Gottlieb: *Foundation of the Entire Wissenschaftslehre*, 24–25; "Lectures Concerning the Scholar's Vocation," 25, 31; letters to Schiller, 47–48, 51–55; "On Spirit and Letter in Philosophy," 11, 21–22, 36, 49–51, 63n2; "On Stimulating and Increasing the Pure Interest in Truth," 22; Schiller's rejection letter to, 21–22, 48–51; on style, 23–24, 35–36; on vocation of the human being, 11
Foundation of the Entire Wissenschaftslehre (Fichte), 24–25
Four Quartets (Eliot), 15, 204, 208. See also *Burnt Norton* (Eliot)
Fuchs, Carl, 90

Gadamer, Hans-Georg: on absolute, 67; on Celan and breathturn, 215–16; on Celan and moment of interpretation, 217–25; on Celan and reserve of the perhaps, 225–28; philosophical hermeneutics by, 9, 16, 231–32; on poetry as truth, 203; *Who Am I and Who Are You?*, 215, 223
The Gay Science (Nietzsche), 88, 102, 116–17
Gedachte, 198
Geheimnis, 227–28
Geist und Buschstabe der Dichtung (Kommerell), 17
On the Genealogy of Morals (Nietzsche), 102
genius, 68, 98–99, 125, 253–54

George, Stefan, 193–94
"Germania" (Hölderlin), 142, 162
Gethmann-Siefert, Annemarie, 67, 82n35
Goethe, Johann Wolfgang von: Hegel on, 66, 73–74; *Meister*, 48; Nietzsche on, 86; Schiller on, 49, 57
"On Grace and Dignity" (Schiller), 26, 27
"The Greek Interpretation of Human Beings in Sophocles' *Antigone*" (Heidegger), 142
Griechische Metrik (Nietzsche), 88

Harnischstriemen, Faltenachsen (Celan), 223–24
Hector, 119, 133n8
Hedreen, Guy, 94
Hegel, Georg Wilhelm Friedrich: on absolute spirit, 65–68, 71–73; *Aesthetics*, 68, 77; on Cervantes's *Don Quixote*, 77–80; Eurocentrism and, 71, 81n21; on Romantic art, 12, 65–77
Heidegger, Martin: *Being and Time*, 14, 161–64, 167–69, 178–79; *Contributions to Philosophy*, 173; on *ethos* as poetic dwelling, 8, 140–45; *The Event*, 191–92; "Hölderlin and the Essence of Poetizing," 14, 160–61, 162–63, 165–69; "Hölderlin's Hymn 'The Ister,'" 13, 142, 152; on Hölderlin's "Remembrance," 172; "Letter on Humanism," 144; on origin of philosophical thinking, 1; "The Origin of the Work of Art," 188, 190, 191, 196; on oxymoron, 148–53; on poetizing and philosophical thinking, 2–3, 4–9; on poetry and modernity, 65; on poietic momentum, 15, 170, 185–98;

Heidegger, Martin *(continued)*
 on Sophocles's *Antigone*, 13, 142, 145–53, 156n46; on uncanniness of the human being, 145–48; *What Is Called Thinking?*, 178, 181n37. *See also* Hölderlin, Friedrich
Heimkehr, 140
heimlich, 227–28
Hera, 119
Heraclitus, 4–5, 139, 197, 202, 208, 209
hermeneutic experience, 217
Hermocrates, 247
heroic ideal and heroism: anti-hero or last hero, 130–33; Homer's legacy on, 115, 119–25; Nietzsche on, 12–13, 116–17, 125–30. *See also* tragedy
historico-geographical stage of art, 71
Hölderlin, Friedrich: "The Archipelago," 160, 180n22; *Bread and Wine*, 65; *Empedocles Poems*, 246; "Germania," 142, 162; *Hyperion oder Der Eremit in Griechenland*, 245–46; "The Ister," 13, 142, 152, 154n13; on language, 8–9; on poetic dwelling, 140–45; "Remarks on Oedipus," 160; "Remembrance," 14, 154n13, 160, 164–67, 170, 172, 175–78; "The Rhine," 162; on time, 160–62. *See also* Empedocles; Heidegger, Martin
"Hölderlin and the Essence of Poetizing" (Heidegger), 14, 160–61, 162–63, 165–69
"Hölderlin's Hymn 'The Ister'" (Heidegger), 13, 142, 152
Holocaust, 9–10
Homer, 119–25, 134n15. *See also* heroic ideal and heroism
hope, 16, 228–31, 234n31

Hyperion oder Der Eremit in Griechenland (Hölderlin), 245–46

Iliad. *See* Homer
imagination, 23–24, 29–36, 43n69, 54, 56, 70
In die Rillen (Celan), 225–26
Innigkeit, 143, 159, 175
"The Ister" (Hölderlin), 13, 142, 152, 154n13

Kant, Immanuel: *Critique of Judgment*, 32–33, 40n28, 43n69; Schiller's interpretation of, 28–29
Kaufmann, Walter, 121–22
"A Kind of Atavism" (Nietzsche), 116–17
Kommerell, Max, 17

Laches (Plato), 120, 134n9
language: art as, 66–70, 75–77; music and, 12, 87–89; poetizing and, overview, 1–11; poietic momentum, 15, 170, 188, 190–98; silence and, 6–8
last hero, 130–33
"Lectures Concerning the Scholar's Vocation" (Fichte), 25, 31
Lectures on Art (Schelling), 77–78
"Letter on Humanism" (Heidegger), 144
Letters on the Aesthetic Education of Humanity (Schiller), 22–23, 25–28, 36, 49
Life as Literature (Nehamas), 85
Lucian, 86
Luyster, Robert, 121–25, 134n16, 135n22
lyric poetry, 12, 91–94, 98–101

Manes, 249–50, 259

Mann, Thomas, 130–31
Meister (Goethe), 48
"Meridian" (Celan), 6
Merkelbach, Reinhold, 96, 97
modernity: Hector and, 133n8; Hegel on art and, 12, 65–66, 70–77; Nietzsche on reason and, 12–13, 125, 129–30, 133
moment of interpretation, 16, 217–25
moral freedom, 11, 25–27. *See also* aesthetic freedom
music and language, 12, 87–89

Nagy, Gregory, 119, 133n8
"On the Necessary Limitations in the Use of Beautiful Forms" (Schiller), 31
Nehamas, Alexander, 85, 87, 101
new souls, 89–92
Nicomachean Ethics (Aristotle), 120, 134n9
Nietzsche, Friedrich: on ancient Egypt, 106n28; on Archilochus, 12, 86, 94–101; on Dionysus, 89, 95, 96; *The Gay Science*, 88, 102, 116–17; on Goethe, 86; *Griechische Metrik*, 88; on heroic ideal and tragedy, 12–13, 86–88, 94–95, 116–17, 125–30, 134n16; "A Kind of Atavism," 116–17; on modernity and reason, 12–13, 125, 129–30, 133; on music and language, 87–89; on new souls, 89–92; on philosophers as poets, 202–3; on silence in language, 6; *Thus Spoke Zarathustra*, 6, 85, 122–24, 254. See also *The Birth of Tragedy out of the Spirit of Music* (Nietzsche)
"Nietzsche's Psychology and Rhetoric of World Redemption" (Crawford), 127

Oedipus Tyrannos (Sophocles), 161
ontotheology, 66–67
"The Origin of the Work of Art" (Heidegger), 188, 190, 191, 196
otherness, 1, 16, 154n13, 230–31
oxymoron, 148–53

Panthea, 249
Parmenides, 139, 145, 197, 201–2, 204
perhaps, poems and the reserve of, 225–28
philosophical thinking and poetizing, overview, 1–11
Plato: aesthetics of, 13; on courage, 120, 133n4, 134n9; on philosophy and poetry, 1, 202; on tragedy, 130
poesie, 187
poet-heroes, 12–13, 125–30. *See also* heroic ideal and heroism
poetic dwelling, 8–9, 140–45, 146–47
poetizing and philosophical thinking, overview, 1–11
poietic momentum, 15, 170, 188, 190–98
primordial sense, 211–12
Prometheus Bound (Aeschylus), 126

rape, 96–97
Reading the New Nietzsche (Allison), 85
reciprocal action, 24–25, 39n27
"Recollection in Metaphysics" (Heidegger), 7
Reinhardt, Karl, 125, 135n31
religion, 66–68, 78, 247
"Remarks on Oedipus" (Hölderlin), 160
remembrance, 14, 148, 153, 170, 172, 177–78, 256
"Remembrance" (Hölderlin), 14, 154n13, 160, 164–67, 170, 172, 175–78

reserve, 16, 225–28
"The Rhine" (Hölderlin), 162
rhythm, 12, 88–89
Rickman, Alan, 91, 101, 107n43
Rilke, Maria Rainer, 9
Ritschl, Friedrich, 85
Romantic art: description of, 70–72; end of art thesis, 12, 65, 72–73; as infinite task, 74–75; language of, 66–70, 75–77, 188–91; as term, 65, 74
Rorty, Richard, 204

Schelling, F. W. J., 74, 77, 98
Schiller, Johann Christoph Friedrich: on beauty, 42n55; on *darstellende Schriftsteller*, 31, 32–34, 41n42; Kant interpretation by, 28–29; *Letters on the Aesthetic Education of Humanity*, 22–23, 25–28, 36, 49; letters to Fichte, 11, 21–22, 23–24, 48–51, 55–62; "On Grace and Dignity," 26, 27; "On the Necessary Limitations in the Use of Beautiful Forms," 31; on reciprocal action, 24–25, 39n27; on style and form, 28–32, 41n52; on vocation of the human being, 11. See also *Die Horen* (publication)
Schlegel, August, 74
Schlegel, Friedrich, 74, 77
Schlegel-Schelling, Caroline, 74
Schopenhauer, Arthur, 99
self-knowledge, 248–49
silence and language, 6–8
Silk, Michael, 86
Sommer, Andreas Urs, 101
Sophist (Plato), 202
Sophocles: *Antigone*, 13–14, 78–79, 142, 145–53, 156n46, 161; *Oedipus Tyrannos*, 161

sorrow, 239–45
speculative impulse, 68–69
spirit: Fichte on, 27–30, 35–36, 51–53; Hegel on, 65–68, 71–73; Schiller on, 27, 30, 49, 63n14
"On Spirit and Letter in Philosophy" (Fichte), 11, 21–22, 36, 49–51, 63n2
Sprich auch du (Celan), 227
Stern, Joseph, 86
Stille, 6
Strong, Tracy, 87
style, 28–32, 41n52, 53–54, 87. See also aesthetic freedom
symbolic art, 71. See also Romantic art

Theatetus (Plato), 1
thinking. See philosophical thinking and poetizing, overview
Thus Spoke Zarathustra (Nietzsche), 6, 85, 122–24, 254
Tieck, Ludwig, 74, 77
time, 160–62, 170–71, 247
tragedy: Aristotle on, 92, 101–2, 130, 136n47; Heidegger on, 145–48; Nietzsche on, 12–13, 86–88, 134n16. See also catastrophe; heroic ideal and heroism
Treu, Max, 94
truth, 67–68, 70, 202–4, 209

uncanniness of the human being, 145–48
unhomeliness, 146–48
unseasonality, 119
Ur-Eine, 98–99

vocation of the human being, 11, 25
Von Ungeträumten geätzt (Celan), 224

Wagner, Richard, 87, 96, 122

On the Way to Language (George), 193
Wege im Schatten-Gebräch (Celan), 227
Weltaufenthalt, 140–41
West, Martin, 97
What Is Called Thinking? (Heidegger), 178, 181n37
"What Is That—Philosophy?" (Heidegger), 1–2
Who Am I and Who Are You? (Gadamer), 215, 223

Wilamowitz (Ulrich von Wilamowitz-Moellendorff), 96, 105n21
wind, 172, 174, 177–78, 182n44, 231
Wirk nicht voraus (Celan), 229
"The Word" (George), 192

"You be like you" (Celan), 6–7

Zarathustra, 6
Zeus, 244–45

www.ingramcontent.com/pod-product-compliance
Lightning Source LLC
Chambersburg PA
CBHW020642230426
43665CB00008B/284